Reinventing Dixie

REINVENTING DIXIE

TIN PAN ALLEY'S SONGS
THE CREATION OF THE MYTHIC SOUTH

JOHN BUSH
JONES

LOUISIANA STATE UNIVERSITY PRESS

BATON ROUGE

Published by Louisiana State University Press
lsupress.org

Louisiana Paperback Edition, 2022

DESIGNER: Michelle A. Neustrom
TYPEFACE: Vulpa

Library of Congress Cataloging-in-Publication Data
are available at the Library of Congress.

ISBN 978-0-8071-5944-6 (cloth: alk. paper) — ISBN 978-0-8071-5945-3 (pdf) —
ISBN 978-0-8071-5946-0 (epub) — ISBN 978-0-8071-7735-8 (paperback)

For John Shelton Reed,
without whose insights, wisdom, wealth of information,
great good humor, and unflagging, enthusiastic support,
this book would have been much more difficult—
and not as much fun—to write.

CONTENTS

PREFACE

I'm not a musicologist, by training or by trade. My degrees and my teaching of university courses for thirty-eight years were in English literature and theatre, mostly the latter, primarily as a theatre historian—especially of musical theatre. But my lack of music education didn't affect my exploration of sixty years of professional songwriting about the South, since most of my emphasis is on the lyrics of those songs, with only occasional remarks about their melodies, musical styles, and related matters. My background in the "content analysis" of literature and plays (including musicals) prepared me to tackle this subject, and I'm no stranger to writing about popular music, considering my *The Songs That Fought the War: Popular Music and the Home Front, 1939–1945* (UP of New England, 2006).

When looking at musicals, songs, or other topics I've written on, such as home front life during World War II, I am by inclination and practice a cultural and social historian, with a penchant for placing what I call the cultural "artifacts" (musicals, songs) in larger historical, cultural, and social contexts to see what sense I can make of them in the aggregate, not as individual items each unto itself. Call me, if you will, an empirical historian, preferring to work with primary materials—in this case the sheet music of the songs— rather than with secondary works, except for historical or biographical background information as necessary. Accordingly, I don't approach a subject I'm working on with a preconceived theory, thesis, or agenda. Instead, I examine each artifact in turn (in this book, the 1,079 "Dixie tunes" for which I found sheet music in various libraries, plus one song only on a phonograph record), "listen" to what each one has to say to me, and then try to tell its story, along with the stories of all the other artifacts, drawing from them a unifying theme, idea, or historical vision. For this book that vision started to come very early in my research while I was still amassing photocopies of sheet music I would eventually write about, and long before I was writing; yet it wasn't a predigested idea of mine, but something that came from the primary material, the songs, I was reading.

I began gathering sheet music at the John Hay Library, the special collections library at Brown University in Providence, Rhode Island, where I live. With its collection of over 140,000 pieces of American sheet music, the John Hay, along with the libraries at UCLA, Duke, and Johns Hopkins, and the Lilly Library at Indiana University, houses one of the largest archives of American song in the United States. Of the 1,079 published songs about the South that I ultimately acquired, about 900 came from the John Hay alone. Without getting too far ahead of myself for what will be the book's major thrust, while at the Hay seeking songs in the boxes of American vocal music arranged only alphabetically by title regardless of date, authorship, or subject, I learned that most of what I call "Dixie tunes," written mostly by northern, urban Tin Pan Alley songwriters, had as their theme the idealizing, glorifying, or romanticizing of the South, and *not* the South of some distant past but the South contemporary with the writing and publishing of each individual song. These songs disseminated, and helped create, a twentieth-century version of the "moonlight and magnolias" vision of an idyllic South that imbued the American popular imagination for over half a century. This was *not* identical with the moonlight and magnolias component of the two nineteenth-century myths created by southerners for southerners, the antebellum Plantation Myth and the postbellum Lost Cause Myth, but something different, as discussed in Chapters 8 and 9. But I learned all that only when I was much farther on in my research and writing.

Since I intend my books more for general audiences than for academic ones, I do not weigh them down with the heavy apparatus of hundreds upon hundreds of endnotes (or footnotes) simply to document my sources. It's my belief that endnotes are best reserved for discursive discussions in scholarly works for scholarly readers, since they often carry the discourse into directions not entirely germane to the main thrust of the book. Since I prefer saying all I have to say in the body of the text, I have no use for such endnotes, and I loathe the thought of having readers, especially general readers, chasing hundreds of superscript numbers to the back of the book only to find a citation to, say, nothing but the place, date, and publisher of a song. So, as in my previous books, also mostly for general readers, I have adopted a slightly modified version of in-text parenthetical documentation as laid out in Chapter 7 of Joseph Gibaldi's *MLA Style Manual and Guide to Scholarly Publishing*, 2nd ed. (New York: The Modern Language Association of America, 1998). I have used such in-text parenthetical citations to identify books and articles, which normally include merely the author's last name and the page reference to the quotation cited or idea discussed, such as (Goldberg 173). A reader may find from just the author's name the full publishing information for his or her book in the Bibliography. If an author wrote more than one book I cite from, a short form of the title is also included, such as (Reed, *Southern Folk* 31). For documentation of sheet music, lyricists and composers of songs are always mentioned in the body of the text, so they don't need to be repeated in the parenthetical. In each instance, the publisher and date are provided, but *not* the page number of quotations, since all the songs run only between two and five pages in the sheet music. For conciseness, I often omit such tags as "& Co." from the name of publishers, and I cite the city of publication only if it is *not* New York. Thus, for example, in the documentation for a quotation from Jack Yellen and George L. Cobb's "Alabama Jubilee," the parenthetical citation would be (Jerome H. Remick, 1915). For a song published elsewhere than New York like "My Girl From Dixie" with words and music by Raymond A. Browne and Robert J. Adams, the form is (Chicago: Sol Bloom, 1900). For the source of quotations or other information I cite from personal e-mails from scholars and other experts in fields germane to the book, the parenthetical gives the last name of the e-mail's sender and a note that the e-mail was sent to me, plus the date, as in (Silber e-mail to the author, December 23, 2011). Silber is identified in the text as Nina Silber, history professor at Boston University and author of *The Romance of Reunion*.

Readers may have noticed that the last title I mentioned was "My Girl From Dixie," not "My Girl from Dixie." It has been the universal practice of American popular song publishers since time immemorial to print sheet music with every word of the title capitalized, including the so-called "little words"—articles, prepositions, conjunctions, and the like. I followed this practice in my book on World War II songs and several articles, and it's one I continue here, if for no other reason than historical authenticity.

In the text I almost invariably follow the order of the published sheet music in citing the name of the lyricist(s) first and the composer(s) second. If the words and music were both by the same team of writers, I specify "words and music by" followed by as many names as necessary, as in the example of "My

Girl From Dixie" above. But if a single person wrote *both* the words and music, rather than writing "'Alexander's Ragtime Band' with words and music by Irving Berlin," I write simply "Irving Berlin's 'Alexander's Ragtime Band.'"

In quoting from lyrics, a frequent exercise throughout the book, I retain all spelling, grammar, punctuation, and other idiosyncrasies of the published texts exactly *as is,* with no attempt to regularize, normalize, or modernize. If some grammatical or spelling peculiarity is especially odd, I follow it with a "[*sic*]" to let readers know I didn't miss something so strange that it needed correction or comment.

Finally, the history of the songs I write about in this book and call Dixie tunes includes not just their publication as sheet music but their recording as phonograph records as well. For those Dixie tunes for which I could find an original phonograph recording made close to the time of the song's writing and publication and reproduced on the World Wide Web or Internet (the term I use in the book for brevity's sake), I indicate that information in the body of the text along with the name of the performing artist, record label, and, when known, the date of the recording session, so that readers might find and listen to the Dixie tunes for themselves and therefore have the full experience of *hearing* these historic pieces and not just reading their lyrics. In most cases, especially for early songs, only one recording will appear, as for, say, the 1906 Bert Williams rendering of "The Mississippi Stoker." Information on the Internet sites I include as of this writing varies from none at all through unreliable to extensive and totally accurate. Most of the "none at all" and "unreliable" information appears with songs uploaded on YouTube; conversely, songs on the National Jukebox site produced by the Library of Congress provide extensive information, including exact recording dates, the personnel of singing groups, and the names of conductors of backup bands and orchestras. Other archival song sites are nearly as good in providing background material. But having the Internet at one's fingertips mostly makes possible hearing many songs, from the early popular recording artist Arthur Collins singing the legend of "Dixie Dan" in 1907, to Jo Stafford extolling Cajun cuisine in "Jambalaya" in 1952.

ACKNOWLEDGMENTS

I'd be exaggerating to say it takes a village to produce a research-based book like this, but it *did* take a far-flung neighborhood of people and places, some of whom and which I never encountered face to face. These included institutions, scholars, nonacademic experts, relatives, and friends. They provided me with everything from materials I worked with, through information, commentary, and opinions, right down to good old moral support and an occasional cheering section when I wondered how I could get through another of my "I should have my head examined" projects involving wading through a thousand or more bits of historical data (whether songs or musicals) to write a book. While I wouldn't think of burdening those good folk with an iota of responsibility for the outcome of my research and writing, I still consider them my partners in the effort, regardless of how great or small a part each may have played. The least I can do is thank them all individually and publicly, which I will do forthwith.

As implied above in the Preface, for researching all my books I count myself geographically fortunate to live in Providence, Rhode Island, where I have access to the wealth of materials in the libraries at Brown University and where the personnel of those libraries treat me like a member of the Brown community even though most of my own university teaching was at Brandeis University some forty-five miles to the north in Waltham, Massachusetts. For this book, Brown's John Hay Library, home of its special collections, was also my virtual home away from home (a five-minute drive from my apartment). It was here that once again the staff let me browse at will the seemingly countless boxes of materials in the vast American sheet music collection, and have photocopies made of anything I chose at the Brown community price rather than the higher price charged to visiting scholars, for all of which I am enormously grateful to the library and its welcoming and helpful staff. I must single out for special mention those with whom I worked most closely, starting with Rosemary Cullen, now retired, but then the curator of the American Literature and Popular Culture Collections, who seemed to know everything about everything in the library and who also pointed out to me why I should take a long hard look at "The Yellow Rose of Texas" as background to some songs in this book (see the section on Southern Belles in Chapter 3). Peter Harrington, curator of the Anne S. K. Brown Military Collection, I again owe thanks to for his expertise in dealing, now, with several songs about Dixie boys going off to various wars. From Reader Services, I owe tremendous debts of gratitude to Kathleen Brooks, Ann Dodge, Andy Moul, and Alison Bundy for retrieving all those boxes of songs from the stacks and photocopying the thousands of pages of sheet music I requested over my nearly daily visits during five months in the Reading Room. Finally, my special thanks not to a professional member of the John Hay staff, but to a young woman who, at the time of my research there, was an undergraduate library assistant, but not one who was merely a desk monitor in the Reading Room. Katherine (a.k.a. Katie) Meyers had a real passion for books and archives and truly knew her way around the Hay's collections; more than once she went above and beyond to locate an obscure document for me, and, when she worked in Reader Services, she facilitated photocopying sheet music I requested precisely to my quirky specifications. After graduating from Brown, Katie followed her passion by earning a master of library science degree with a concentration in archives management, at Simmons College in Boston. As I write this she is the collections assistant and archive specialist at the Intrepid Sea, Air, and Space Museum aboard the aircraft carrier Intrepid moored at Pier 86 on the Hudson River in New York City.

Other Brown libraries also proved useful for this project. The Rockefeller Library, the university's main library, is also its microform repository. There I spent literally months spinning through interminable reels of microfilm of the entertainment trade papers *Variety* and *Billboard* for not just articles about Dixie tunes, but also publishers' ads hawking them to entertainers, and rudimentary "charts" of the songs' popularity on the vaudeville stage, in their sheet music form, and, eventually, as phonograph records. Since I generated so many pages of information from the trade papers, I am grateful that "The Rock" no longer charges a fee for printing paper copies from its microfilm reader-printers! Brown's Orwig Music Library provided a good deal of background material for me, both in its reference collection and in its extensive holdings of books about American popular music, through which I was guided by Orwig's knowledgeable then-music librarian, Ned Quist, who later rose to the post of associate university librarian for research and outreach services. While I was writing the book, the new music librarian, Laura Stokes, was equally helpful on my frequent fact-checking forays to Orwig.

Beyond Brown, other Providence libraries aided my research. Thanks to its music librarian, Margaret Chevian, I learned that the Providence Public Library has a small but interesting archive of sheet music, and, given full access to it, I unearthed and photocopied a number of Dixie tunes not in the John Hay collection. Also, the James P. Adams Library at Rhode Island College was my source for a periodical the Brown libraries don't subscribe to, the *Southern Speech Communication Journal,* which contains Stephen A. Smith's useful article on country music that I discuss in the Epilogue.

Between the John Hay and the Providence Public libraries, I acquired photocopies of over nine hundred Dixie tunes professionally written and published between 1898 and 1958, the years during which Tin Pan Alley produced such songs. Yet this fell short of my goal of at least a thousand such representative songs as my corpus to work with, so I turned to other library collections, and did this without ever leaving Providence, thanks to the Internet. Rosemary Cullen at the John Hay had told me of a tremendously useful website, the Sheet Music Consortium—said consortium consisting of the libraries at UCLA, Indiana University, Johns Hopkins, and Duke, and also including entries from "The Maine Music Box" comprising the Bagaduce Music Lending Library in Blue Hill, the Bangor Public Library, and the University of Maine's Fogler Library. In the old version of the Sheet Music Consortium I used while researching in 2010 (its "Advanced Search" option superior to the new version of the site that has supplanted it), each participating library not only gave full information on the sheet music in its collection, but also provided digitized reproductions of all sheet music in public domain that could be copied free online. The site's "Advanced Search" allowed one to find songs by author, composer, publisher, title, keyword, date, or any combinations thereof. Using primarily the keyword option for names of southern states, towns, and rivers like Swanee (lots of those!), or things like steamboats, cotton, and barbecue, from home I found and photocopied another roughly 110 pre-1923 Dixie tunes using the Sheet Music Consortium. So I want to thank the great libraries from coast to coast that participate in the Consortium, which significantly augmented my Dixie tunes collection, even though I never walked into any of their actual brick-and-mortar facilities.

There remained the problem of songs still in copyright that I did not find in the John Hay, where I could have any songs regardless of their dates photocopied since they were for research purposes. I went back to the online Consortium with my keyword checklist again, found only thirty such post-1922 songs, and discovered the Lilly Library at Indiana University held all of them. I dashed off an e-mail to the Lilly and got an almost immediate and welcoming reply from the library's reference librarian, David K. Frasier, saying that if I would send to his attention a list of the songs with the full collection information for each he would facilitate my request.

Two other libraries and one person at each, deserve a special singling-out and thank-you, for tracking down one song apiece for me. The online Consortium didn't list any of its participating libraries as having Benny Davis and J. Fred Coots's 1936 "Alabama Barbecue." I discovered on the Internet that the University of Mississippi had a copy and sent off an e-mail query about it. In reply, Greg Johnson, blues curator in Archives and Special Collections at the J. D. Williams Library, sent me a digitized copy of the song, which I readily copied. Also, although I had Johnny Mercer's lyrics for "Dixie Isn't Dixie Any More" from Robert Kimball's book of Mercer's song lyrics (see Bibliography), the entry gave no information on the song's publisher. I therefore sent an e-mail to the special collections department at Georgia State University, which houses a remarkably full collection of Mercer's songs and other papers. I received what I needed from popular music and culture archivist Kevin Fleming, whose reply let me know from the sheet music that the publisher was Robbins Music, and its date of publication 1937, contrary to Kimball stating it was 1939. This experience shows why I prefer working with primary source materials.

Turning now to individuals not connected with institutions, I must begin by thanking, as I have before, Amanda Dupuis, my informal Mac guru, who I swear knows more about Microsoft Word than Bill Gates. Amanda extricated this low-tech person from more than his share of embarrassing to near-fatal computer disasters. Similarly, my nonmusical side thanks concert pianist, professor of music, artist-in-residence at Rhode Island College, and friend Judith Lynn Stillman, for informally serving as my music consultant and playing "on demand" some Dixie tunes I needed to hear but for which I found no recordings on the Internet. Also, my Cajun friend from Lafayette, Louisiana, Michelle Menard, whom in earlier books I thanked for computer assistance and southern cuisine, I now thank for her using her uncanny computer skills to dig up an arcane bit of southern geography that elucidated a line in one Dixie tune I discuss, Alfred Bryan and Harry Tierney's 1916 "She's Dixie All The Time."

As for all my books since *Our Musicals, Ourselves,* intellectual properties attorney Jerry Cohen, a partner in the firm of Boston's Burns & Levinson and a nationally recognized authority in copyright law, was again invaluable in providing me with sound guidelines and strategies for keeping within the bounds of fair use in reprinting song lyrics still in copyright. This allowed me to sidestep costly permission fees and avoid copyright infringement and possible litigation.

I owe particular thanks to four authors whose books provided me with information useful to my preparing this one, taking time from their own pursuits to reply to my e-mailed queries exploring matters their books didn't cover as extensively or specifically as I had hoped they might. Their helpful replies ranged from just one or two return e-mails to, in some cases, a quite lengthy "e-correspondence." I acknowledge the specific contributions of each of them within the text, but they deserve mention here as well, in the only order I deem fair—alphabetical: Philip Furia, professor of creative writing, University of North Carolina Wilmington, and author of *The Poets of Tin Pan Alley;* James N. Gregory, demographer, professor of history, University of Washington, and author of *The Southern Diaspora;* Nina Silber, professor of history, Boston University, and author of *The Romance of Reunion;* and Stephen A. Smith, professor of communications, University of Arkansas, and author of *Myth, Media, and the Southern Mind.* The e-mail correspondence of two other authorities helped me greatly with specific aspects of my research and writing. Fred R. Shapiro, editor of the authoritative *Yale Book of Quotations,* went to some lengths to dig up early newspaper quotations using "Tin Pan Alley" to describe not just New York's popular music publishing trade but things in other cities too, and Michael Lasser, host of public radio's award-winning *Fascinatin' Rhythm: Songs from the Great American Songbook,* used his vast knowledge of popular music to shed some light on sticky matters concerning how to interpret certain lyrics from decades past in their historical contexts.

Moving from the very specific assistance of this group of scholars and other authorities (with more at the end of the Acknowledgments), I swing a full 180° to the intangible support of a wide, far-flung circle of caring relatives and friends who had my back during my multi-year adventure of researching, writing, and revising this book. To begin, there was, as with my previous books, my son, Carson, my daughter-in-law, Dawn, her mother, Sheri Pollock, and *her* mother, Shirley Tepper, as warm an extended family as anyone could wish for, with the added plus for this book that Carson and Dawn enlightened me about some recent rock bands and songs about which, I admit, I knew nothing (largely by choice!). Three students I taught at Brandeis regularly kept in contact from distant corners of the land by e-mail or phone—Helen Lewis in Boston, Adina Conn in Florida, and Laura Lee Bahr in Los Angeles. My dear friend since high school, Deborah Dashow Ruth, a poet and playwright living in Kensington, California, stayed in touch by e-mail about our writing projects and other mutual interests. Closer to home, I want to thank for their continued support two long-time friends in the Boston area whom I see or talk to whenever I can, Jon Goldberg and Claudia Novack, and, in Providence, George Goodwin, Peter Borgemeister, Amy Rittenhouse, my two longest-standing and closest friends, Bob and Elva Mathiesen, and, finally, my loving and lovable long-haired orange cat, Marmalade, whom I can even forgive when he takes it into his furry head to tap-dance on the keyboard when I'm trying to write.

Finally, to rather skew the meaning of the Book of Matthew's "So the last shall be first," in all my Acknowledgments I leave for last the person or persons first in importance for making each book happen. For *Reinventing Dixie* I have a "final four" of indispensable contributors, starting with my editor Rand Dotson at the Louisiana State University Press, whom I thank for believing in this project, being my "point man" for getting the approval of the LSU Publications Committee to have the book accepted for publication, and for working so closely and congenially with me in all we did together.

Al Pavlow, whom I previously acknowledged for his assistance with *The Songs That Fought the War,* is the author/compiler of the self-published twenty yearly volumes of *Hot Charts* for 1940 through 1959, which meticulously detail the popularity of phonograph records month by month for each year of those volumes, as well as his *Big Al Pavlow's The R&B Book: A Disc-History of Rhythm & Blues* (Providence, RI: Music House Publishing, 1983).

Al is a living, breathing encyclopedia of the recording industry and the popular music business generally. He acquired his storehouse of knowledge not academically but "in the trenches," so to speak, as the former owner of a record store first in Central Falls, then later in Providence, Rhode Island, dealing with people in the record trade, and, on his own, collecting records, books, discographies, trade and popular magazines, and other charts and indices of phonograph recording popularity; says Al, "I don't live in a house, I live in a library." And a mighty well organized library it must be. In contrast to Al's help with my book on popular songs associated with World War II in which he taught me volumes about the recording business at the time and how to interpret contemporary popularity charts, for this book Al has been most specifically my discography authority. Whenever I phoned him for the date and/or record label of a Dixie tune record I found on the Internet that lacked such information or, worse yet, had erroneous information—whether I reached Al or left a message on his voice mail with what I was looking for—within hours he invariably called me back with the accurate, authentic data I needed. There's some irony in this since, as near one another as we live, Al shared all his knowledge for both books by phone, until to repay him in some small way I finally took him to lunch in 2012 and we chatted for hours face to face. Beyond just providing factual discographic information for *Reinventing Dixie,* Al taught me to appreciate the talents of some of the early recording artists whose records of Dixie tunes I found on the Internet, including Henry Burr, Ada Jones, Vernon Dalhart (both before and after he turned to country music), Marion Harris (who sounds like an early Ethel Merman), Arthur Collins and his frequent comic duet partner Byron G. Harlan, the Peerless Quartet, and the American Quartet, whose lead tenor Billy Murray was also one of the early twentieth century's most popular solo recording artists, and whose tenor voice is so distinctive that, thanks to Al, I learned to identify his singing as easily as I can recognize Bing Crosby. My appreciation again goes to Al Pavlow, not just for materially supporting this book but for enriching my awareness of the artists who brought Dixie tunes to life via recorded sound.

My continuing friend and former colleague at Brandeis, professor of American studies Stephen J. Whitfield, also did much to help make this book happen, as he has done before just by his support and enthusiasm for my projects. During my research and writing, Steve and I met about quarterly for lunch, talking as much as eating, brainstorming about Tin Pan Alley, Dixie, and their intersections, with Steve often asking me pointed, useful questions about just what I was doing. It was Steve who recommended James Gregory's book on migrations from the South mentioned above and also advised that I e-mail Fred Shapiro about Tin Pan Alley—both very fruitful suggestions. Most materially, Steve photocopied for me his article about Jewish songwriters of southern songs, "Is It True What They Sing About Dixie?" (see Bibliography). This article proved to be the jumping-off point for some ideas of my own in *Reinventing Dixie,* even though I pointed out to Steve a factual error in his piece, which he took with his usual good humor, just as I had done when he found a gaffe of mine in *The Songs That Fought the War* despite a glowing review he wrote of it for a French historical journal. But far and away, the most singular thing Steve did for me occurred precisely on September 22, 2010, when I was still in the early stages of my research. I admit that going into this project I knew more than my share about popular music but absolutely nothing about southern studies, so when confronted with the question of where barely high school–educated early Tin Pan Alley songwriters came up with the detailed southern imagery for their lyrics, I was stumped. I contacted colleagues and friends in the music and American studies departments at both Brown and Brandeis, all to no avail, until I e-mailed Steve. Steve was stumped too, but he sent me an e-mail introduction to a southern studies specialist friend of his, and that introduction was a game-changer for the entire book.

The man Steve introduced me to wasn't just *a* southern studies specialist, but the *best*—John Shelton Reed, professor emeritus from the University of North Carolina, founder of the journal *Southern Cultures,* and author of numerous books and articles in the field of southern studies (and barbecue). Within two days of my e-mailing him, Professor Reed (soon to be John) wrote me a thoughtful reply. From the single answer to that one still not wholly answered query, John has remained my unflagging southern studies consultant, "walking bibliography," and delightfully humorous commentator, as well as an enthusiastic booster of my work, yet still a critic when criticism is due. More than once while I was writing and testing out ideas on him, John saved my (fill in whatever body part you like) with words like—my paraphrase—"Don't you *dare* write that, or you're gonna look mighty foolish, sir." Over the course of my research and writing, John was virtually my collaborator, for without his knowledge of the South and his depth of wisdom on how to treat the issues I deal with in this book, I fear I would still be seeking a path to enlightenment in unfamiliar territory. Small wonder I dedicated *Reinventing Dixie* to John Shelton Reed, since I don't exaggerate when I say I couldn't have written this study of Tin Pan Alley's Dixie songs without him. I can only add that what I'm most grateful for are, first, this distinguished scholar's belief in my project and its value for the fields of popular music and southern studies, and second, the fact that, though my entire acquaintance with John, as of this writing, has been only via hundreds of e-mails, he has made me feel he's a friend I've known all my life. Thanks, John.

Reinventing Dixie

PROLOGUE
Why Dixie?

In 1898 the yet unknown 26-year-old composer Harry Von Tilzer and 24-year-old lyricist Andrew B. Sterling wrote a typical Victorian/American sob-ballad, "My Old New Hampshire Home." In the song a young man bids a temporary farewell to his young virginal sweetheart, only to find on his return that in his absence she has died—one in a legion of similar tearjerkers in the late nineteenth century that spilled over into the early twentieth. Von Tilzer and Sterling thought themselves lucky to sell the piece outright to New York publisher Wm. C. Dunn & Co. for the less than princely sum of $15.00. In no time their song's sheet music was selling like proverbial hotcakes, along with phonograph records (these had become commercially available in 1897), notably, a Columbia disc by the popular Irish tenor George J. Gaskin. The sheet music of "My Old New Hampshire Home" sold over two million copies, and it was the largest-selling recording of 1898–1899. Yet Von Tilzer and Sterling got little of what should have accrued to them. In 1899, out of shrewd business sense, the publishers Shapiro and Bernstein bought out Dunn, mostly for the rights to "My Old New Hampshire Home," paid Von Tilzer and Sterling $4,000 in royalties, and made Von Tilzer a partner in the firm, now called Shapiro, Bernstein & Von Tilzer. Sterling came along as a lyricist in Shapiro and Bernstein's "stable" of writers.

Despite "New Hampshire" catching fire with the public, it didn't spark a blaze of more songs with New England settings or stories. But the same year it took off, publishers in what would come to be called Tin Pan Alley (see Chapter 1) produced at least three songs about the South; in 1899, eleven; six in 1900; and between 1901 and 1909, from ten to fifteen each year. Then in 1910 came twenty-three songs about Dixie, and the numbers stayed in the twenties or higher till 1928, only starting downward during the Great Depression in the early '30s and finally fading away in 1958.

1

Some words of explanation: I said "at least" just above regarding the numbers of Dixie tunes because I found and photocopied 1,079 of them written and published by Tin Pan Alley songwriters and publishers between 1898 and 1958 in the library archives of sheet music of American popular song that I listed in the Preface and Acknowledgments—plus one unpublished song I located only on a phonograph recording. Yet there may be even more since even the best libraries do not consciously build collections of popular music on *any* theme or topic; rather, they take individual songs or collections that are donated to them on a random, haphazard basis. This was borne out as I went through microfilms of *Variety* and *Billboard* (early on called *The Billboard,* but for convenience I use the trade paper's modern name), just between 1910 and 1932—the heyday of Dixie tunes. I found in publishers' ads and popularity charts another 128 titles of songs for which I never turned up sheet music. Yet this doesn't mean they don't exist; some ads name the songwriters, and some of these tunes are mentioned in places like the song lists for writers on the Songwriters Hall of Fame website, a usually, though not always, reliable source of information. I decided, however, that since I already had over a thousand southern songs to work with in discussing the Alley's sixty-year output of southern songs, the time spent trying to find two or three more would be an exercise in diminishing returns and would not change my conclusions much if at all. So when in this book I refer to, say, Irving Berlin's 19 Dixie tunes or the roughly 225 pieces about someone traveling back to the South, those numbers refer *only* to songs for which the concrete evidence of the sheet music exists in library repositories and of which I have photocopies.

Just as "My Old New Hampshire Home" didn't raise a public hue and cry for more songs about New England (see Jones, "Sing Two Songs"), I also found that no other regions of the United States inspired songwriters or their publishers to produce anywhere near the number of songs as those about Dixie. For a while I kept a list for each region, but once I'd gotten through song titles beginning with the letter "I," I found that the Midwest had 32 (largely because of all the tunes about Chicago), whereas at that point in the alphabet the South already had 445! Curiously, of all geographic areas the runner-up to Dixie was—Ireland! So, the question is: "Why Dixie?"

There are three approaches to this question, all fairly speculative: from the perspective of the music or content (theme, story, setting, and/or imagery) of the songs themselves; from the perspective of the songwriters; and from the perspective of publishers and audiences, or, in other words, the commercial perspective. Trying to account for the popularity of Dixie tunes on the basis of their music is the riskiest approach, since they shared the same musical styles with other songs of their day, and they lasted for so many years that their musical styles shifted over time. For example, when Dixie tunes first emerged in 1898 and ragtime was in vogue, no songs about the South published in the next few years were in ragtime, but by and large were sentimental ballads in waltz time and other American/Victorian musical modes. Only around 1910 did ragtime Dixie tunes begin to appear, and only in 1911 was the term first used in Dixie song titles with Irving Berlin's "Alexander's Ragtime Band" (Ted Snyder, 1911) and "That Carolina Rag" with lyrics by Maurice Burkhart and Jack Coogan and music by that one-name wonder, Violinsky (Chicago: Will Rossiter, 1911). So the ragtime rage of the first half-decade of the twentieth century had nothing to do with the initial popularity of Dixie songs.

Looking at the songs' themes, stories, and especially their settings and imagery is a far safer bet for examining the immediate popularity of Dixie tunes when they first came on the market. During their first five years (1898 through 1902), professional popular song publishers in New York, Chicago, and Milwaukee (home base of the eminent Charles K. Harris, lyricist and composer of the runaway hit "After The Ball," who would later move his offices to New York) published forty Dixie tunes *in toto,* and their subject matter ranged widely. Only some of the topics or story lines, such as traveling home to Dixie (five of these), a northern boy marrying a southern girl (three), the singer (white or black) idealizing his Southern Belle (the largest group with nine), or one remarkable descriptive song in 1902 that virtually encapsulates the vision of an idyllic South, are totally tied to Dixie. That song, now long forgotten, is "Under Southern Skies (A Song Of The South)" with words by Al Trahern and music by Lee Orean Smith (Vandersloot Music Co., 1902), from a play of the same name. The first verse and chorus are a virtual microcosm of what has come to be called the Moonlight and Magnolias Myth of the South, to which we shall often return (see, especially, Chapter 9):

> The sweet magnolias are in bloom, the fields are white as snow,
> The air is filled with rare perfume, the sky is all aglow,
> Far o'er the hills the setting sun, is sinking bright and clear,

The darkies gather round and hum the songs they love to hear,
Beneath the shadow of the pines, a lad of seventeen,
Is swinging in the ivy vines beside his ideal queen.
He whispers to her soft and low, she timidly replies,
"I will always love you dear, under southern skies."

You'll hear the darkies singing,
The songs they love the best,
You'll hear the banjos ringing,
While the old folks rest.
The pickaninnies dancing,
To see who'll win the prize,
In the evening by the moonlight,
Under southern skies.

I must make it clear that the thoroughly romantic and idyllic tone of this lyric precludes "darkies" and "pickaninnies" from being pejorative terms for African Americans. This is true both for this song as well as subsequent Dixie tunes. These terms should not be considered politically incorrect in the contexts in which I use them throughout this book. In my eyes these people of color were as much an image of the idealized South for the songwriters as were the Southern Belles and Gentlemen who also populated the virtually mythic, idyllic Dixieland the lyricists were writing about and glorifying. To refer to the darkies in the majority of the songs as blacks would do a disservice to the historical authenticity of Alley songwriting. By contrast, when I treat the few realistic songs about the South, including those with three-dimensional black personae singing them (such as "Ol' Man River"), not to mention the Alley's songwriters who were persons of color, I refer to them as African Americans or blacks. I consider these matters at greater length when discussing the nature and significance of the idealized, mythic South that permeates most of the Alley's songs about Dixie, as well as the counterbalance of the small body of realistic songs about the region.

To return to the themes and subjects in the first five years of Dixie tunes, aside from those *directly* tied to the South noted above, the others could have been rooted in any region of the country or none in particular, like nostalgia for one's childhood home (four), a boy wooing and wedding his sweetheart

(three), homesickness (three), love songs to the singer's actual or desired beloved (three), and six sob-ballads of virginal young women dying between
the time their beaus had to go away for a while and their return to marry
them. Clearly, then, it was not the subjects, themes, or scenarios of the songs
alone that first drew very early twentieth-century audiences to Dixie tunes,
but something else about the lyrics. At least that's my best guess.

That something was the atmosphere created by the words in those forty
songs, words that shaped the sights and sounds of a place exotically distant
from the mostly urban northern songwriters who wrote them and their mostly
urban northern listeners, who bought their sheet music and phonograph records in the early years of the twentieth century. Without citing all of the more
than fifty such images and phrases evoking the South that I found in the first
five years of Dixie tunes (1898–1902), what follows is a representative list of
them, which deliberately includes some similar ones to show how often key
images were repeated: "where the meadow grass is blue"; "where the Southern Sun is shining"; "I hear the happy darkies singing"; "beneath the sunny
Southern sky"; "sunny Tennessee"; "far across the fields of cotton"; "the Mobile waters gently glide"; "we'd listen to those darkies sing in chorus gay and
light"; "among the Southern pines"; "the old cane brake"; "where the sweet
magnolias bloom"; "where the grass is always blue"; "the sun that's ever shining"; "tall palmettos"; "the mockingbirds are singing sweet and gay"; "the
whippoorwill's soft whistle thru' the night air"; "my old plantation home";
"where the cotton blossoms grow"; "a field of snowy white"; "hear the darkies
singing soft and low"; "beneath the southern skies"; "in that sunny land call'd
Dixie"; "where the skies are ever fair"; "the moon is gently stealing from
behind the southern hills"; "the mockingbird does sing"; "'midst the sugar
cane and corn"; "stars are ever shining"; "by the Suwannee river where orange blossoms bloom"; "magnolia's sweet perfume"; "'neath the pines in dear
old Dixie"; "I hear the darkies croon"; "beneath the Southern moon"; "the
honeysuckle breathes its rare perfume"; "hear the darkies singing gaily"; "my
dear old southern home"; "the sweet magnolias are in bloom"; "the fields are
white as snow"; "you'll hear the banjos ringing"; "when the moon is brightly
shining, in sunny Tennessee [Really? Both at once?]"; "when the fields are
white with cotton"; and "'neath the moon's fair light." Then just the twelve
Dixie tunes of 1903 overflowed with another thirty-one such phrases, adding into the mix for the first time such iconic southern images as "on a cot-

ton steamer [boat]"; "moonlight on the Mississippi"; "hear the old steamboat a-blowing"; "where the bayou breezes blow"; "where the palm trees bend and sway"; "upon the Mississippi shore"; and "when it's moonlight on the levee." These frequently used images built up an ever-fuller picture of an idyllic South during the first decade of twentieth-century Dixie songwriting.

Such imagery depicts a world apart from the cold, industrialized urban North of the songs' creators and their audiences, so it's no wonder Dixie tunes appealed to listeners' fancies for a more bucolic life and a warmer place to live it in. Or, as Isaac Goldberg put it in his 1930 book on Tin Pan Alley, "Paradise is never where we are. The South has become our Never-never Land—the symbol of the land where the lotus blooms and dreams come true" (Goldberg 46).

Such images of a Golden Land in the Dixie tunes written in the first decade of the twentieth century may have played a role in the proliferation of southern songs when seen from the perspective of at least some songwriters who wrote them. In a thoughtful article on the Jewish contribution to Dixie tunes through 1936, Stephen J. Whitfield soundly suggests that in the early decades of the century so many Jewish lyricists wrote of the South, and especially about traveling home to family in a bucolic setting, because "the pastoral ideal . . . was historically so bewitching" to young immigrants or sons of immigrants who had mostly left shtetls in agrarian eastern Europe for the crowded Lower East Side of New York City (Whitfield 17). Whitfield goes on to say that

> in the Tin Pan Alley studios . . . the South remained handy as a fantasy of a social order that immigrant songwriters never knew and could easily sentimentalize; in no way could the Gowanus Canal be made as enchanting as the Suwannee River. Historians should not find it too much of a stretch to grasp why the idea of the South seemed so alluring to songwriters who were immigrants or the sons of immigrants, why it conjured up a yearning among Jews to return to a comforting home. Left only with legs after centuries of exile, here was a way to establish roots. These craftsmen might pretend that life could be unbroken, love could be unconditional, families protected and united. (17–18)

Whitfield's remarks are useful for explaining the increase in Dixie tunes by Jewish songwriters—but only starting around 1910. Though New York publishers combined to produce 134 southern songs between 1898 and 1909, their lyrics were almost all by non-Jews. In my database for those years, only seven lyricists are positively identifiable as Jewish, and of those only Charles K. Harris and Charles Horwitz wrote more than one song apiece. In addition to them, the list includes Gus Edwards (born Gus Simon in Germany), Robert Levenson, Jerome Kern (yes, he wrote lyrics early on), Joe Schwab, and Al Jolson. Further, only Edwards and Jolson can be described as "immigrants or sons of immigrants." So, although Jewish lyricists contributed greatly to the proliferation of Dixie tunes, most were relatively late bloomers, only getting into the act during the 'teens of the twentieth century.

When these second-decade Jewish songsmiths *did* get started, they didn't do so just to express their personal fantasies of returning to a congenial family and agrarian homeland. Let's face it, these guys, like all popular songwriters of the day, weren't lyric poets like Keats and Shelley warbling their odes to the woodland wild. Nosiree, they were commercial hacks, cranking out buckets of songs with their composing partners just to make a few bucks (and hopefully more than a few). This motive is of prime consideration for understanding the huge proliferation of Dixie tunes from the perspective of songwriters, Jewish or otherwise. Jack Yellen (born in Poland), one of the Jewish sons of immigrants and a prolific writer of Dixie tunes and other songs, who came to the United States in the early 'teens as did Irving Berlin (born in Russia) and L. Wolfe Gilbert (born in Ukraine), later in life expressed why so many young lyricists got on the southern song bandwagon, apparently influenced by tunes from the first decade of the century: "Dixie songs were then the craze, and like all other writers of our limited talents . . . [ellipsis in Cox's text] we started out by imitating" (Yellen, Reminiscences of Jack Yellen, Columbia University Oral History Collection, 1958, quoted in Cox 9). When these young songwriters saw their Dixie tunes were catching on, they naturally kept writing more of them. From the perspective of the men (and some women) who wrote the lyrics, Yellen's brief remark is almost enough to explain the torrent of 392 Dixie tunes that burst from creative Alley minds in the years between 1910 and 1919. The numbers kept increasing throughout the 1920s.

Yet there were more pragmatic reasons to write southern songs than mere imitation of what others had done or were doing. Gus Kahn, author of "Carolina In The Morning," suggested there were so many Dixie tunes "because Southern place-and-State names lent themselves to rhyming" (Goldberg 46).

Two more reasons were well expressed in the 1926 *Billboard* article "Senti-mental Songs Live Longest," by L. Wolfe "Wolfie" Gilbert, writer of many southern songs, including the lyrics to the early hit "Waiting For The Robert E. Lee" (1912) and both the words and music of the later smash "Down Yon-der" (1921). Some of what he says reads like advice to young or prospective songwriters, and while he doesn't directly allude to Dixie-tune-making, his points apply to that branch of the popular music craft: "Personally, I prefer to write heart-interest [i.e., sentimental] ballads, but after all is said and done, a professional songwriter has little to say in the matter, for if he wants to keep in the front line and earn a livelihood he must follow the style of songs that please the public" (Gilbert 78). Ergo, as long as Dixie tunes are in vogue, write 'em! Wolfie maintains that songwriters must keep an eye out for what's popular on the sheet music market, since "Approximately 95% of popular music is purchased by or for young women, hence when a professional song-writer starts to write a song he consciously or unconsciously keeps before him the likes and dislikes of young women" (78). On top of songwriting, Wolfie became a publisher, so such advice makes a good segue to looking at prolifer-ating Dixie tunes from the perspective of publishers and audiences.

About a third of the way through his book, which generally exudes a love for Tin Pan Alley, Isaac Goldberg writes with sadness, bitterness, almost ran-cor, of the commercialism of the popular song industry: "It does not mean what it says or sings. It is the paradise of the Pseudo. Songs are not made, primarily, to sing; they are made to sell. Happy? Sad? Profit is the wind that fills the sail and points the weathervane. In the Alley, song becomes synthetic; one weeps, one laughs, at so many percent" (Goldberg 140). Yet closer to the book's end, Goldberg modifies his view of the trade to say something positive about its "product": "The Alley is an industry, tainted by commercialism and insincerity. In this respect it differs not a jot or tittle from other industries the world over. . . . And [yet] one thing the Alley achieves that has yet to be paral-leled by the humorless 'art' songs of the conservatories: it manages, stammer-ingly yet at times inimitably, to speak the yearnings, the sorrows and the joys of a new, an emergent folk, different from any other people in the world" (320).

Sixty years later, in *The Poets of Tin Pan Alley*, Philip Furia encapsulated Goldberg's description of the Alley with total objectivity and not a shred of pejorative comment or regret for its practices: "One of the earliest indus-tries geared to standardization and mass marketing, Tin Pan Alley quickly evolved a rigid formula for popular songs" (Furia 13). This formula, which came along later than the early period of Dixie tunes, is the AABA (stanza-stanza-bridge *or* release-stanza) structure for the chorus of almost all songs from the late 'teens through the 1940s. But even before then publishers imposed another formula for their writers to follow.

From the beginning there always were freelance popular tunesmiths. But alongside them, the major publishers—M. Witmark & Sons; Jerome H. Remick & Co.; Waterson, Berlin & Snyder; Shapiro, Bernstein & Co.; Leo Feist; and others—had in their offices "stables" of staff composers and lyricists who wrote songs to be published exclusively by the companies they worked for. Often publishers' ads in *Variety* and *Billboard* proudly listed the creative talent in respective stables and even occasionally proclaimed bragging rights that a certain lyricist or composer now worked for a certain firm. Since these stables of writers wrote for particular publishers, their employers could dictate the kinds of songs they wanted them to write. Throughout the long history of the Alley, most of those songs, as Furia reiterates frequently, were generic love songs, most of which weren't tied to anything topical or geographical, except for such occasional things as the spate of Hawaiian and other South Sea ballads just before and during the early 'teens. The simple reason that love songs always dominated the output of the Alley is that love songs are largely what the sheet music and record–buying public bought the most of. The one great and long-lasting sixty-year exception to this is, of course, the Alley's tremendous output of Dixie tunes. Small wonder, with shrewd and savvy publishers keeping their eyes on how southern songs were continually becoming hits or at least selling well enough to encourage their stables to keep cranking out yet more. The publishers' formula was simplicity itself: as long as consumers kept buying Dixie tunes, Tin Pan Alley kept writing and marketing them. *That's* what accounts for proliferating Dixie tunes from their publishers' perspective.

What accounts for it from the audience standpoint is more problematic and conjectural. One clue to the songs' decades-long popularity is the same as something already mentioned that impelled at least some songwriters to keep writing southern songs—the images of a land more tranquil than the overcrowded, industrialized northern cities in which most of the hearers and buyers of those songs lived. In other words, the songs' content gave their listeners some escape from the worst elements of modernity, if but a fleeting one. Another aspect of the theme or storyline of Dixie tunes was an even more powerful draw for their longevity and virtually universal popularity across America. Of the 1,079 catalogued southern songs written and published between 1898 and 1958, those about homesickness, traveling home, or nostalgia for one's childhood home comprise 491 or 45.5 percent of them, and as Jack Yellen said in his reminiscences, "Nostalgia gives a song a quality that nothing else can give it" (Yellen 24; quoted in Cox 32). Add to these 110 songs in which the singer idealizes the South or expresses love for a special spot in Dixie, and the grand total of "homing" songs rises to 601, or 56 percent of the documented Dixie tunes.

In his Stephen Foster biography with the wonderful title *Doo-Dah!,* Ken Emerson made an observation about homesickness with respect to "Old Folks At Home," which Foster wrote in 1851: "One reviewer called the 'homely tune' a 'catching, melodic *itch* of the time' . . . and nearly everyone scratched, be they Irish or German immigrants feeling homesick for the old country, frontiersmen or forty-niners pining for the folks they had left behind in the East or African Americans forcibly separated from their birthplaces and families. 'Old Folks at Home' was all things to all people" (Emerson 182). So too, songs like "Swanee" (1919), "Carolina In The Morning" (1922), "Alabamy Bound" (1925), "Georgia On My Mind" (1930), and "Chattanooga Choo Choo" (1941) evoked feelings of homesickness in Americans regardless of where they were born, where they were when they heard the tune, or where they were trying to get back to, even though all the songs were specifically about Dixie.

Such anecdotal evidence is nice, but I wanted something more solid to explain the proliferation of Dixie tunes from the audience perspective. I stumbled on it inadvertently while doing collateral reading in preparation for writing this book. One book that seemed from its title to be of some use was the late Jack Temple Kirby's 1978 *Media-Made Dixie: The South in the American Imagination.* As it turned out, it wasn't. The media Kirby focused on were almost entirely film and literature, with just a few pages on country music and a single glance at Tin Pan Alley, likening it to the country music of the 1930s as being "simply and properly nonintellectual" (90). Yet one statement of Kirby's early in the book startled my mind into churning about just when Dixie tunes were most popular, which in turn led me to even more speculative thoughts on matters of demographics and song popularity. Following a lengthy chapter on D. W. Griffith's epic (and racist) silent film *The Birth of a Nation* and his other shorter films about the South, Kirby writes that after those motion picture successes "the South began to suffer the indignity of silence. From 1916 through 1928, not a single book on a southern subject appeared on annual best seller lists. Virtually no notable film concerned the region either—except Buster Keaton's hilarious (if silent) 1926 classic, *The General*. . . . It was a cynical age" (Kirby 44). Those words had me leaping for my database of Dixie tunes where I found, to my delight and a bit of surprise, that the inclusive thirteen years of 1916 through 1928 of Kirby's "cynical age" had produced 519 Alley southern songs, or 48 percent of all those created in its sixty years of spinning out such tunes. It's a safe bet the hearers and buyers of the sheet music and records of those songs totaled more people than all the audiences for *The Birth of a Nation* and the readers of novels set in the South through those dates. Moreover, the Alley's songs weren't cynical, but idyllic portraits of an idealized South. With the almost single exception of John Shelton Reed, Kirby was just one of many southern studies scholars who have erred by ignoring the presence and power of the Alley in shaping Americans' imaginative picture of Dixie during the first half of the twentieth century. (I hardly dare mention in the same breath Reed and Professor Karen L. Cox, whose chapter "Dixie in Popular Song," in *Dreaming of Dixie* [2011], is so littered with misstatements and factual errors as to render it almost useless as a serious treatment of the subject.)

Still, what to make of the 519 Dixie tunes between 1916 and 1928? Since so many of the songs had as their primary emphasis homesickness and its cognates, possibly population shifts out of the South helped account for both the songs' number and success. I was already familiar with the Great Migration of blacks from the South that began during World War I; however, blacks, whether in the North or South, were not the primary buyers of Dixie tunes. But I knew nothing of the southern white exodus that began around the same time except for the single remark in *1001 Things Everyone Should Know About the South* by John Shelton Reed and Dale Volberg Reed that "over the next decades more whites than blacks left the South" (109), so I consulted demographer James N. Gregory's 2005 *The Southern Diaspora: How the Great Migrations of Black and White Southerners Transformed America*. During what Gregory labels the "first phase" of white migration "thanks to the job opportunities of World War I. . . . By 1920, southerners living outside their home region numbered more than 2.7 million and in 1930 more than 4 million" (Gregory 12). These years nearly embraced those of the rush of 519 Dixie tunes between 1916 and 1928. Gregory further points out that "war production created in excess of 3 million new manufacturing jobs while immigration [from abroad] dropped from 1.2 million in 1914 to only 110,000 in 1918," helping account for the white and black exodus from the South, since "Newspapers helped spread the word that there were jobs with high wages in the northern industrial workforce" (24). On top of "young people with blue-collar skills . . . following industrial pathways that led out of the South" (26), "in this first phase were southern whites with money, special ambitions, and education. They included salesmen who thought that Chicago, Detroit, or New York were the right markets for their skills and professionals who jumped at the chance to work for a big firm in a big city" (27).

Gregory's remarks about the number and nature of the former southern whites now in the North, especially in terms of the kinds of employment they had, and, one might assume, their disposable income, led me to think there might have been a correlation between the terrific outrush of the Alley's Dixie tunes, especially of the homesick type, and this newly transplanted market for such songs. So I sought the opinion of Professor Gregory, a professional demographer. The day after I e-mailed him, I received a kind though not unexpectedly cautious reply that read in part, "I'd guess that migrating southerners were not a critical commercial audience for or inspiration for the homesick songs of the 1920s. White migrants remained pretty invisible in the North until the 1930s" (Gregory e-mail to the author, October 29, 2010). I would agree that from our hindsight of decades later the southern migrants probably do seem "invisible," although I wonder about those in the business and professional classes. And I have a hunch that to the sharp eyes and shrewd minds of those canny creatures, the Alley music publishers of the late 'teens and '20s, they were anything but. Leaving aside publishers like Harry Von Tilzer, Irving Berlin, and Jack Yellen who began as songwriters and continued to be songwriters even after they entered the publishing game (always with a businessman as an associate), most of the Alley's big-time publishers were first and foremost *businessmen,* many of whom started out in other trades before publishing songs. Edward B. Marks was a notions salesman; Jerome H. Remick, a graduate of the Detroit Business University, ran a lumber firm in that city; and Leo Feist was the sales manager of a corset company, to name three. These men and other Alley publishers had to keep a lookout on the market for whatever they were selling, be it cosmetics, corsets, or sheet music. So if during and after World War I, the papers were full of ads urging southerners to come north for work, Alley publishers would have seen or gotten wind of those ads and capitalized on the increased market potential for their sheet music sales, with a special eye to homesickness Dixie tunes. I'm sure the more affluent migratory southerners in business and the professions Gregory writes of didn't stay invisible for long, so there's a chance the first phase of the white migration helped explain the huge swell in Dixie tunes between World War I and the year prior to the Crash of '29.

A few southerners, white *and* black, came north to the Alley itself, both as songsmiths and as publishers: more about them and the other Alleymen in Chapter 1. But for now . . .

Why Not Dixie?

No, this sub-heading isn't intended to balance the first section by discussing what *deterred* the proliferation and popularity of Dixie tunes during their sixty-year output from the Alley, since apparently there were few deterrents until the 1940s and '50s. Instead, this section of the Prologue discusses my reasoning for two intentional omissions from "my" Dixie. So here come two reasons why some songs aren't in this book about the Alley's Dixie tunes.

The first is purely geographical and unlikely to be too controversial. While a great number of Dixie tunes are geographically generic, making reference to the South in general, an equally large or larger number are about a specific state, city, or locale like the Swanee River or Shenandoah Valley. Accordingly, I confronted the question of precisely which states to include from among those that Alley songwriters wrote about. Naturally, I began with the eleven states that comprised the Confederate States of America, but—and here is my big omission—I dropped Texas even though it had been in the Confederacy. Alley songs about Texas didn't read or sound southern. They all had an Old West look and feel to them, quite different from the "Moonlight and Magnolias" quality of the idyllic South of true Dixie tunes. All, that is, but one, which I do include, "A Boy From Texas—A Girl From Tennessee," with words and music by Joe McCarthy Jr., Jack Segal, and John Benson Brooks

(Shapiro, Bernstein, 1948), with the lead recording by Nat "King" Cole. But you can bet if the song had been "A Boy From Texas—A Girl From Michigan" it wouldn't have made the cut! Not in *my* Dixie.

On the other hand, though Kentucky was never a Confederate state, it was southern for Stephen Foster, for the Alleymen, and it is for me, along with West Virginia, which didn't exist as a state during the Civil War but was a part of Virginia. As for Maryland, which like Kentucky remained part of the Union during the War between the States even though it was a slave state, the tiny number of Tin Pan Alley songs about it (mostly about the high-steppin' town of Baltimore) have so little of a southern feel to them that I have omitted Maryland along with Texas from my Dixie mix.

Second, I decided to omit from my discussion of Dixie tunes the entire genre known as coon songs even though some readers might object to this. And note that I do not put coon songs within quotation marks as some writers do because coon songs were what they were unabashedly called when they were written and performed, and to call attention to them within quotation marks is, as I see it, squeamish and dishonest.

For readers unfamiliar with the term or the phenomenon, coon songs—written by both blacks and whites—had their heyday on the vaudeville stages of the Gay Nineties and continued to be performed, though with waning popularity, in those venues during the first two decades of the twentieth century. They were vehicles for a solo performer (less often a duet), sometimes a man, but more often a voluptuous woman, black or white with an hourglass figure, who came to be called a "coon shouter," epitomized by white May Irwin, who sometimes performed in blackface and was considered the finest coon shouter of them all. Even the great (or notorious, depending on your point of view) Lillian Russell occasionally got into the coon shouting act. How coon shouters got that moniker was probably from the musical quality of coon songs themselves, which "possessed a strong beat and marked syncopations, [were] in a quick tempo, and demanded a loud robust delivery" (Ewen 102).

The personae of the characters singing and depicted in coon songs, and these songs' content, point of view, and above all, their tone, are the reasons I have left them out of this book on Dixie tunes. But before turning to those intrinsic reasons, another reason for their omission here is simply that coon songs have already been treated fully and intelligently elsewhere, as in the article by James H. Dorman and the book by Lynn Abbott and Doug Seroff (see Bibliography).

The nature of coon songs says they just don't belong in a treatment of Alley tunes glorifying and idealizing Dixie. The kinds of African Americans who are the personae singing a coon song or are the characters being described by a coon shouter are almost never the happy southern darkies who populate Dixie tunes and who were described earlier in this Prologue. Rather, they are almost always citified northern blacks, the men typically being gamblers, con men, and, primarily, profligate womanizers or at least two-timers; and the women, gold diggers in metropolitan Darktowns epitomized by the singer of black songwriter Ernest Hogan's coon song classic, "All Coons Look Alike To Me" (M. Witmark, 1896), who can only see the color of her admirers' money, not distinguish their faces.

To be sure I was on solid ground, I sought some "second opinions" on coon songs' exclusion, first from Philip Furia, a fine scholar of American popular music. I laid out my reasons for wanting to omit coon songs, stating I would explain those reasons in a long paragraph (which has become several paragraphs). Phil replied, in part, "If it's a good paragraph, you can get by with leaving 'coon songs' out" (Furia e-mail to the author, July 31, 2011).

The best argument for keeping coon songs out of the book is the *tone* of their content. Even in comic Dixie tunes in which the protagonist is a particularly skillful ladies' man—such as Jack Yellen and Milton Ager's "Lovin' Sam (The Sheik Of Alabam')" (Ager, Yellen & Bornstein, 1922)—and the "hero" just happens to be a southern darky, the character is being comically *idealized* for his prowess in his ways with the ladies. In other Dixie tunes where happy darkies appear, they are treated with respect, are not caricatured, and absolutely are never the object of racial derision. These qualities of the Alley's southern songs set them entirely apart from the caricatured quality of the characters and racist tone of coon songs. Furia uses the terms "racist," "caricature," and "caricatured" a total of nine times in describing coon songs in his discussion of them on pages 26 through 29 of *The Poets of Tin Pan Alley*. When I pointed this out to him, Phil replied, "Okay, I'm not going to argue with my own text" (Furia e-mail to the author, August 4, 2011). So ended the question of whether coon songs should be omitted here as far as Philip Furia was concerned.

Thinking I should also get an opinion from the southern studies side of things, I presented my arguments for leaving out coon songs to my guide in all things southern, John Shelton Reed. My e-mail coon song exchange with John was much briefer than that with Phil Furia. I just laid out my rationale for wanting to leave coon songs out of the book, and, typically, John's reply embodied not just his wisdom but his succinctness and wry, sly humor as well: "I'd do whatever I had to do to leave them out. You'll be criticized for it, but that's a small price to pay for the relief of not having to deal with them" (Reed e-mail to the author, August 5, 2011).

For me that was the final nail in the coffin for coon songs in this book. Except perhaps for minimal references to them in order to point out why a particular Dixie tune is *not* one, the subject of coon songs is, then, dead and buried. Now we can get on to what *is* in the book, starting with who wrote all those Tin Pan Alley songs of the South.

THE ALLEY AND ITS DENIZENS

In many ways this book is about myths. That's myths *plural,* not just *one* myth, as might be expected in a look at Americans' perception of the South in the first half of the twentieth century as filtered through popular music. The book looks at yet other myths, including earlier ones about the South created by southerners in the nineteenth century, specifically the Plantation (a.k.a. Old South) Myth before the Civil War and the Lost Cause Myth after the Confederacy was defeated (see especially Chapter 8). Other myths surrounded the popular song industry, the makers of those songs, and the geographic hub where many of those songs were published in the early days. Portions of one of these myths remain intact, but I will debunk considerable parts of it, after which I will debunk a second widely held myth wholesale.

A Local Habitation and a Name

What became known as Tin Pan Alley was never one fixed locale. The popular music publishing industry was analogous to Nathan Detroit's legendary "oldest established, permanent, floating crap game" in the musical *Guys and Dolls,* with firms moving their offices to various spots in New York City most advantageous to their trade. The first significant gaggle of publishers clustered around Union Square on East 14th Street near Tony Pastor's music hall in the 1880s to take advantage of peddling their songs to singers performing there and in other nearby vaudeville houses. Publishers' offices often followed the theatres, accounting for their gradual movement uptown over time. Around the turn of the twentieth century (hereafter to be called just the turn of the century), the favored locale for several major firms (though with little connection to the city's theatrical life) became West 28th Street between

Broadway and 6th Avenue. The publishers moved on later, but here the myth of Tin Pan Alley's naming occurred.

Precisely when the naming legend began to circulate isn't known, but what is known is when that single block of West 28th Street began to be familiarly called Tin Pan Alley. According to Fred R. Shapiro, editor of the authoritative *Yale Book of Quotations,* other than a quite nonmusical reference to "a rumpus among a number of women in Tin Pan Alley . . . [which] branches off from Wallace Street" in New Haven, mentioned by that city's *Evening Register* on August 8, 1890 (e-mail to me on September 6, 2011), the first known print mention of the Alley as New York City's "publisher's row" appeared on page 4M of the Metropolitan section in the Sunday edition of the *New York World* on May 3, 1903, in a piece by Roy L. McCardell titled "A Visit to 'Tin Pan Alley,' Where the Popular Songs Come From" (e-mail of July 27, 2011). McCardell first says that the Alley "Gets Its Name from the Jangling of Pianos That Are Banged and Rattled There Day and Night as New Songs are Being 'Tried On.'" Two short paragraphs later the writer reiterates his point with little variation or elaboration: "It gets its name from the tinpanny sounds of pianos that are banged and rattled by night and day as new songs and old are played over and over into the ears of singing comedians, comic opera prima dinnas [*sic*] and single soubrettes and 'sister teams' from vaudeville." He goes on to assert, "Now, 'Tin Pan Alley' is considered a term of reproach by the Tin Pan Alleyites. They prefer to designate it as 'Melody Lane.'" My research didn't confirm this, but I did notice, when I started looking at every issue of *Billboard* and *Variety* starting in 1910 for evidence of the popularity of Dixie tunes, that "Tin Pan Alley" was used familiarly, and in a nonpejorative way, as it has been ever since. One point the article indirectly made is that if people, even if just in the music trade, were familiar with the term "Tin Pan Alley," the name must have been coined at least a few years before the article's date for it to have become current by 1903.

The Alley's pianos may have sounded like so many tin pans clanging together, but the question remains as to who dubbed the Alley thus and when. Isaac Goldberg's *Tin Pan Alley,* published in 1930, tells the tale with just a slight bit of wavering. Goldberg takes pride in his source of the story, Harry Von Tilzer, music publisher and composer of maybe more than three thousand songs (most likely by his own account), including such million-plus sellers as "A Bird In A Gilded Cage," "Wait Till The Sun Shines, Nellie," and "I

Want A Girl Just Like The Girl That Married Dear Old Dad." Yet Goldberg suspects what others knew—that Von Tilzer, on top of being a successful songwriter, was a shameless self-promoter. So Goldberg hedges his bets: "It is *probably* [my emphasis] in his office, early in the 1900's, that Tin Pan Alley received its name. Here is the story as I received it from Harry himself" (Goldberg 173). Still, as we shall see, Goldberg lent more credence to the self-promoting Von Tilzer's tale than he probably should have.

According to "Harry," "It was Von Tilzer's custom, when playing the piano in his office, to achieve a queer effect by weaving strips of newspaper through the strings of his upright piano. It was not a musical effect; it is wispy, sometimes mandolin-like, and blurs the music just enough to accentuate the rhythms" (173). In the Von Tilzer/Goldberg rendition, a frequent visitor to Von Tilzer's office was Monroe H. Rosenfeld, also a songwriter as well as newspaperman. To let Goldberg tell the rest in his own words, one time Rosenfeld "had just finished an article upon the music business—perhaps for the *Herald*, on which he worked for a number of years—and was casting about for a title. Harry happened to sit down and strum a tune, when Rosenfeld, catching the thin, 'panny' effect, bounced up with the exclamation 'I have it!' It was another 'Eureka!' 'There's my name! exclaimed Rosenfeld. Your Kindler and Collins [piano] sounds exactly like a Tin Pan. I'll call the article Tin Pan Alley!'" (173).

Now, gentle reader, if you believe all of Goldberg's story and I tell you Harry Von Tilzer opened his own music publishing firm at 42 West 28th Street only as late as 1902, perhaps you'll allow me to sell you a certain Brooklyn Bridge, considering the fact that the 1903 *New York World* article makes it clear that by that year, the term "Tin Pan Alley" was already in common usage for that block of publishers' offices on West 28th Street. Of course Rosenfeld could have frequented Von Tilzer's office when Harry was still a partner in the firm of Shapiro, Bernstein & Von Tilzer from 1900 to 1902, but it's doubtful the two respectable, established former gentlemen would have wanted their young new partner tinkering with his studio's piano so that odd sounds wafted from it to the possible chagrin of their clientele. Also, the subject of Rosenfeld's article was to be the popular music business being established on West 28th Street and, as such, was a phenomenon that had begun only in 1900 when both Shapiro & Bernstein and Leo Feist moved onto the street. So if Rosenfeld did write such an article—and in all likelihood he did—it had to have been in 1900, or at the very latest 1901, well before Von Tilzer set up shop on his own.

Isaac Goldberg seems to back off the whole matter slightly in his concluding remarks about the naming of Tin Pan Alley: "There are those who doubt Rosenfeld's invention. The pianos of the professional parlors in those days, they will assure you, sounded so unmistakably like tin pans that the metaphor must have occurred to hundreds of listeners simultaneously. Yet, to those whose curiosity has extended to Rosenfeld's articles and verses, and to inferences as to his peculiar personality, it is easily credible that he was just the kind of man to name Tin Pan Alley" (173–74). Perhaps Rosenfeld was, but not necessarily under just the circumstance Goldberg narrated, planting the original seed of the naming myth. Other variations seem more plausible, or further call into question Goldberg's account.

In all four other published versions, Monroe Rosenfeld was consistently the star performer, with Harry Von Tilzer getting into the act only as a secondary player in three of them. Looking at those involving both men, one of the most impossible was an online teaching tool I bumped into when I was doing my initial research for my Dixie tunes project. A website called "Music 273: Survey of American Popular Music" contained the course syllabus for a class by that name at the Richmond campus of Eastern Kentucky University, taught by one Larry Nelson sometime in the early to mid-1990s. Only a skeleton of the site now remains, but when I found it I captured the whole outline for the discussion of Tin Pan Alley, where it noted, among other things, "In 1899 the *New York Herald* hired Monroe Rosenfeld (also a part-time composer) to write a series of articles on the flourishing business. . . . Rosenfeld visited the offices of Harry von Tilzer, one of the publishers located on West 28th St. He compared the sound of so many pianos banging out tunes to tin pans and coined the phrase 'Tin Pan Alley' to describe West 28th St., the home of so many music publishers." The syllabus deserves at least a B for pointing out that the *Herald* specifically hired or commissioned songwriter Rosenfeld to write such an article, as opposed to Goldberg's contention that he had been a staff member of the paper for a number of years, for which there is no evidence at all; and maybe even an A—for suggesting it wasn't Von Tilzer's wacky piano but the cacophony of tinny uprights in many studios that inspired Rosenfeld to come up with the sobriquet "Tin Pan Alley" for the block. *However,* and it's a mighty big however, the events couldn't have played out as Instructor Nelson states they did. The *Herald* couldn't have asked Rosenfeld for a piece on 28th Street publishers in 1899 since as of that year there were none there, least of all Harry Von Tilzer, who didn't become a partner with Shapiro and Bernstein until 1900 or open his own firm until 1902. For this impossible dating of the Alley's naming, I give the syllabus an F.

Conversely, except for a single gaffe, one of the more plausible renditions of the story is one of the more recent, appearing in the Introduction to David A. Jasen's *Tin Pan Alley: An Encyclopedia of the Golden Age of American Song* (2003). Jasen wisely begins with the phrase "According to legend" before stating, "The naming of Tin Pan Alley came at the turn of the twentieth century, when Monroe Rosenfeld, a prolific composer-lyricist, wrote a series of articles for the *New York Herald* on the new and energetic popular-music business. For research, he visited the office of Harry Von Tilzer, located at 42 West Twenty-eighth Street, between Broadway and Sixth Avenue" (ix). Usually a careful recorder of the dates when publishers opened their offices, Jasen should have looked back at what he had written. Von Tilzer set up shop in 1902, two years *after* the turn of the century, depending on how literally Jasen meant "at the turn of the century." Ignoring Von Tilzer's oddball piano, Jasen notes, "Rosenfeld heard the din of competing pianists as he left Von Tilzer's office, and he recorded that this street, with dozens of demonstrators working at the same time, sounded like a bunch of tin pans clanging. He characterized the street where all of this activity was taking place as 'Tin Pan Alley.'"

Finally, Kenneth Aaron Kanter in *The Jews on Tin Pan Alley* (1982) more or less subscribes to the Goldberg variation but with a few original twists, one of which truly damns Von Tilzer as the self-promoter that he was. For Kanter, Rosenfeld was describing publishers' row in a magazine piece, not a newspaper article or series of articles, but still visited Von Tilzer, where Harry "had wound pieces of paper over the strings of a piano to make it give off a tinny sound that he was fond of. . . . Rosenfeld heard the piano, which gave him the title for his article, 'Tin Pan Alley'" (24). Kanter points out, and rightly so, "From that time on, the area, and eventually the American music business in general, was known as 'Tin Pan Alley.'" And since it was known as that with no tone of disparagement, Kanter finally notes, "Later on, Von Tilzer claimed that he had coined the name"—a self-promoter to the end.

One version of the Alley's naming keeps Von Tilzer out and is simple, direct, and plausible in everything including the date. It appears early in Philip Furia's *The Poets of Tin Pan Alley* and is brief enough to bear quoting in full:

> In 1900 songwriter Monroe H. Rosenfeld was commissioned by the *New York Herald* to do a story on the new sheet music publishing industry that had emerged at the end of the nineteenth century. Rosenfeld went to the tiny stretch of West 28th Street between Broadway and Sixth Avenue, where most of these publishers had their offices. There, out of the windows of the closely packed buildings, came the din of dozens of upright pianos —a din made even more tinny by weaving strips of newspaper among the piano strings to muffle the sound. The racket, so the story goes, reminded Rosenfeld of rattling pans and inspired him to christen the street "Tin Pan Alley." (19)

Could anything possibly be simpler than that to explain the origin of "Tin Pan Alley"? Yes, in fact. There *is* a simpler explanation, and one that very likely may still put Monroe Rosenfeld center stage as the perpetrator of the name, but with the setting for the deed not West 28th Street at all, but in the quiet of his own sitting room (or anyplace else) as he was writing his commissioned piece for the *Herald.* Rosenfeld didn't need to hear the cacophony of publishers' pianos to remind him of tin pans clattering. Remember Rosenfeld was both a sometime journalist and, first and foremost, a prolific writer of popular songs, both lyrics and music. According to the *Oxford English Dictionary* (second edition), "tin pan" had been current American slang for "a cheap 'tinny' piano" at least as far back as 1882. As such, the expression may have been in Rosenfeld's active vocabulary and ready for him to incorporate in the body of his article or use as his title without a trip to West 28th Street at all. Yet since "tin pan" for a tinny-sounding, cheap piano had been in the air for at least eighteen years before popular music publishers began moving into the brownstones on West 28th Street, it is also possible that the nickname for the block just evolved over time, not attributable to any one person.

But if Rosenfeld wrote his Tin Pan Alley article, why has no one discovered and discussed it? I can't speak for previous writers on Tin Pan Alley's history who may have not cared enough or have been too lazy to look for it. But I can at least offer my own *mea culpa* for not following the lead until I cornered my prey or finally backed off with only negative results—my usual *modus operandi*. When I decided to undertake my Dixie tunes project, I was no longer affiliated with any institutional library where I had interlibrary loan privileges, nor was I within convenient and reasonably inexpensive striking distance of a library that had either the paper copy or a microfilm of the 1900 *Herald* I could peruse from one year's end to the other at my leisure for what is, in the last analysis, little more than a footnote to this study of Dixie tunes. So I leave that adventure to some other interested party.

More to the point of the publishing of all those Dixie tunes, West 28th Street may have been the New York hub of the popular music trade early in the twentieth century, but it wasn't too long until Tin Pan Alley became a long and winding thoroughfare. There were successful publishing houses in such far-flung cities as Chicago, Cleveland, Detroit, Cincinnati, St. Louis, Kansas City, and distant San Francisco. In time some firms moved to New York (Jerome H. Remick from Detroit and Sam Fox from Cleveland, to name but two), but others, like Chicago's Harold Rossiter, Kansas City's J. W. Jenkins & Sons, and San Francisco's Sherman, Clay & Co., stayed put and stayed afloat in a ruthlessly competitive business that grew more and more Manhattan-centered with each passing year, at least until the 1930s when some Hollywood motion picture studios began to buy up New York publishers, after which popular music publishing became somewhat bicoastal. But even then most studios' publishing operations remained in New York.

The Numbers Game

It is demonstrable that between the early 1920s and late 1960s, roughly 90 percent of the lyricists, composers, and, to a slightly lesser extent, book (i.e., script) writers for Broadway musicals were Jewish, meaning ethnically Jewish, not necessarily observant Jews in their religious practices (see Jones, *Our Musicals* 205). Over the years a virtual myth blossomed that Jewish songwriters also dominated or even monopolized popular songwriting in Tin Pan Alley. Well, the one-word reply to that belief or myth, as the hard numbers will show, is simply "Wrong!" This erroneous belief has not just been "in the air," but has affected the thinking and writing of otherwise careful scholars. Stephen J. Whitfield, author of "Is It True What They Sing About Dixie?," is

Jewish, as am I despite my WASP-like name (for its roots, see Jones, "Contradictions" 143–44). Yet Whitfield falls into the trap of the myth at the end of an otherwise flawless description of the Alley just after the turn of the century: "The populace of Tin Pan Alley—the owners of the music publishing houses, the creators of the record companies, the song pluggers and writers—were overwhelmingly Jewish immigrants" (Whitfield 9). Up to "and writers" Whitfield is right on the money (pun intended) in saying that the business end of the Alley was almost solidly in Jewish hands. Other than a few non-Jewish holdovers from the nineteenth century such as Howley, Haviland and Co., and T. B. Harms (taken over by Jewish Max Dreyfus in 1904), the publishing houses that ruled the Alley from 1900 on were the Jewish-owned firms of Leo Feist; Shapiro, Bernstein & Co.; Jerome H. Remick and Co.; M. Witmark and Sons; Harry Von Tilzer; Sam Fox; Joseph W. Stern (succeeded by his partner Edward B. Marks); Waterson, Berlin & Snyder; Broadway Music Corp. (owned by Will Von Tilzer, one of Harry's brothers); York Music (founded by two more Von Tilzers, Albert and Jack); and, starting later than the others in 1922, Robbins Music Corp.

But to return to the dominance of Tin Pan Alley by Jewish lyricists and composers, it just ain't so. To the contrary, the figures reveal objectively that Jews represented quite a small minority in both categories of creative talent, at least among Alley writers of the words and music of Dixie tunes between 1898 and 1958. That was practically everybody who was anybody in the Alley during those years—especially through 1936, when the bulk of southern songs were written. As a Jew myself, I can spot Jewish or Jewish-sounding names with at least 95 percent reliability. But when I thought I found a Jewish writer but wasn't entirely sure, I consulted one or more relatively reliable print sources, including the *ASCAP Biographical Dictionary,* biographical entries in Jasen's *Tin Pan Alley,* and Internet websites for individual Alley writers.

Here, then, are the raw figures and percentages of Jewish lyricists and composers of the Alley's Dixie tunes between 1898 and 1958: of 426 lyricists only 83, or a mere 19.5 percent, were Jewish; Jewish composers made a more respectable showing, with 119 among the 434 in all, or 27.4 percent.

Despite their tiny numbers compared to non-Jewish Alleymen, Jewish writers of Dixie tunes—both composers and lyricists—wrote more songs than their non-Jewish brethren and, of those, far more big moneymaking hits. Modifying this disparity a bit is the fact that the Alley was "ecumenical," with a considerable number of songwriting teams, whether for a few songs or the long term, consisting of one Jew and one non-Jew. Also, throughout the history of the Alley, white and black lyricists and composers often teamed in racial and creative harmony, a topic to be treated more later on.

In rough chronological order, here are some of the prominent Jewish/non-Jewish collaborations. Jewish wordsmith Jack Yellen scored big with non-Jewish ragtime tunesmith George L. Cobb four times in three years with "All Aboard For Dixie Land" in 1913, followed by "Listen To That Dixie Band," "Alabama Jubilee," and "Are You From Dixie? ('Cause I'm From Dixie Too)," all in 1915; while Canadian-born Catholic lyricist Alfred Bryan wrote six songs idealizing Dixie with Hungarian-born Jewish composer Jean Schwartz, all in 1919, best typified by "You're Living Right Next Door To Heaven When You Live In Dixieland." In the 1920s, German-Jewish lyricist Gus Kahn wrote five Dixie tunes with Brooklyn-born composer (and occasional lyricist) Walter Donaldson, not a Jew, including their virtually iconic 1922 "Carolina In The Morning." Mitchell Parish, a Jew who wrote lovely lyrics to such songs as "Stardust," teamed up with non-Jewish composer Frank Perkins six times between 1932 and 1935 to write a group of southern songs that includes "Stars Fell On Alabama" (1934), arguably the most breathtakingly beautiful song about the South ever written. And, from 1941, "Chattanooga Choo Choo" had words by Polish-Jewish Mack Gordon, and tune by Italian-American Harry Warren. With this list one might start to wonder where all the Jewish composers were. Some, like Irving Berlin, composed the melodies to their own lyrics, while many others most often teamed with Jewish lyricists in the production of Dixie (and other) songs, one example being that of composer George W. Meyer working for years with the lyric-writing duo of Sam M. Lewis and Joe Young; this trio turned out one of the highest volumes of Dixie tunes ever produced in the Alley. Still, however productive and successful the Jewish wordsmiths and tunesmiths in the Alley were (and they *were*), the myth that they dominated the output of all other Alleymen by their sheer numbers remains just that—a myth.

"I'll Sing You A Song About Dear Old Dixie Land"

I chose the title of this 1919 Dixie tune with deliberate irony to head this chapter's section that begins by listing typical features of early Alleymen's backgrounds, since *atypically* the song's lyricist Henry Creamer and composer Turner Layton were black. Also, Creamer was born in the South, and, unlike most barely high school–taught white Alleymen, Layton had studied dentistry at Howard University.

The characteristic white Alleyman portrait runs like this: Most of the composers and lyricists, like Stephen Collins Foster, born just outside Pittsburgh long before them, were white northerners, mostly born and raised in or near large metropolitan centers like New York City, Philadelphia, Chicago, and Milwaukee; but some, like Ballard MacDonald, hailed from as far away as Portland, Oregon, still urban but Pacific northwestern. And too, especially in the early years, other urban songwriters were European immigrants, most arriving in the United States as infants or young children with their parents. Many but not all of these were Jews, most of the Jewish ones settling into the Lower East Side of New York. Over the years, a few white songwriters also found their way up to New York from the South, starting in the very early years with Monroe H. Rosenfeld himself, born in Richmond, Virginia, and up to, much later on, Johnny Mercer, born and raised till he was ten in Savannah, Georgia. Most of the southern-born Alleymen wrote very few Dixie tunes. When I mentioned this to a cynical friend, he remarked, "That figures. Those southern lyricists saw too much up close of what the South was *really* like to try writing songs glorifying Dixie!" Perhaps there's a modicum of truth in that. Over twenty-five black Alleymen also wrote Dixie tunes, including some who came from the South, but their backgrounds and contributions are so singular compared to those of their white cohorts that I save my initial discussion of them for the following section.

Very few white northern-born-and-bred Alleymen had more than a high school education, if that. (Harry Von Tilzer, while still Aaron Gumm back home in Indianapolis, at age fourteen ran away and joined the circus, not typical behavior for a nice Jewish boy.) As lyricist William Jerome astutely observed in a 1916 *Billboard* article, "Strange to say our best songs come from the street. Art knows no age, it knows no class, and song writing is an art that even Yale or Harvard have never mastered" (46). Two of the few early exceptions to the "high school at most" portrait of the early Alleyman were both halves of the Jack Yellen/George L. Cobb team, the former a graduate of the University of Michigan, the latter of Syracuse University. Another was Oregonian Ballard MacDonald with his Princeton degree. But they were rare birds in the Alley. Finally, as far as can be determined, few northern-born Alleymen ever traveled farther south than Atlantic City until after they had written all or most of their Dixie tunes. The few exceptions might have been vacations by train of the more affluent tunesmiths like Irving Berlin to spots like Palm Beach and Miami. But there are some who argue South Florida is too far south to count as Dixie, though for this book it certainly *does* count since plenty of songs romanticized it, even before Edgar Leslie and Joe Burke's 1935 mega-hit "Moon Over Miami."

Before discussing, or even speculating on, the still unsettled question of where the first half-decade (1898 to 1902) of the Alley's generally undereducated and untraveled lyricists came up with their images for songs about an idyllic South, I should state that from this point on I will emphasize almost exclusively the words of Dixie tunes, since the texts, not the music, convey the stories, themes, ideas, and values that their lyricists wanted listeners to take away with them.

When I began this project by finding and having photocopies made of every Tin Pan Alley Dixie tune in the sheet music collection in the John Hay Library, I soon discovered a disconnect between the Alley's output beginning in 1898 and southern songs earlier in the nineteenth century. With few exceptions there is no continuity between the kinds of imagery of the South in southern songs before 1898 and the imagery of those that professional Alley lyricists employed from that date forward. Whether the earlier songs were from the tradition of blackface minstrelsy, the so-called "plantation songs" of Stephen Foster and others, or the few rare other songs about the South, almost none contained the sorts of pastoral, idyllic images seen in Alley tunes between 1898 and 1902, some of which I already listed in the Prologue. And, too, Alley songs typically idealize the South of the here and now. If a song, say, was written in 1912 or 1936, it's the 1912 or 1936 South that's being glorified, or, in a nostalgia piece, maybe reflexively from the singer's younger days, but almost *never* the antebellum South. Yet, nineteenth-century southern songs—such as Foster's "Massa's In De Cold, Cold, Ground"—often were nostalgic pieces about life before the Civil War. Moreover, southern darky dialects dominated most plantation songs and those from minstrel shows, a comparative rarity among Alley songs about Dixie. All of this raised for me, as well as for other scholars I consulted, a baffling question: If not earlier songs, what were the sources of southern imagery these generally poorly educated, lowbrow, untraveled, mostly northern urban lyricists used in their Dixie tunes? In brief, where did they *learn* about the real or imagined South they were singing of?

Before attempting to tackle this question, let me try to answer an even more unanswerable one—*why* was there a sudden burst of Dixie tunes beginning in 1898? The best thought I came up with is that, in the late nineteenth century, there was among the northern public a renewed interest in things southern, and the commercial minds of what became the Alley latched onto the marketability of that interest.

One index of public interest in the South was songs in which a northern boy woos and weds a southern girl, getting (often begrudgingly) the permission and even blessing of the girl's father, in some cases a Civil War veteran. This motif had been popular in travel literature, novels, magazine stories, and plays from the late 1860s through the early 1890s, as Nina Silber discusses in *The Romance of Reunion: Northerners and the South, 1865–1900* (see Chapter 2). Like those prose and stage works, the songs symbolized for popular consumption the reconciliation of sectionalism after Reconstruction, but they were a long time coming. I found nothing like them after the end of the Reconstruction era in 1877 until the first of their kind in 1899, "My Little Georgia Rose," with lyrics by Robert F. Roden and music by Max S. Witt. This was followed in 1900 by "My Girl From Dixie," with words and music by Raymond A. Browne and Robert J. Adams, and in 1901 by Martin Bowes's "A Little Southern Bride" and Willie Wildwave's "She's Kentucky's Fairest Daughter." More songs of sectional reconciliation through courtship and marriage were published as late as 1915 (see Chapter 2).

Keeping with my half-decade for exploring where Alley lyricists got their Dixie images, another indicator that songwriters were riding the commercial coattails of public interest in the South around the turn of the century is that, between 1898 and 1902, they wrote six sob-ballads like those popular during the nineteenth century in which a virginal young woman dies between the day her beau must leave her for a while and the time he returns to marry her; but now all six songs have southern settings for no good reason. Chronologically they are "The Girl I Loved In Sunny Tennessee" (1899), words by Harry Braisted and music by Stanley Carter; "Savannah Lou" (1899), words by Fred Raymond, music by Harry S. Marion; "In Alabama" (1900), words by Carroll Fleming, music by Chas. B. Lawlor; Gus Edwards's "Where The Mississippi Flows" (1901); Tony Stanford's "She Rests By The Suwanee [*sic*] River" (1901); and Charles K. Harris's "In The Hills Of Old Carolina" (1902). Other than "In Alabama," whose lyric contains only generic imagery, all the rest include at least one or two of the kinds of images I list in the Prologue to give an air of the South or romanticized local color to the bittersweet (or, if you prefer, maudlin) tales the songs are spinning (more about these and later ones of their ilk in Chapter 2).

This is the best I can do to try to answer *why* Dixie tunes began to be written and to proliferate beginning in 1898—primarily to capitalize on what seems to have been among urban northerners a growing interest in, fascination with, and/or curiosity about the South around that time. Nina Silber in *The Romance of Reunion* points to northerners' earlier romanticizing and sentimentalizing of the South going back to the Reconstruction period and up to 1900, but little of this could or would have directly influenced Alley songwriting starting in 1898 (see especially Silber 66–92, wherein she treats northern tourism in the South). Perhaps that kind of interest had been spurred by the 1896 publication of northern travel writer Julian Ralph's accounts of his meanderings in the South in *Dixie; or Southern Scenes and Sketches,* which had earlier appeared as a series of articles in *Harper's Weekly* (Cox 4); and previously by the many successive editions of Joel Chandler Harris's popular *Uncle Remus: His Songs and His Sayings,* which was first published in 1880; plus Chandler's later Uncle Remus publications. Then, too, on the stage were dramatist Augustus Thomas's 1891 hit *Alabama,* in which love triumphs over sectionalism, and playwright/actor William Gillette's 1896 Civil War melodrama *Secret Service,* which had the impressive New York run for a nonmusical play back then of 176 performances. These books and plays suggest that there was a taste for the South among northern audiences and readers of the time. With a keen eye for such things, the Alley's songwriters and publishers were ready to give that public Dixie songs to sample along with the other southern fare they had before them.

To return to the main point about the origins of idyllic southern imagery in Dixie tunes between 1898 and 1902, very little in them was similar to what's found in southern songs written earlier in the nineteenth century. Still, it's not unlikely that as public schoolboys in the 1880s and '90s a good many future Alleymen sang some of the occasional nineteenth-century songs that *did* include the southern images they themselves would later incorporate into their own Dixie songs. Highest on the small list of writers of such songs was, of course, Stephen Foster, yet despite his large output of popular songs during his very short life, only a comparative few were of the "plantation song" variety, a great many more being typical Victorian-American "parlor songs," including some of the dead-virgin species. Of the dozens I read of Foster's plantation songs—many in darky dialect—only four contained the sorts of images used wholesale by later Alleymen. Two remain familiar and widely sung (and were common fare in music classes during my own "grammar school" days in the mid-1940s), the other two less so, but this doesn't mean all four might not have been sung in 1880s and '90s schoolrooms.

The first four lines of "My Old Kentucky Home, Good Night" (the original title of the song, which Foster didn't write in dialect) are a virtual compendium of some images most used later in the Alley's Dixie tunes: "The sun shines bright in the old Kentucky home, 'Tis summer, the darkies are gay, / The corn top's ripe and the meadow's in the bloom / While the birds make music all the day." Sunshine, summer, happy darkies, fertile fields, and singing birds formed the ambience surrounding the central spot in many Alley songs about the South—home, and Foster may have planted these visions in the minds of young would-be lyricists at an early age. From the less remembered "Down Among The Cane-Brakes" came the single image "Down among the cane-brakes on the Mississippi shore"; and "The Glendy Burke" (about a steamboat) offered the whole conceit "My lady love is pretty as a pink; I'll meet her on the way; / I'll take her back to the sunny old south / And there I'll make her stay." Foster also may have unwittingly given budding young lyricists a scattering of Dixie images throughout the verses of "Old Folks At Home," which was published in nineteenth-century songbooks both in its original heavy darky dialect and in a normalized English rendition (which I am using here). Either way, it's a popular song that was most probably sung in public schools and contained such familiar southern phrases and images among its three verses as "Way down upon the Swanee River"; "Still longing for the old plantation"; "Oh, take me to my kind old mother!"; and "When will I hear the banjo strumming, / Down in my good old home?" Foster's entire theme is homesickness, the driving force of a large percentage of the Dixie tunes Tin Pan Alley would produce during the entire history of the song type.

Homesickness also pervaded two songs by other writers almost surely sung in public schools attended by future Alleymen. Black songwriter James Bland packed his 1878 "Carry Me Back To Old Virginny" with images of "where the corn and taters grow," "where the birds warble sweet in the spring-time," and "in the fields of yellow corn." And there's no denying that despite its rousing up-tempo melody, Dan Emmett's 1859 "Dixie's Land" (better known as just "Dixie"), with its opening line of "I wish I was in de land ob cotton," is a homesickness tune right from the get-go.

This meager handful of nineteenth-century southern songs, perhaps sung in their childhood or teenage years by future professional songwriters, could not have been enough to supply them with sufficient images for their Dixie tunes. So, at the suggestion of Steve Whitfield, I contacted southern studies specialist John Shelton Reed. John recommended southern studies books for me to read, and I occasionally carried on e-mail correspondence with those authors still living.

I ruled out as a source of Alleymen's southern imagery anything pretending to the name of "literature" about the South, whether "plantation novels" or the poetry of southern ladies rhapsodizing on the landscapes within which they dwelled. I reasoned these rudimentarily educated "lowbrow hacks" (as I first described Alleymen to John) may be presumed to have read little beyond the daily paper and an occasional popular magazine like *Collier's* or *Saturday Evening Post* (John's suggestions in his reply), perhaps finding odd bits of Dixie stuff in the stories, articles, or ads. Nor may it be supposed they were familiar with antebellum culture as found in the Plantation or Lost Cause Myths, or had even heard of these myths at all. Perhaps, as Stephen A. Smith, author of *Myth, Media, and the Southern Mind,* suggested to me, a few college-educated or other literate lyricists may have read Henry W. Grady's description of an ideal yet simple southern farmer's home and its residents in his speech "The Farmer and the Cities," delivered at Elberton, Georgia, in June 1889 (see Harris, *Grady* 176–78). One would like to think so, since it epitomizes the idyllic image of a Dixie home and family, which lyricists shaped into hundreds of songs over the years. But that, too, can only be guessed at, not proven.

These speculations on *verbal* southern imagery in songs or prose that future or young Alleymen may have read weren't very productive. A more fertile field of images for the lyricists' own verbal facility was, not improbably, *visual* rather than verbal depictions of the South. These ranged from such artifacts as engravings, daguerreotypes, and photographs of Dixie scenes on travel brochures found at the turn of the century on racks in railroad stations, to reproductions of the popular Currier & Ives lithographs that could be bought or simply viewed in shop windows up and down Broadway and elsewhere.

While today we think of Currier & Ives as the master lithographers of winters in New England and sleigh rides and skating in Central Park, they in fact also produced a vast number of color lithos of southern scenes. These included not just their magnificent depictions of Mississippi River steamboats both at rest being loaded with firewood or cotton (often with the darky stevedores singing or dancing as in later Alley songs), or racing one another, but all manner of domestic scenes as well. The latter always showed perfect harmony between white southern planters, their wives, and the happy darkies in their employ, whether in the home or in the fields. The lithograph "A Cotton Plantation on the Mississippi" is rich in such detail; in the foreground are a white man and woman talking next to a mule-drawn cart laden with cotton bales, in the middle distance darkies picking cotton, and in the far distant background the River with a steaming sidewheeler—enough to give a few Alleymen material for at least three or four good lyrics. "Low Water in the Mississippi" depicts not just the River with two steamboats and a raft afloat, but of special interest to lyricists, on the left bank in the background the "big house" of a plantation, and up close in the foreground, a cabin in front of which are very happy darkies, dancing and singing to a banjo one of them is playing. Other Currier & Ives prints depicted actual southern spots Alleymen went on to sing about: "Natural Bridge / In the 'Blue Ridge' Region, Rockland County, Va." and "Lookout Mountain, Tennessee / And the Chattanooga Rail Road," to name only two. Still others showed southern black/white harmony up close, as in "The Old Barn Floor": In a barn a darky plays the banjo and a pickanniny dances, while a young white farm family—mother, father, and young child—happily watch the impromptu entertainment. "My Cottage Home," drawn by Fanny Palmer, who drew many Dixie scenes for Currier & Ives, depicts a modest southern house in an idyllic setting of southern pines and foliage, the young mistress of the house with her dog gazing fondly on her abode from the garden gate. In many ways, Fanny Palmer in her day resembled the Alleymen of a later era; this talented artist of southern scenes was born in England, lived in New York, and never traveled in the South. But at least it's known that Fanny got *her* inspiration for her drawings of southern scenes from daguerreotypes and engravings in books. And, too, beyond Currier & Ives, there were lesser lithographers and engravers creating scenes of the South during what was a period of interest in that region among northerners in the late nineteenth century. So Alleymen or soon-to-be Alleymen had much to see when it came to idealized images of Dixie. Yet it must be recalled that even this lies largely in the realm of conjecture. So where the first half-decade of Alleymen got their southern images still remains in great part an open question.

Some readers must wonder about my insistence on referring to and discussing lyricists who created songs in only the first half-decade of the professional writing and publishing of Dixie tunes, 1898 through 1902. The reason is that forty professionally written and published Dixie tunes appeared during this half-decade, which seemed like a workable number of songs to handle in my chase for antecedents of their images. After reading over all of them, I discovered these songs in the aggregate contained a wide array of idyllic southern images, an extensive selection of which I listed in the Prologue. With these Dixie images at hand I could search for their nineteenth-century sources. I rarely found them, but I discovered other valuable things.

The lyrics of the forty songs were written by a total of thirty-three different writers; Andrew B. Sterling was guilty of six of them, and Charles K. Harris and five lesser-known writers wrote two apiece. This information was helpful for trying to determine how many of the first half-decade Alleymen were northerners born and bred, as opposed to who, if any, might have come to the Alley from the South—not an easy task considering the paucity of biographical information for popular songwriters in the very early years. Of those lyricists who wrote multiple songs, five were definitely northerners: Harris and his friend Charles Horwitz, both from Milwaukee; Sterling from New York City, as well as Harry Braisted (pseudonym for comedian Harry B. Berdan); and Will D. Cobb from Philadelphia. Nothing is known about the origins of Robert F. Roden and Tony Stanford. As for the other twenty-six lyricists, I found data on where only ten were either born, grew up, or both, but it never was in the South. Wm. H. Gardner was born in Boston; Joseph E. Howard and Raymond A. Browne were from New York City; Jas. O'Dea came to New York from Canada; Robert B. Smith was born in Chicago; Gus Edwards, born Gus Simon in Hohensalza, German Empire, grew up in the Williamsburg section of Brooklyn; Stanislaus Stangé hailed from Liverpool, England, coming to the States when he was nineteen; Max Hoffmann, born in Gnesen, Poland, was raised in St. Paul, Minnesota; and William Jerome was born William Jerome Flannery of Irish immigrant parents in Cornwall-on-Hudson, New York. All that's known about Al Trahern (lyricist of the richly detailed "Under Southern Skies" quoted from in the Prologue)—according to a brief 1903 piece about him in the *Music Trade Review*—is that before coming to New York to write songs for musicals and the Alley, he "began his career as a newspaper reporter 'in the West.'" Whether he was a southerner or northerner is anyone's guess, and the same may be said for the other sixteen Dixie tune lyricists between 1898 and 1902 for whom no biographical data has surfaced. Yet the wise money says most if not all were northerners, as would be most Alleymen thereafter.

The output of the forty Dixie songs filled with southern imagery in those five years, many of which were commercial successes familiar to audiences and other songwriters alike, became a veritable storehouse of source material from which other later lyricists could borrow (or cannibalize, if you wish) as many images as they chose to use, alter, tweak, or expand upon in their own Dixie tunes—all for the taking, free of charge. Not only could they, but they clearly *did*, as even a casual glance at Dixie tune lyrics down through the years makes apparent. This isn't to say that all Dixie lyrics look alike or they all look swiped from a single source. Not at all. Many, if not all, Alley lyricists were creative craftsmen who knew how to manipulate this store of images in fresh, original ways. And too, they added to their songs more detail such as southern place-names, whether of cities, as Jack Yellen did in his and Milton Ager's 1923 "Louisville Lou (The Vampin' Lady)," or rivers other than the Mississippi and Swanee, as Cab Calloway, Guy Wood, and Jack Palmer did in "Ogeechee River Lullaby" in 1942.

A source of amusement, and a sign that some Alleymen were untraveled northerners, is the odd places where some of them put the Mississippi and Suwannee (Swanee) rivers in their songs, showing these men to be geographically challenged. Only one lyricist, L. Wolfe Gilbert, made a huge gaffe about the Mississippi. The first line of Wolfie's hit with Lewis F. Muir's ragtime melody, "Waiting For The Robert E. Lee" (F. A. Mills, 1912), is "Way down on the levee in Old Alabamy," but, as Stephen J. Whitfield points out, "that state is located about 150 miles east of any levees" (11), and, by implication, of the Mississippi River itself.

Many more lyricists tossed the poor old Suwannee—or, since Stephen Foster, in song almost always just Swanee—River all over Dixie. But before getting to them, for readers who may have forgotten or have never known just where this fairly obscure river actually belongs, here's a brief refresher course: The Suwannee flows out of the Okefenokee Swamp in southern Georgia through northern Florida, where it empties near the town of Suwannee into the Gulf of Mexico, more or less bisecting the peninsular from the panhandle sections of that state. Irving Caesar, lyricist of "Swanee," with George Gershwin's music and sung by Al Jolson, which became one of the biggest hits for all three of them, in his later years offered a more subjective description of the river in a video interview on the Internet as of this writing: "Most of the boys who'd written about Dixie had never been to Dixie at the time and neither had George nor I been down South. After the song became a hit we took a trip to Florida, and crossing the border from Georgia into Florida, there's the Suwannee River. The conductor or the porter on the train, who knew something about what we were up to, said, 'Boys, there's that river you wrote about.' We looked down, and there was this nice muddy little stream. I said to George, 'It's a good thing we wrote the song first.'" One can hope Caesar and Gershwin's Florida trip was before 1923, or that Caesar later forgot he'd seen the Swanee in Florida, since he became one of the lyricists guilty of juggling the river all over Dixie. In "Nashville Nightingale" (Harms, 1923), which the two wrote about a black female blues singer, Caesar wrote, "Sing a little tune for me, Croon for me. . . . 'Neath the Swanee moon / My Nashville Nightingale." But Caesar wasn't the first.

It began in one of several Dixie tunes associated with the Great War (now World War I). In "It's A Long, Long Way To Dixie" (Chicago: Tell Taylor Music Pub. Co., 1917), with lyrics by Taylor (a Chicago lyricist and publisher) and music by Earl K. Smith, lines echoing Stephen Foster contain this geographic nonsense: "I'm going way down south to my Old Kentucky home. . . . Way down upon the Swanee River where I long to stray." In 1919, Louis (later just Lou) Herscher—who went on to a long, successful career as both lyricist and composer—wrote the words and music of a cute song whose conceit played on southern place-names that contain multiples of a single letter, such as the two G's in Georgia, four A's in Alabama, and so forth, its title being "There Are Just Two I's In Dixie (Two Blue Eyes That Mean The World to Me)" (Philadelphia: Emmett J. Welch, 1919). Yet in the midst of this fun is the geographical goof, "You'll find four S's in Mississippi / Where the Swanee River flows."

"Old Plantation Blues" (McKinley Music, 1922) was the product of two Chicagoans who rarely went anywhere else, lyricist (and sometimes tunesmith) E. Clinton Keithley and hugely prolific ragtime and popular music composer F. Henri Klickmann. Here they revealed their midwestern insularity by declaring, "I long to be / In Alabamy with my Mammy on the Swanee Shore." And the prolific Dixie tunes team of Sam M. Lewis and Joe Young ought to have known better by 1930 when they got together with composer Harry Warren to write in the otherwise moving "Cryin' For The Carolines" (Remick Music Corp., 1930), "Lord, take me away from the Hudson / Good Lord oh let my troubles flow / Good Lord take me back to the Swanee / That's the place where sinners go. . . . I'm cryin' for the Carolines."

Nor were black Alleymen, including those from the South like Richmond-born Henry Creamer, immune from plopping the Swanee down in strange places, as he did in "Dear Old Southland" (Jack Mills, 1921), with music by his frequent collaborator Turner Layton: "How I long to roam back to my old Kentucky home . . . / And I long just to see once more / The land I love—the Swanee shore." Even one of the truly great black lyricists, Andy Razaf, misplaced the Swanee in the area known as the "Mississippi Basin" in his song by that name (Joe Davis, 1933), although in fact the river is nowhere near that huge land mass. Still, the song's homesick singer laments, "If my eyes could see that river, Swanee scenes I've known. . . . Wanna take my rightful place in that MISSISSIPPI BASIN back home."

Yet whatever these lyricists, white and black, may have lacked in their knowledge of southern geography, they and hundreds more who wrote Dixie tunes excelled in painting vivid, luxurious, romantic, and even comic scenes mostly glorifying the South, real or imagined. And though they were comparatively few, black Alleymen through the years would write a significant number of songs idealizing Dixie, as paradoxical or oxymoronic as that notion may first appear.

"I Never Had The Blues (Until I Left Old Dixieland)"

Andy Razaf more than made up for his gaffe about the Swanee being in the Mississippi Basin with another Dixie tune that became an iconic expression of idyllic southern comfort, country style, "That's What I Like 'Bout The South." Yet the tale of that tune is so complex it's best told in Chapter 9, with the other songs focusing on idealizing the South. Besides, to say more of Razaf here would be to start almost at the end of the story of blacks in the Alley. Well before there *was* an Alley, New York's music trade was virtually color-blind. Prior to the turn of the century blacks were writing everything from Gussie Davis's sob-ballads to Ernest Hogan's coon songs, not to mention full-scale black musicals performed largely for white audiences (see Jones, *Our Musicals* 31–36). Publishers, whether Jewish like Joseph W. Stern and M. Witmark & Sons, or not, like Howley, Haviland, and Co., eagerly accepted top-notch material by talented writers regardless of race, especially encouraging work by black lyricists and composers. Still, some black writers wanted a publisher to serve the creative output of their own. Thus, out of two smaller attempts starting in 1903, in 1905 Richard Cecil McPherson and Will Marion Cook merged their individual efforts into Gotham-Attucks Music Company, the first major black-owned song-publishing house in New York (see Jasen 163). No other significant black publisher came to the Alley until 1918, when Harry Herbert Pace and bluesman W. C. Handy moved their firm Pace & Handy from Memphis to New York. Later, two more black bluesmen got into publishing—Spencer Williams briefly, and, for much longer, Clarence Williams (no relation), who brought the firm he founded as Williams and Piron in New Orleans in 1915 to the Alley as Clarence Williams Music Publishing Company in 1921; his outfit lasted until the 1940s.

To return to black songwriters, and specifically, those who wrote Dixie tunes, it's possible to create a profile of them similar to that for their white brethren above, and some of the differences between the profiles are striking. First, and so obvious it's hardly worth saying, the total number of black lyricists and composers is much smaller than either category of white Alleymen alone. Thus I grouped them into a single list, admittedly perhaps missing one or two. Still, the total I came up with is twenty-seven black writers of Dixie tunes between the earliest in 1903 and the latest in 1942. Most variant from white lyricists and composers is that twelve of the black ones came to the Alley from the South, and, of primary significance for Dixie tunes, eight of those wrote lyrics about an idyllic Southland. Also, in the early years, black Alleymen were better educated than the white. Some had just a public school education (a few composers had extra private music study), but ten—both lyricists and composers—had college degrees or attended a college or conservatory for a time, some at historically black institutions, others at places like New York University, Cornell, and the New England Conservatory of Music. A far different portrait from that of white Alleymen in the early years of Dixie tunes.

Three salient characteristics of black songwriters' output are worth glancing at here to round out this initial picture of their presence in the Alley. First, and perhaps paradoxically, many Dixie tunes by black Alleymen were remarkably similar to those by whites, notably those idealizing the South, especially when the lyricist was a black southerner, as in the case of Bob Cole, born in Athens, Georgia, and raised in Atlanta. Cole wrote the words of "Moonlight on the Mississippi" (Jos. W. Stern, 1903), the earliest Dixie tune by blacks, with music by [J.] Rosamond Johnson, born in Jacksonville, Florida, himself, and one couldn't wish for a more idyllic vision of a southern scene, as the chorus alone attests:

> Moonlight on the Mississippi
> And all around is very peaceful and serene,
> Moonlight on the Mississippi
> And ev'rything is lending beauty to the scene;
> Hear the old steamboat a-blowing
> And hear the echo that comes floating down the stream;
> Hear the old shanghai [i.e., rooster] a-crowing,
> Darkies are a-singing,
> Banjos a-ringing,
> Moonlight on the Mississippi.

Set against other similar songs of its day, no one would have suspected two of those "darkies" wrote it!

Cole and Johnson weren't the only black Alleymen to idealize the South, nor did this occur just in the Alley's early years. To cite only one familiar later example, in 1922 lyricist Henry Creamer and composer Turner Layton wrote the still-perennial favorite of Dixieland jazz bands that glorified one special cosmopolitan southern spot, in "'Way Down Yonder In New Orleans" (Shapiro, Bernstein, 1922): "There is heaven right here on earth / With those beautiful queens, / 'Way down yonder in New Orleans." Creamer wasn't the first, nor would he be the last lyricist, black or white, to compare Dixie or parts thereof to heaven—the South often coming out more favorably in the comparison!

The mention of "'Way Down Yonder in New Orleans" leads to the second distinguishing feature of Dixie-tune-writing African Americans—the relatively large number of *hits* they had (as well as non-Dixie hits) considering how few such songwriters there were. To take them in rough chronological order, although W. C. Handy's biggest all-time seller was and remains his non-Dixie "St. Louis Blues," two of his pieces about southern locales, "The Memphis Blues" (the version with lyrics by white George A. Norton, published in 1916) and "Beale Street Blues" (with Handy's own lyrics, 1917), achieved hit status as well. In 1919 black composer Maceo Pinkard collaborated with white lyricist William Tracey on his first million-seller, "Mammy O' Mine." Pinkard worked almost entirely with white lyricists throughout his career and had many more million-selling songs, but only one of those was another Dixie tune with words by the barely known Ken Casey, the 1925 smash "Sweet Georgia Brown," a tune still remembered if for no other reason than as the theme of the Harlem Globetrotters basketball team. Lyricist Noble Sissle and composer Eubie Blake mostly wrote songs for all-black musicals, but several of them became hits on their own, including two Dixie tunes from their 1921 hit show *Shuffle Along,* when both "In Honeysuckle Time" and "Bandana Days" had considerable success outside the theatre. Yet that success was only modest compared to the national craze created by wordsmith Cecil Mack and tunesmith Jimmy [James P.] Johnson in 1923 thanks to a Dixie dance tune they wrote for their musical *Runnin' Wild,* the name of which most people get wrong by trying to insert "The" before its actual one-word title, "Charleston." Also in 1923, in a very different vein, Clarence Williams's "Gulf Coast Blues" attracted great attention thanks to Bessie Smith's recording. Just when Spencer Williams wrote the words and music of what became his biggest hit and most famous song, "Basin Street Blues," remains unclear, but its probable first publication was by Mayfair Music Corporation in 1933. And, finally, we come full circle to Andy Razaf's "That's What I Like

'Bout The South," mentioned at the top of this section, which Razaf most likely wrote in 1933 but which only achieved coast-to-coast popularity in the 1940s thanks to Phil Harris's radio performances and recording of the song.

The third and final salient feature of the work of some black lyricists is as seemingly paradoxical as their writing songs idealizing an idyllic, romantic Southland. Like many white songwriters, some black ones wrote of homesickness for the South, but in most of the black songs, there is a subtextual genuineness in these sentiments, as if the feelings were the personal expression of the actual lyricist, not of a persona created by him for the purpose of the song alone. These black-written homesickness songs thus appear to be more than mere commercial copycats in that genre. They articulated real sentiments of many southern blacks displaced in the North that despite discrimination, poverty, Jim Crow laws, and even lynchings, they still felt the South to be a more congenial comfort zone—or, in other words, a *home*—than the cold, impersonal North. Blacks wrote several songs from this seemingly unusual point of view, but it was perhaps no more sincerely expressed than in New Orleans–born Spencer Williams's lyric for his 1919 Dixie tune with music by white Charley Straight, the apparently genuine title of which heads this section: "I Never Had The Blues (Until I Left Old Dixieland)" (Pace & Handy, 1919). Much more on this theme appears in Chapter 7's first sub-section: Displaced Darkies.

Dixie Mills

To say some lyricists and composers of Dixie tunes were prolific would be an understatement. This is why I created the term Dixie Mills for Alleymen who seemed to ceaselessly grind out such songs. Nor were they just prolific in churning out Dixie tunes but in their entire output of popular songs, for none of these wordsmiths and tunesmiths made a career of writing just about the South. They were as unstoppable in spinning out their share of love songs, novelty songs, dance tunes, and whatever else was in fashion or they thought they could make fashionable at the time. Such productivity is illustrated by Gus Kahn, who in 1922 alone wrote the words for the blockbuster "Carolina In The Morning" (music by Walter Donaldson) and two other Dixie tunes, "Dixie Highway" (music also by Donaldson), and "Southern Memories" (music by Phil Goldberg and Frank Magine), while in the same year penning the lyrics for three non-Dixie hits, "Toot, Toot, Tootsie, Goodbye" (music by Ernie Erdman et al.), "My Buddy" (music by Donaldson), and "On The Alamo" (music by Isham Jones).

I admit my single criterion for being a Dixie Mill—writing or composing a minimum of *six* Dixie tunes—is arbitrary, but that number seemed sufficiently large to indicate said Alleyman was assiduous enough at the task of cranking out southern songs to be worthy of the title. Yet I allowed for some slight flexibility. In a few cases, if an Alleyman turned out only five Dixie tunes in a compact span of time, he could also qualify as a Dixie Mill. I say "he" strictly from the facts of the matter, since no Alleywoman ever turned out more than four, that singular woman being Grace Le Boy, Gus Kahn's earliest Dixie-tune composer and, soon after, his wife. Many other Alleymen wrote multiple numbers of Dixie tunes below my qualifying cutoff figure, but no group of lyricists and composers of southern songs than the Mills themselves better illustrates the plethora of such songs that came from the Alley between 1898 and 1958. Hence, it seemed fitting to highlight this by ending this chapter containing profiles of Alleymen with alphabetical lists of Dixie Mill lyricists and composers, with those who wrote both words and music included in one list only, except for Walter Donaldson—which I explain in notes after each list.

Dixie Mill Lyricists

NAME	NUMBER OF SONGS	INCLUSIVE YEARS
Irving Berlin	19	1911–1940
Lew Brown	13	1912–1934
Alfred (Al) Bryan	19	1907–1929
Irving Caesar	7	1919–1936
Grant Clarke	15	1914–1929
Henry Creamer	10	1918–1927
Benny Davis	6	1922–1930
B. G. (Buddy) De Sylva	16	1909–1928
Walter Donaldson	10	1916–1931
Raymond B. (Ray) Egan	8	1916–1925
Cliff Friend	8	1919–1939
Harold G. (a.k.a. Jack) Frost	7	1905–1920
Clarence Gaskill	5	1920–1923

(*continued*)

Dixie Mill Lyricists (*continued*)

NAME	NUMBER OF SONGS	INCLUSIVE YEARS
L. Wolfe Gilbert	13	1911–1929
William Jerome	8	1902–1927
Howard Johnson	7	1915–1929
Earle C. Jones	6	1906–1913
Gus Kahn	21	1913–1934
Edgar Leslie	11	1909–1940
Sam M. Lewis	22	1913–1932
Ballard MacDonald	14	1911–1920
Jack Mahoney	10	1911–1920
Stanley Murphy	14	1912–1917
Mitchell Parish	9	1921–1935
Harry Pease	5	1923–1928
Andy Razaf	9	1928–1939
Billy Rose	6	1925–1935
Fred Rose	6	1925–1931
Noble Sissle	6	1919–1925
Andrew B. Sterling	11	1899–1922
William Tracey	8	1916–1927
Jack Yellen	23	1912–1935
Joe Young	24	1912–1933

Dispelling the popular notion that Irving Berlin was the most prolific purveyor of words in Dixie tunes, the list of lyricists shows top dog in that department was Joe Young with twenty-four, beating out Jack Yellen's second-place twenty-three by just one song. Young topped them all only because, though he normally wrote Dixie tune lyrics in tandem with Sam M. Lewis, he also wrote a few on his own. The gifted Walter Donaldson, both as a lyricist and, mainly, as a composer, was the most prolific non-Jewish Alleyman of his day, and not just of Dixie tunes. His ten lyrics in the above list were sometimes set to melodies of his own composition, but he also wrote words to other people's tunes, and, as will be seen in the ensuing list, the same held true for Donaldson's melodies for southern songs.

Dixie Mill Composers

NAME	NUMBER OF SONGS	INCLUSIVE YEARS
Milton Ager	6	1922–1929
Harry Akst	10	1922–1936
Eubie Blake	6	1919–1925
Harry Carroll	8	1912–1920
George L. Cobb	6	1912–1916
Walter Donaldson	26	1915–1934
Gus Edwards	6	1899–1910
Albert Gumble	19	1909–1919
Ray Henderson	8	1923–1926
E. Clinton Keithley	6	1905–1925
F. Henri Klickmann	6	1919–1922
Arthur Lange	5	1915–1917
Henry I. Marshall	12	1913–1916
George W. Meyer	15	1907–1925
Halsey K. Mohr	6	1914–1921
Lewis F. Muir	5	1912–1914
Frank Perkins	5	1932–1934
Maceo Pinkard	6	1919–1927
Jean Schwartz	17	1902–1927
Abner Silver	6	1918–1925
Harry Tierney	7	1916–1930
Egbert Van Alstyne	9	1903–1925
Albert Von Tilzer	10	1909–1925
Harry Von Tilzer	8	1899–1922
Harry Warren	7	1924–1952
Richard A. Whiting	12	1916–1925

What's notable in the list of Dixie Mill composers is that two of them, Lewis F. Muir and Frank Perkins, are not only the five-song exceptions, but virtually all of those songs were *hits* with their respective lyricists L. Wolfe Gilbert and Mitchell Parish in extremely short periods of time, 1912–1914 and 1932–1934, respectively. Also, Walter Donaldson's high-scoring twenty-six melodies were almost all for Dixie tunes with lyrics by writers other than himself.

With this chapter's overview of the Alleymen who wrote the songs behind us, the ensuing chapters will examine the multifarious themes and subjects of the sixty years' worth of Tin Pan Alley Dixie tunes. We'll also look at the roles they played in forming and disseminating the American public's imaginative visions and images (or myths, if you will) of the American South during roughly the first half of the twentieth century.

2

WEEPY TIME DOWN SOUTH
Early Sentiment and Sentimentality

Even before there was a Tin Pan Alley in name, sentiment accounted for much of the stock-in-trade of the popular song industry in the United States. And if it was a hot commodity in vocal music generally, imagine how much sentiment figured in Dixie tunes with their emphasis not only on romance, but on homesickness, nostalgia, and the idyllic word-pictures of what lyricists considered to be the real or imagined South. While heavy sentiment was largely the product of the Alley's early years—say, before 1915—sentiment to some degree was endemic to many Dixie tunes right to their demise in the Alley in the 1950s, after which Nashville took over writing, publishing, and recording country tunes of homesickness for the South.

Sentiment is not a pejorative term or negative thing, though it has been devalued in recent decades, mostly among the young, whose musical tastes run more to the cynical, violent, and anti-nearly everything. (Relevant titles are Tina Turner's 1984 classic "What's Love Got To Do With It?" and, perhaps less familiar, yet still far from anything resembling sentiment, songs by the rock band Extreme between 1992 and 1995 like "Cupid's Dead," "There Is No God," "Leave Me Alone," and, of course, "Cynical," as well as much of the current genre of rap music.) In popular music, then, far from being bad, and deriving from the dictionary definition, sentiment is the *neutral* nomenclature for the appeal of a song based on *emotion* rather than on reason or intellect. While many recent and current rock and rap numbers appeal to emotions (albeit negative ones) rather than to reason or intellect, they assuredly are not sentimental.

Things get sticky and turn pejorative when people confuse sentiment with sentimentality, and the problem isn't made any easier since both nouns share the same adjective—sentimental. It's mostly agreed that sentimentality—meaning excess sentiment sinking into bathos and/or mawkishness—is a negative trait of popular songwriting. That agreement goes back a long time, although the two terms are still confused. An early advocate of drawing the line between acceptable sentiment and unacceptable sentimentality was the great southern writer of the Uncle Remus stories and other works, Joel Chandler Harris, who in 1898 pronounced, "In the great majority of cases sentiment develops into a sentimentality that is sometimes maudlin, sometimes officious, and frequently offensive" (Harris, *Grady* 34). Although during the sixty years of the Alley's Dixie tunes, sentiment was generally kept reined in within proper bounds, for the period during which Harris wrote he was absolutely correct. The writers of the earliest southern Alley songs apparently never read, or if they read, never heeded Harris's words, for—in the main— from 1898 through the Great War, maudlin sentimentality ruled the day in Dixie ditties, and it's with these treacly tunes that this chapter largely concerns itself.

Hypersentimental writing and audiences marked the earliest Dixie tunes as holdovers from the American Victorian era, in which popular "literature" was filled with sensational and sentimental triple-decker novels and their equivalents in multi-versed songs about young girls wronged, lovers parted by shipwrecks or fires, and innocent waifs abandoned, all oozing sticky sentimentality from their cover-art engraving to the last notes of their final chorus. One popular song-type in the mid-to-late nineteenth century was what I can only call dead-baby songs. The covers featured an engraving of a young mother, and sometimes a father too, either kneeling by an empty cradle, or standing outdoors by a tiny grave. What was beyond the covers I had not the stomach to find out without an insulin shot. I can take just so much gratuitous sentimentality; perhaps Americans of the Victorian era were made of stronger stuff than I, or maybe they just loved to wallow in such goo. Attesting to that are the many songs that were the flipside of dead-baby tunes—ones to be sung by a very young child whose mother has died, with such titles Isaac Goldberg noted as "Hello, Central, Give Me Heaven," "My Mamma Lives Up In The Sky," and "There's Another Picture In My Mamma's Frame" (Goldberg 94–95).

Dixie tunes never exploited babies and children for the sake of such cloying sentimentality, although they appear in a few songs in which their mammy is singing them a lullaby and even fewer in which they wish their mammy, now dead, was still on earth to sing them to sleep or care for them. Such songs are sentimental, as are all mammy songs, but they don't cross into gratuitous sentimentality. In fact, I had originally thought to include the genre of mammy songs in this chapter, but realized that the multidimensional mammy figure is so closely allied to feelings and images of nurturing and home in the South that such songs would be best deferred to Chapter 7, which is on the themes of home and homesickness. Besides, mammy songs mostly came later than the songs of treacly sentimentality that this chapter discusses.

Some lines of lyrics and summaries of the scenarios of three typical early Alley songs will show how heavy sentimentality played a role in Dixie tunes of the day. In the first year of such songs, a former slave tells a rare tale of the Civil War years in an Alley tune in "Way Down In The Old Palmetto State" (Chicago: Frank K. Root, 1898), with Clara Scott's words and Paul B. Armstrong's music. When Yankee troops "swarm'd the old plantation" of his "kind old master," a handsome northern soldier "stole the love of sweet Miss Fay," the plantation owner's daughter, and the two ran off, shortly after which both the old man and his wife died of grief. The song's refrain captures the sentimentality of the whole: "From the rice fields come the sounds of birds a-singing, / All around the dear old home it's sad and still, / Thro' the pine-tree tops the winds are softly sighing, / Where sleeps the kind old Master on the hill; / My heart is sad when thinking of the old home, / With its tumbling roof, its broken fence and gate, / Oh, to breathe the breath of sweet Magnolia blossoms / 'Way down in the old Palmetto State!"

In 1903, Andrew B. Sterling (words) and Harry Von Tilzer (music) wrote a piece, published by Von Tilzer, the egregiously sentimental "Down Where The Swanee River Flows," in which a boy returns to his southern home too late after his mother has died. Sterling's lyric sinks into bathos by his writing it in the first person, as the song's second chorus illustrates: "Where the sweet magnolia blows, there the Swanee River flows, / There's a lonesome little cabin on the hill, 'Tis the old home of my birth, but no fire burns on the hearth, / No mammy's there, the place is cold and still; / On the mantlepiece [sic] unread, lay the note in which I said, / 'Mother darling I am coming, wait for me'; / But I found a vacant chair, standing by the fireside there, / And I knelt and said a prayer on bended knee."

Herbert H. Taylor's "My Rose of Tennessee" (Chicago: Will Rossiter, 1907) is an archetypal tearjerker. A young man weds a girl from Tennessee with her mother's blessing, the mother only wishing they won't be living so far away. The second stanza tells the rest and reveals the sentimentality of the lyric's diction: "One short year soon passed away, We were coming home one day, / Just to cheer that mother as in days of yore, / Flowers blooming just as fair, birds sang sweetly everywhere, / But no mother came to greet us at the door. / By the dear old rustic seat, / Where as lovers oft' we'd meet / When the evening sun-beams set the West aglow / Just a little grassy mound was the message that we found, / And it seemed to speak those words of long ago"— "those words" being the refrain in which the mother described her daughter as "the fairest flower that blossoms 'mid the cotton and the corn."

Lest one think sentimentality occurred only in Dixie tunes of loss or death, rest assured it was also the stuff of early twentieth-century Alley songs of romance down south, including some by writers as gifted and prominent as the prolific team of Irish-American lyricist William Jerome and Jewish-Hungarian immigrant composer Jean Schwartz in their "My Lady of Kentucky" (Jerome H. Remick, 1905). Just Jerome's first verse and chorus, using some archaic diction and syntax, illustrates how stickily sentimental Dixie love songs could get back then: "Through a garden in Kentucky underneath the harvest moon / Two fond lovers singing love songs wend their way, / Little thinking of the morrow, hearts as true as stars in June, / Now and then the lad would kiss his queen and say— . . ." But for all the sentimental Dixie love songs in general, hyper-sentimentality was mostly reserved for two genres of Dixie tunes, one which began later than one would logically think and continued many years beyond when one would imagine it could have attracted an audience, and the other localizing dead-virgin songs in the South.

Sectional Reunion Sentimentalized

Nina Silber's *The Romance of Reunion* examines not how northerners viewed the South politically during and after Reconstruction, but how they felt about it sentimentally, even romantically, through works of fiction and nonfiction, civic pageantry, minstrel shows, and other popular cultural events up to and just past the turn of the century. Silber observes that throughout the 1870s, '80s, and '90s, nearly up to the Spanish-American War, in the northern imagination the North was portrayed as masculine and the South as feminine: hence the scenario of the northern boy courting and "winning" the southern girl with her southern (sometimes Confederate veteran) daddy's permission and occasionally even blessing "in scores of novels, plays, and popular songs" that appealed "mainly to middle- and upper-class northerners" (Silber 95). While she cites a number of novels, plays, stories, and travel accounts containing this motif, Silber never again returns to the matter of popular songs. Curious about this and why the earliest one I found was dated 1899, long after the vogue for this brand of sentimental story-telling had passed, I e-mailed Silber, a history professor at Boston University, and received an almost immediate reply, which, if not precisely answering my questions, was enlightening on its own.

Silber began her e-mail "with the confession that since I did the research for The Romance of Reunion [her earliest book] some twenty years ago, my recollection of all my findings will inevitably be a bit dim" (Silber e-mail to the author, December 23, 2011, as are all further quotations from her). She notes, as I just did, that the "pattern of the northern boy courting the southern girl was the predominant narrative in much of the fiction, theater, and travel accounts I surveyed from the 1870s and 1880s." Silber also mentions she did most of her popular song research at the Library of Congress and the Performing Arts Division of the New York Public Library, so one might assume that if any songs with this boy-girl motif existed before the turn of the century, she would have found and mentioned them in her book, considering how detailed her presentation is of the prose and theatrical works telling such tales. But she doesn't. Yet, "Right around the Spanish American war I was struck by a new theme that was less about romance and more about . . . the manly reunion of northern and southern white men." In her last chapter, "New Patriotism and New Men in the South," Silber treats manliness and northern admiration for it in southern men, especially after Teddy Roosevelt recruited so many for his Rough Riders in 1898. Yet at the same time my group of Alley northern-boy-woos-southern-girl songs began to emerge, seemingly anachronistically.

After addressing this point by saying to me, "what you describe is curious," Silber offered an intriguing hypothesis for these sentimental boy-girl songs coming so late when the general run of positive sentiments about the South starting at the time of the Spanish-American War had shifted to an appreciation of the manliness of white southerners: "Maybe these songs were already being nostalgic about the 'romance of reunion' sentiment? Indeed, I do think that songs seeking to promote a sentimental, nostalgic sensibility would absolutely work better telling this story about the romance of southern women than a story that celebrated southern manhood." Whether such nostalgia was a deliberate harking back to the popular scenario of stories, novels, and plays from the 1870s and '80s by lyricists, or merely their unconscious penchant to write in a sentimental fashion, it's impossible to say, since so little is known about the early Alleymen who wrote these songs. But either way, for me Silber's theory goes a long way toward explaining the writing and popularity of this little group of songs from 1899 up to the Great War.

Only three of these songs, all among the earliest, conform precisely to the North-South courtships in the prose tales and plays of the 1870s through early '90s. Despite the joyousness of the intersectional romances themselves, two of these Dixie tunes are written like Victorian-American sob-ballads—bittersweet to the point of being lugubrious, the third just sweetly sentimental. Most striking about Robert F. Roden's lyric for the earliest of these songs, "My Little Georgia Rose," with Max S. Witt's music (Jos. W. Stern, 1899), is the speed with which the girl's father, seemingly not an ex-soldier, accepts the northern lad's proposal: "My boy, / May your lives be filled with joy." Yet with his next breath he starts turning on the guilt even before the first verse is over: "Tho' 'twill break my heart, this plan that you propose; / All the sunshine in my life will depart when she's your wife, / When you carry North my little Georgia rose." In the second verse we find that for a while the girl's doting father wrote letters to the young couple, but in time they "seldom came, his love to tell." Learning his health is failing, the young man and his bride return South to see the old man "for one long, last farewell." When they are at his bedside, Roden turns on a final outpouring of lugubriousness (and guilt) in Daddy's last words: "'Life seems so empty now,' he said, 'Since my darling child is wed, / Tho' her happiness I never would oppose; / From the day her mother died, She was always by my side, / 'Till you took away my little Georgia rose.'" Though Wolfie gets his song order a bit out of whack, L. Wolfe Gilbert in his 1926 *Billboard* piece on sentimental songs notes from a distance of twenty-seven years that "My Little Georgia Rose" was a great sentimental hit in its day (Gilbert 78), suggesting that other tunes about intersectional romances may have also done well.

Willie Wildwave's sweetly sentimental "She's Kentucky's Fairest Daughter" (Helf and Falke, 1901) recounts how "an old Kentucky colonel" gives his permission and unspoken blessing to his daughter's match when he says to her, "'You know I want to keep you here, but still I've naught to say, / Just let your heart decide, and thus be led. / A daughter of Kentucky can never go astray' / Then as he joined their hands, once more he said: / 'She's Kentucky's fairest daughter, with her mother's laughing eyes, / She's Kentucky's fairest daughter, born beneath the southern skies, / She's a daughter of Kentucky, she is staunch and true and plucky, / If you've won her heart, you've won a prize.'" Sentimental, yes, but never going over into the cloying or bathetic. Yet this isn't a true song of North-South reconciliation, since Kentucky remained a state loyal to the Union during the Civil War.

The last song conforming to all aspects of the North-South courtship motif is Martin Bowes's "A Little Southern Bride" (Richard A. Saalfield, 1901), a tearjerker combining the worst kinds of excessive sentimentality with dolefulness that makes "My Little Georgia Rose" look cheerful by comparison. Written in the first person, the song tells of a northern boy who "To a grand old southern home I once did stray." There he met and fell in love with Molly, the daughter of a father "who for the southern cause had bled," and the boy courted her for a number of years. When the young man finally told Molly's father that he wished to marry her, "These are the words the brave old soldier said" (which is the chorus to each of the song's two stanzas): "'Molly is a Southern girl, her father wore the gray, / You are from the North my lad your father wore the blue, / She's been my joy for years,' and his old eyes filled with tears, / 'But if she dearly loves you and you'll be kind and true, / Then take her lad, protect her, my only child my pride, / Take her to your Northern home, a little Southern bride.'" In the second verse the lad does so after the two are wed "from her grand old southern home," and Molly's father writes weekly letters to the young couple. Then a message comes "Bidding us for the last time to seek his side." When they are by him, at long last—having only given them *permission* to wed before—"his fond eyes with pain were dim / But he gave his father's blessing ere he died." The chorus repeats, the song ends, and, presumably, there's not a dry eye in the house.

The remaining eight songs sentimentally or romantically celebrating the North and South forming a more perfect reunion are more upbeat than these. Several are too similar to discuss individually, but pointing out the highlights of a few shows how some were variations on the common theme. "My Girl From Dixie," with words and music by Raymond A. Browne and Robert J. Adams (Chicago: Sol Bloom, 1900), is a cheerful tune in which the

Yankee singer idealizes the Southern Belle he's about to marry, taking time out to declare, "It will be a union of the Blue and Gray upon our wedding day / When I wed the girl from Dixie who has won my heart away." On December 12, 1901, Silas Leachman recorded the piece for Victor Monarch Records, and it's on the Internet. Two 1910 songs have ungainly titles but are interesting for quite different reasons. "When A Boy From Old New Hampshire Loves A Girl From Tennessee" has lyrics by William Cahalin and Robert F. Roden and music by J. Fred Helf (J. Fred Helf, 1910). The piece celebrates one of the most amicable reunions of North and South through marriage in song, since not only does the boy travel to Dixie for the wedding, but a whole trainload of his relatives arrives from New Hampshire too, all warmly greeted by the girl's kin in Tennessee! The second is "Don't Forget Your Northern Lad When You Go Back To Dixie," with lyrics by Monroe H. Rosenfeld and music by Harry I. Davis (Jos. W. Stern, 1910). It's a reunion song, but the northern man doesn't want his southern sweetheart to forget, when she returns to Dixie, the promises they made each other about future plans while she was visiting up North. The song is curious for two reasons. First, Rosenfeld was a rare southern Alleyman, born and raised in Richmond, Virginia, yet this is the *only* Dixie tune this writer of over two hundred popular songs ever wrote. Second, the lyric is unusual since the northern singer so adores his southern fiancée that he says, "In Georgia land I'll take my stand, / If you'll give me your heart and hand," rather than asking her to move north with him.

Three other songs stray far from the norm. In Herbert Ingraham's "Dixie Belle" (Maurice Shapiro, 1911), the girl's father is adamant in refusing to let his "Southern flower" wed her "Northern beau." But this flower is no shrinking violet. She had promised the boy to marry him, and marry him she will, so she contrives to elope: "While her dad was sound asleep, / She said I feel bad for my contrary dad, But my promise I must keep"—one feisty belle for 1911!

In the unique "When Northern Eyes of Blue (Surrendered To The Southern Gray)," with Thomas Hoier's words and James Morgan's music (Chicago: Will Rossiter, 1915), the northern blue eyes belong to a woman, and the southern gray ones to a man, as the final words of the chorus say: "He fought her with love, and with kisses / Till at last her poor heart gave way / I know it's true, those Northern eyes of blue, / Surrendered to the Southern gray." Whether Hoier was trading on the new appreciation of southern manliness or just looking for an original angle by having the South "win" after over fifteen years of the same motif, it's impossible to say, but the lyric is a striking departure from others in the group.

One song, earlier than this, deserves mention, partly because it's by the only two writers of such songs who achieved lasting name recognition, lyricist William Jerome and composer Jean Schwartz, and partly because it's the one song that generalizes the sectional reconciliation theme into something of a national patriotic display, sentimentally perhaps, but rather charmingly, too. "Dear Old Dixie Land" (Jerome H. Remick, 1905) portrays reunion between the North and South in bold strokes. To cite just three of them, including the chorus: "Miss Dixie and her Uncle Sam are strolling arm in arm . . . / Miss Nancy's fixing up the place, just gaze inside and see, / The pictures hanging on the wall are Lincoln, Grant, and Lee. / Way down South in Dixie, Dear old Dixie land / The Blue and Gray are marching, Brothers, hand in hand / Stars and stripes a-flying united now we stand, / It's all forgotten in the land of cotton, Dear Old Dixie land." Jerome's lyrics may have been trading on the new patriotism and new manliness in the air in both the North and South after the Spanish-American War.

Dead Virgins in Dixie

Part of me truly believes that Edgar Allan Poe would have thought twice before stating in his 1846 essay "The Philosophy of Composition," "The death . . . of a beautiful woman is, unquestionably, the most poetical topic in the world" (qtd. in Emerson 167) if he could have foreseen that in its wake (pun intended?) would follow the legion of mawkish, second-rate songs on that topic that poured forth during the rest of the nineteenth century and the first decade of the twentieth, Stephen Foster guilty of some of them. Written by lesser lights than he, songs in which a virginal young woman dies before marriage proliferated down through the decades of Victorian and Edwardian America, their sheer quantity indicative of how the public ate up these weepers, along with the dead-baby songs noted earlier. (Seemingly, in music lovers' hearts back then, egregious sentimentality and morbidity went hand in hand.) In most dead-virgin songs, no locale is named, the emphasis being put on a person, not a place. That changed in 1899 with Sterling and Von Tilzer's multimillion seller "My Old New Hampshire Home," discussed in the Prologue, and in that same year the rash of dead-virgin songs set in Dixie broke out and spread through eleven such tunes by 1909, after which the disease shriveled and died.

In his 1926 *Billboard* piece on sentimental songs, L. Wolfe Gilbert suggested reasons for the popularity of dead-virgin tunes in their day, and nailed down the features of their usual "plot.": "Years ago, when divorce and running away with another's sweetheart was not a sort of national pastime, lovers were rarely separated, so far as the average person knew, except by death or a lovers' quarrel. So when the songwriter sang about lovers, he parted them either by death or a quarrel and the public got 'My Old New Hampshire Home,' 'The Girl I Loved in Sunny Tennessee' and 'She Rests by the Swanee River.' In practically every song of this type one found the lover returning to his home only to discover that his sweetheart had passed away during his absence" (Gilbert 78). Note that two of the three dead-virgin songs Wolfie cites as public favorites were Dixie tunes. Given how young girls were betrothed back then, the frail things in these songs must have been between sixteen and twenty. Only one song names the cause of death—a fever; for the rest, some safe bets are consumption, pellagra, or cholera.

Seven of the eleven dead-virgin Dixie tunes follow the scenario Gilbert sketched, either fully or in a truncated way. The first, "The Girl I Loved In Sunny Tennessee," with Harry Braisted's words and Stanley Carter's music (Jos. W. Stern, 1899), is a truncated one. Rather than having a first verse in which the boy proposes and says good-bye to his girl as he goes off to war or some other calling, Braisted's lyric begins with him "speeding on a train" homeward to see her after an absence of "a few short years." The joyful tone abruptly shifts when he arrives to find friends, neighbors, and his own mother in tears, but his intended absent from the scene. "As I whispered, 'Mother dear, / Where is Mary? She's not here!'" his mother wordlessly "pointed to a spot, / In the churchyard's little lot / Where my sweetheart sleeps in sunny Tennessee."

To go into all the particulars of the other six overly sentimental songs with the same or similar plots would be simply redundant, if not bathetic, so I'll just hit the highlights of three that stand out for various reasons. It's possible that in "In Alabama," with words by Carroll Fleming and music by Chas. B. Lawlor (Lyric Music Publishing, 1900), the man's sweetheart may have been older than the norm for virginal victims when she died, for we learn that after he went off to war he was "For many years a captive, held upon a foreign strand," so there's no telling how long he was away from his Dixie darling. Still, by the time he returned, in the second verse, he sings, "I'll ne'er forget the greeting of her mother old and gray, / My loving heart was breaking as I heard her sadly say, / We've laid her in the garden 'neath the roses fragrant bloom, where the odor of the lilac fills the air with sweet perfume." "In The Hills Of Old Carolina" (London: Chas. K. Harris, 1902) had both words and music by the acknowledged Alley turn-of-the-century Schmaltz King Charles K. ("After The Ball") Harris, and its treacly mawkishness measures up to anything else he ever wrote. As shrewd a songwriter as a publisher, Harris knew the dead-virgin market was a bandwagon worth jumping on. In the song, the boy says good-bye to his girl to go fight a war in which "the Blue and Gray join hands," most likely a reference to the recent Spanish-American War, which lasted only a matter of months. But "When I came to claim my bride, / She was sleeping side by side, / With the old folks on the hills so far away." Much of the song's sentimentality comes in the chorus: "In the hills of old Carolina, Stands a dear old southern home / Where 'oft in childhood days we used to play, / Now the one I loved so well, Sleeps where weeping willows dwell / In the hills of old Carolina, far away."

One song contains both a lovers' quarrel and a death—"The Heart You Lost In Maryland You'll Find In Tennessee," with Arthur J. Lamb's words and Alfred Solman's music (Jos. W. Stern, 1907). The story is quickly summarized: The boy and girl live in Maryland (considered part of Dixie in this song); they quarrel and she moves to Tennessee. After a time the girl regrets her harsh words and writes to the boy to join her there, but as the boy arrived, "His sweetheart's mother met him in the doorway, / And when he saw her eyes with sad tears fill, / She whispered: 'In another land she'll meet you.' / Then she pointed to the churchyard on the hill." For me that gets the bathos prize, hands down.

Other songs in the dead-virgin group stray slightly from the usual plot pattern or discard it entirely in interesting ways. In Tony Sanford's "She Rests By The Suwanee River" (F. A. Mills, 1901)—which L. Wolfe Gilbert wrote as "Swanee" and which should be "Suwannee"—the boy doesn't go anywhere; the girl simply dies before the two can wed, and she does so in the first verse. On February 16, 1901, Joseph Natus recorded that verse and the chorus for Victor Monarch Records, as may be heard on the Internet. In "Where The Mississippi Meets The Sea," one of the rare early Alley songs by a female lyricist, with words by Rose Bradley and music by Carl F. Miller (Melville Music, 1906), the young man also doesn't return from a journey and the young woman who dies, in this case of a specified fever, is African American. And in "When The Birds In Georgia Sing Of Tennessee," with lyrics again by Arthur J. Lamb and music by Ernest R. Ball (M. Witmark, 1907), we are actually witness to a dying girl in Tennessee taking comfort in the love letters she receives from her sweetheart in Georgia.

Modern sensibilities may find the sentimentality of dead-virgin songs hard to take, but there was a positive side to some of their lyrics—evocative descriptions of Dixie scenes, creating images of the idyllic South much of this book focuses on. Two samples will illustrate this.

German-Jewish-born Alleyman Gus Edwards gained most fame as a composer ("In My Merry Oldsmobile," "School Days," "By The Light Of The Silvery Moon"), and as the producer of the vaudeville act "School Boys and Girls," for which he "discovered" and directed such future personalities as Eddie Cantor, Walter Winchell, Groucho Marx, Lilyan Tashman, and Ray Bolger (see Jasen 127). But occasionally he turned his hand to lyric writing, as in the mostly descriptive first verse of his dead-virgin song "Where The Mississippi Flows" (Haviland & Dresser, 1901): "As the golden sun goes down in a little southern town, / On a quaint old fashioned home it sheds its glow; / As it sinks behind the hill, then the mocking birds are still, / And my thoughts go back to days of long ago. / When the moon in splendor grand rises o'er the lovely land, / Then I seem to roam again with sweetheart Rose; / And I hear her say one word, sweetest that was ever heard, / 'Mid magnolias, where the Mississippi flows." The Dixiescape (to coin a word) that forms the refrain in Tony Sanford's "She Rests By The Suwanee River" portrays an equally lush bucolic South as a northern Alleyman conceived it: "She rests by the Suwanee River Where the orange blossoms bloom / Where the air is always scented With magnolia's sweet perfume— / Where the Mocking birds are singing In the tree-tops all the day, / She rests by the Suwanee River—Far, far away." One can't tell if the song's final words are a deliberate echo of Stephen Foster's "Way down upon the Swanee River, far, far away," but such descriptive passages in dead-virgin songs lead naturally to the final topic in this chapter.

Nostalgia Isn't What It Used To Be

When novelist, editor, and all-around wit Peter De Vries coined that phrase, it's almost certain he didn't base his observation on any decreasing degree of nostalgia in Dixie tunes down through their history, if indeed he based it on anything at all. But the fact is that, with few exceptions, in the Alley's southern songs where the theme is the singer's nostalgic longing for times, places, or people he loved long ago, the sticky sentimentality is laid on more thickly, as if with a trowel, in those written from 1899 through the 'teens than in those of the 1920s and '30s. After that, such nostalgic pieces fizzle out entirely. One reason for this might be that as time went by, the Victorian/Edwardian sensibilities for extravagant sentiment, which wallowed in nostalgia, gradually gave way to the good-time-Charlie mindset of the '20s Jazz Age and then, when that party was over with the Crash of '29 and the Great Depression, to the cynicism and despair of the '30s. Yet this hypothesis won't work, since other kinds of Dixie tunes remained as lushly romantic, idyllic, and filled with sentiment as were the songs of earlier decades—and just as popular too—some, in fact, even more so. No other explanations for the demise of Dixie nostalgia in Alley songs come readily to mind; it just happened with the end of the '30s.

I didn't select the fifty-seven Dixie tunes lumped under this heading because their theme of nostalgia equals the first, preferred Merriam-Webster definition of "homesickness." If they did, these songs would appear not here but in Chapter 7 with the hundreds of genuine homesickness songs and those about people acting on their homesickness and traveling back to Dixie. No, the nostalgic Dixie tunes in this group are a special breed, precisely conforming to the second Merriam-Webster definition of "a wistful or excessively sentimental sometimes abnormal yearning for return to or of some past period or irrecoverable condition." The key points are two: the excessive sentimentality aligns these songs with the other types discussed in this chapter, and the singer yearns for the irrecoverable, unlike in actual homesickness songs where there is always a chance of going home. The tone here is one of stasis: for whatever reason, you can't go home again; or, what you long for—a childhood home, a deceased spouse, sweetheart, or mammy—is no longer there to return to. These songs contain not just heavy sentimentality but futility too, something absent from straightforward homesickness and "traveling home" songs.

From the earliest—Charles K. Harris's "'Mid The Green Fields of Virginia" (Milwaukee: Chas. K. Harris, 1898)—to the latest—Al Trace's "Little Sweetheart Of The Ozarks" (Chicago: M. M. Cole, 1937)—all the Alley's nostalgic Dixie tunes share two features. Not surprisingly, they are written in the first person, and the gender of that person is invariably male, though a few of the lyricists were women. One other shared aspect of twenty of the fifty-seven nostalgia songs is more unusual, as if the lyricists impossibly were in collusion about how to begin their first verses. In each of these songs, spread out from 1899 through 1921, the singer's nostalgic reverie begins either at twilight or in the first hours of darkness after dusk. Other than these hours suggesting a quiet time for solitude and reflection after the business of the day, I find no good reason for beginning these nostalgic Dixie tunes in the early evening.

Broken down by what the songs' singers are nostalgic for, just two are for Dixie melodies heard long ago, excluding lullabies sung by southern mammies. The earliest, "Chattanooga Blues" (Seidel Music Pub. Co., 1916), with music by the publisher, I. Seidel, has a lyric by Maceo Pinkard, who later became one of the Alley's great black composers ("Sweet Georgia Brown," to name just one of his Dixie tunes), and it's not hard to understand why he stopped writing lyrics after this uninspired 1916 effort at wistful longing for a song "From dear old Tennessee."

Seven of eight longings for the irrecoverable return to the warmth and lullaby-crooning of a long-gone black mammy—whether one's own mother or a nursemaid from a white singer's childhood—express purely personal emotions, as do virtually all Dixie nostalgia songs. Yet Ballard MacDonald went beyond the norm by turning a personal mammy song into a lament for the passing of a simpler age into one much less so when he wrote "At Mammy's Fireside," with Harry Carroll's music (Shapiro, Bernstein, 1913): "Times are diff'rent since the bygone days, / They don't seem the same as before, / Folks are diff'rent and they've changed their ways, / They don't seem the same no more; / They've machines to pick the cotton that they used to pick by hand, / The darkies who played banjos all belong to someone's band; / They serenade by phonograph, not like I won my bride, / At Mammy's fireside."

A populous group, with thirteen songs, has the least to do with Dixie since these are all singers' reveries about long-lost loves, usually sweethearts, although sometimes wives, and the fact that the two of them lived in Dixie or that the woman died there is incidental. Since the focus is on the personal relationship between the still inconsolable singer and his beloved lover from the past, the locale in these songs could be transferred to almost any region, or none in particular, and the substance of the nostalgic lyric would not change significantly. Only one of these songs, "Dreamy Florida," with lyrics by Leavenworth McNab and music by Salvatore Tomaso (Chicago: Frances Clifford Music, 1921), briefly paints a fairly detailed landscape of a specific section of the South: "Dreamy Florida / Where the orange trees, / Scent the balmy breeze, / And the Southern moon shines drowsily."

Such writing belongs more properly to the fourth and largest group of thirty-four nostalgia songs, in which the singer longs for a familiar place from his past. The place is either a childhood scene replete with friends and family long gone or a Dixiescape of special meaning to the singer but one to which he can never return. Rich descriptive passages are the life of the best of such songs (as are good melodies), for the better the landscape painting, the more effective the nostalgia (and the better the songs will sell).

Illustrative of the last two points is the earliest of the type, the enormously popular "'Mid The Green Fields Of Virginia" by that past master of sentimentality Charles K. Harris (Milwaukee: Chas. K. Harris, 1898), which L. Wolfe Gilbert in his 1926 *Billboard* article cites as one of the great sentimental turn-of-the-century favorites. Harris's ability to capture specifics rather than write in generalities must have been one of the keys to his success: "'Mid the green fields of Virginia, In the vale of Shenandoah / There's an ivy-covered homestead that I love; / With its quaint old-fashioned chimney, and its simple homelike air; / 'Twas the home of my dear parents now above. / Though I'm living in a mansion grand, With wealth at my command, / I'd give it all for just a single day, / To play with my young comrades, and to see my mother dear / 'Mid the green fields of Virginia far away." The earliest recording of the tune on the Internet is S. H. Dudley and Harry Macdonough's on a 1904 Monarch Record. They sing only the first verse quoted above and the chorus, but these alone capture Harris's brand of nostalgia.

Other writers of songs in which the singer futilely longs for a past time and place may not have penned as sustained descriptive passages as Harris, but even their briefer snippets were building blocks for shaping the idyllic image of the South that Alleymen together created over the decades. Just a few will show their variety. In a rare early Dixie tune with both words and music by a woman, Mary S. Knight's "'Neath The Blue Kentucky Skies" (Chicago:

McKinley, 1909) sketched some images nearly as precise and detailed as Harris's: "In childhood's hours 'neath the blue Kentucky sky / It was there the birds sang sweetest in the morn, / It was there the flow'rs bloomed by the way; / It was there the crimson clover mingled its perfume / With the odor of the fragrant new-mown hay."

In *The Yeomen of the Guard*, W. S. Gilbert had the jester Jack Point say, "For, look you, there is humour in all things." Whether consciously or not, lyricist Harold Atteridge took Point's words to heart in a *comic* nostalgia tune with Harry Carroll's music published the year Prohibition went into effect titled "Give Me The Moonshine Of My Old Kentucky Home" (Waterson, Berlin & Snyder, 1920). Despite its copyright date, the tune was probably written the previous year, since it debuted in the Broadway show *Fifty-Fifty, Ltd.*, which opened on October 27, 1919. The piece is a riotous bit of nostalgia sung by a man who sorely misses his family still in the hills of Kentucky, as seen in just the chorus: "Oh! My heart's in the heart of old Kentucky, / For I still am dreaming of that still; / Where the roses 'round the door, / Seemed to say "let's have one more," / Till we couldn't hear the whistling of the whippoorwill. / Oh! what thrills in the hills of old Kentucky— / In the still of the ev'ning we would roam. / And tho' I dearly love the sunshine of Virginia, / Give me the moonshine of my old Kentucky Home."

More in the mainstream of later nostalgia are bits of Larry Yoell's lyric to "Rock-A-Bye My Baby Blues," with music by Billy Hill (San Francisco: Sherman, Clay, 1923): "Shadows softly falling / 'Round the cabin door / Nightingale is calling / Down the Swanee shore / Moon is slowly creepin' in the evenin' sky"; and, its words expressing futility over the inability to recapture the past—from "Louisiana Days," with words and music by Eddie Elliott and W. Max Davis (Jerome H. Remick, 1927), "Louisiana days back in the long ago—Louisiana days I loved them so— / Cotton fields white, Southern moonlight / Banjos strumming sweet and low— / Dreamy nights down on the levee— / Memories that will forever last / Oh! I am longing for the things I love in vain— / Louisiana days that have passed."

Sentiment would continue in Dixie tunes as long as Alleymen wrote them, chiefly as a component of the huge bloc of homesickness songs. Yet in these, the core was the comforting images of home, not the unhappiness of the singer as in nostalgia songs. As Victorian/Edwardian sensibilities drained from American tastes in popular song with the passing of the first three decades of the twentieth century, heavy-handed sentimentality gradually but finally disappeared from Dixie tunes along with potential audiences' desire for it. Henceforth (and even in the "sob-ballad decades"), the Alley's Dixie tunes would be, generally speaking, much more celebratory in nature, as the remaining chapters will reveal.

3

TYPECASTING—SOUTHERN SOCIAL AND ETHNIC, THAT IS

Southern folk never had to wait for Yankees or residents of other sections to sling catchy epithets at them. At least since the mid-nineteenth century, Dixie's denizens called each other names in abundance, and many of those sobriquets permanently stuck as labels for clearly describable southern types, both male and female, white and black. The earliest compilation of a good number of these labeled groups was Daniel R. Hundley's 1860 *Social Relations in Our Southern States.* Hundley was "an Alabama lawyer" whose "family's roots were in Virginia," "a patrician who believed one's highest calling was to be a gentleman" (Hobson 63). He met all the qualifications for being a Southern Gentleman, according to his description of the type in his book, and was, overall, "an Alabamian who sometimes wished he were a Virginian" (Hobson 64), since the "special habitats" of Southern Gentlemen "were Virginia and South Carolina" (Reed, *Southern Folk* 25). If an Alabamian couldn't *be* a Virginian, at least he could marry one, which is what Hundley did in the person of a "wealthy first cousin," Mary Ann Hundley, and together they had seven children. But after Hundley and his brood returned from moving to Chicago, where he worked for his father-in-law and wrote his book, he and his family lived out their lives in Alabama, not in Virginia at all (Hobson 63; Williams).

The title of Hundley's book is a misnomer since the author never discusses *relations* or interactions between or among the groups of southerners he writes of. Instead, each chapter discretely describes the characteristics of just one group. John Shelton Reed correctly states, "Hundley meant his book to be a serious ethnography, describing these different sorts of Southerners" (Reed, *Southern Folk* 24), but he was ill-equipped for the task, not being anything like Reed himself—a sociologist by education, profession, and inclination. More accurately, Hundley's book is a descriptive *catalogue* of southern social types. As Reed points out, "What Hundley called 'classes' he saw as fixed and rigid categories, virtually as castes, not as the combination of social role and observer response that I [Reed] have been using the phrase 'social type' to convey" (*Southern Folk* 24–25). After a preface, Hundley's table of contents divides the book into eight chapters, each dedicated to one specific group (for Hundley a class; for us a social type), in an order essentially from high to low, as follows: the Southern Gentleman (the longest chapter, at seventy pages), the Middle Classes, the Southern Yankee, Cotton Snobs, the Southern Yeoman, the Southern Bully, Poor White Trash, and the Negro Slaves (Hundley [iii]). Not all these types survived beyond the Civil War, others didn't survive into the period of Tin Pan Alley's Dixie tunes, while yet others survived although their names morphed into new ones with the passing years. Twentieth-century southerners came up with some new labels like hillbilly, good old boy, and redneck that to some extent fit Hundley's older types with a little tweaking. Except for Poor Whites, Hundley spent no words on types of southern women, although some had distinguishing labels (such as the Southern Lady and the Southern Belle) dating back to his day. Others existed then but unlabeled, only to get their sobriquets much later (such as the Steel Magnolia—whose name entered the scene *after* the Alley wrote of Dixie). Also, Alleymen borrowed a label from elsewhere to name a southern female type, and I filched a rhyming equivalent for her male counterpart. But that's getting too far ahead of the story of Dixie portrait painting in popular song.

A Paucity of Gentlemen, a Plethora of Belles

In some snippets of his lengthy description extracted by John Shelton Reed, Hundley's Southern Gentleman has "a natural dignity of manner" and "the utmost self-possession—that much coveted *savoir faire,* which causes a man to appear perfectly at home, whether it be in a hut or a palace." He is "remarkably easy and natural, never haughty in appearance, or loud of voice—even when angry rarely raising his voice above the tone of gentlemanly conversation" (qtd. in Reed and Reed, *1001 Things,* Item #933). Moreover, it can be gleaned from numerous actual and fictional accounts that with regard to his interactions with the ladies, the Southern Gentleman is characterized by impeccable manners, a modest and polite but not self-deprecating bearing, and a mode of behavior best described as chivalrous. These qualities were not just the traits of the antebellum Southern Gentleman but ones he carried over past the Civil War and into his few appearances in Tin Pan Alley and other songs of the early twentieth century.

"Few appearances" is a bit hyperbolic, since my explorations for Dixie tunes turned up only three in which the Southern Gentleman makes any appearance at all, and, based on very little evidence, that the man in one of those is a Southern Gentleman is rather conjectural on my part. To begin with that song, "Good Bye Virginia," with music by Jean Schwartz (Waterson, Berlin & Snyder, 1915), had lyrics by the tremendously skillful Grant Clarke. His name never became a household word, but in his short life (1891–1931) Clarke wrote the lyrics of such enormous hits as "Ragtime Cowboy Joe," "Second Hand Rose," and "Am I Blue?" as well as the popular Dixie tune of 1918 (still remembered by some), "Everything Is Peaches Down In Georgia." Born in Akron, Ohio, once he arrived in New York Clarke early on was one of those Alleymen whose careers began as a staff writer for various music publishers. He caught a break by writing special material for some of the biggest stars of the day, including Bert Williams, Fanny Brice, Eva Tanguay, Nora Bayes, and Al Jolson (*ASCAP* 88). As an urban Alleyman, Clarke undoubtedly came to know the ways of northern males, gentlemen and otherwise, and it seems to me that the portrait he paints of the man in "Good Bye Virginia" doesn't fit any kind of gentlemanly northern type at all; he is far too gallant for that. While Clarke's lyric doesn't specify where the man comes from, the lady named Virginia lives in the state with the same name. Early in the song the man falls instantly in love with this winsome woman, but "He saw a ring on her finger, / Just as he reached for her hand" and backed off, pursuing his amorous advances no further. This kind of behavior, it strikes me, is something in the repertoire of the chivalrous Southern Gentleman, being mindful of the lady's married state, whereas a less refined and delicate—or, let us say, perhaps, a more crass—northern chap might continue his pursuit, hoping for an extramarital assignation. In the rest of the song the man sings goodbye to Virginia, both the woman and the state, in various elegant ways, since he knows he must leave each of them, brokenhearted after losing their beauty and charm. As I said, the evidence is slight, but Clarke's lyrics often worked by innuendo and verbal sleight-of-hand, so I stand by my conjecture that the man in "Good Bye Virginia" is in fact a Southern Gentleman.

There's no argument that the two men delineated in Jack Yellen (lyrics) and George L. Cobb's (music) "Are You From Dixie? ('Cause I'm From Dixie

Too)" (M. Witmark, 1915) are southerners. The only question might be whether they are true Southern Gentlemen. Although the language of the younger one who does all the singing is rather more exuberant than the gentlemanly speech described by Hundley, in other respects both men fit the bill nicely, with a little help from the sheet music's cover art depicting a youngish man in a fashionable suit, hat, and spats of the day, and an older one equally fashionable but wearing what might be called a "plantation suit" of long coat and waistcoat, string tie, and broad-brimmed hat; the two are about to shake hands. Behind them are southern blacks picking cotton, and, in the far distance, the "big house" of a plantation. Yet in the lyric the two men meet not on a cotton plantation but in a northern railway terminal. Clothes may make the man, but the lyric doesn't describe either man's natty apparel, so when the song was performed in vaudeville or played on a phonograph without benefit of illustration, the younger man apparently spotted the older one as a fellow southerner not by any distinctive garb but by other ineffable qualities that told him they shared a common heritage, not just as southerners, but perhaps as Southern Gentlemen: "Hello, there, stranger! How do you do? / There's something I'd like to say to you— / Don't be surprised, — / You're recognized! — / I'm no detective but I've just surmised / You're from the place where I long to be, — / You're from my own land, / My sunny homeland, / Tell me can it be?" In the second verse, the singer unambiguously identifies himself as a patrician who, years ago (like Hundley working for his father-in-law's Chicago real estate firm), went north to make his fortune, but is now eagerly planning to return to his family's ancestral home: "It was away back in eighty-nine / I crossed the old Mason Dixon line— / Gee! but I've yearned, — / Longed to return—To all the good old pals I left behind—/ My home is way down in Alabam' — / On a plantation near Birmingham." The case isn't rock-solid, but the men Yellen created seem to fall into the type of the Southern Gentleman. Recording artist tenor Billy Murray recorded the song in 1916 on an Edison Blue Amberol cylinder, and it may be heard on the Internet.

There's no ambiguity at all about the third and final Southern Gentleman song, especially since the title of this 1907 piece, with lyrics by John De Witt and music by W. H. Bontemps, is "I Am A Southern Gentleman." The only quibble is that this tune in all likelihood did not come out of Tin Pan Alley, not even if we take the Alley in its widest sense to include far-flung professional publishers in such cities as St. Louis, Detroit, and Columbus, Ohio.

The truth is that I have no idea where the song was published nor the name of the publisher, since I've never seen the actual sheet music. My acquaintance with the piece is from an excerpt I found on p. 175 of Nina Silber's *The Romance of Reunion,* and endnote 27 on p. 222 gives only the song's author, composer, and date. In our e-mail correspondence, Silber said she checked some files that might have some notes on the song, but her search came up empty. Between her discovering the song either at the Library of Congress or the Smithsonian and the internal evidence of the excerpts Silber quotes, my guess is that "I Am A Southern Gentleman" was written by southerners, and published by a regional, most probably southern, publisher: "I am a Southern gentleman, with gracious mien and air; / I love to serve my mistress sweet, with manners debonair. / I doff my hat and wait on her, Obedient to her will, / For I'm a Southern gentleman, Yes, I'm a Southern still." As if the archaic diction and turned syntax ("mistress sweet," "manners debonair") do not bespeak a southern line of thinking on their own, the final phrase, "I'm a Southern still," in which "Southern" is used as a noun, is something no Alleyman or other Yankee songwriter would ever have come up with. Silber also quotes another single line that nails down the piece as southern-written and most probably southern-published: "The days of knighthood now are past, yet still the knight am I." Even without seeing the song's remaining stanzas, one must wonder if the character spouting such braggadocio qualifies as a Southern Gentleman at all.

Comparatively, Southern Belles were a more popular subject for Dixie tunes than Southern Gentlemen, but this chapter looks at only a small number of songs that directly describe and/or idealize a belle (or belles as a type). The majority of pieces in which a man serenades his belle in direct address via a love song appear in Chapter 5: Dixie Is for Lovers. What, then, is it about the Southern Belle that makes her so idealized and adored? In *1001 Things Everyone Should Know About the South,* through insights, whimsy, humor, and quotations, John Shelton Reed and Dale Volberg Reed largely answer that question, first prefacing it by describing what the Southern Belle will eventually become when she matures into the (usually married) Southern Lady (the subject of *no* Alley songs), who was described in 1891 by Wilbur Fisk Tillett as a type of woman who excelled "in native womanly modesty, in neatness, grace, and beauty of person, in ease and freedom without boldness of manner, in refined and cultivated minds [sic], in gifts and qualities that shone brilliantly in the social circle, in spotless purity of thought and character, in laudable pride of family and devotion to home, kindred, and loved ones" (*1001 Things* Item #944). The Reeds whimsically begin Item #946 with "The Southern belle, the Southern lady's larval form, has been particularly celebrated," after which they let quotations carry much of her description. The first is from Francis Pendleton Gaines: "Beautiful, graceful, accomplished in social charm, bewitching in coquetry, yet strangely steadfast in soul, she is perhaps the most winsome figure in the whole field of our fancy." The Reeds conclude the Southern Belle item in their own voice: "The belle, all too aware that she has to turn into a Southern lady, is known for her frivolity, which may or may not be a put-on, and which has often been deplored, grudgingly admired, or eagerly imitated." Although in the popular, mostly northern, imagination Southern Belles are usually thought of as creatures of the antebellum South, Nina Silber dispels that myth with brief quotations from two late nineteenth-century travel writers' accounts of the droves of them that frequented the lavish spas in West Virginia. Mary Dodge wrote of White Sulphur Springs in 1872, "It is a paradise indeed for unmarried belles, who rule there with a sway undivided by their Benedictine sisters, such as queen it at Saratoga or Newport." In 1875 Edward King described a dinner at the Greenbrier at which "hundreds of beautiful girls from every part of the South, clad in ballroom costume, are seated at the round tables in the long hall" (both qtd. in Silber 87). (One assumes these young ladies came to posh watering holes with at least one parent or a chaperone, but neither Silber nor her sources address this point.) To show the Southern Belle lived into the twentieth century (and most likely lives into the twenty-first), the Reeds' Item #946 includes a toast from an Alabama fraternity dance in the 1930s recorded by Carl Carmer: "To Woman, lovely woman of the Southland, as pure and chaste as this sparkling water, as cold as this gleaming ice, we lift this cup, and pledge our hearts and lives to the protection of her virtue and chastity." No Dixie tunes focus on these frigid attributes of the Southern Belle!

Some readers may be surprised—although they shouldn't be, considering their two fairly well-known antebellum ancestors—that three early Tin Pan Alley Southern Belles were persons of color. The earliest pre–Civil War song about such a lady was written by Stephen Foster himself. His "Lou'siana Belle" (Cincinnati: W. C. Peters, 1847) was, as the sheet music states, "Written for and Sung by Joseph Murphy of the Sable Harmonists," an all-black minstrel troupe. The first verse unambiguously states, "Oh! Lou'siana de same old state, / Whar Massa us'd to dwell; / He had a lubly cullud gal, / 'Twas the Lou'siana Belle," and each refrain ends with the singer declaring, "Oh! Belle, de Lou'siana Belle, / I's gwine to marry you Lou'siana Belle."

Explaining the other ancestor of the Alley's black and mixed-race Southern Belles takes a bit more doing, since the anonymous "The Yellow Rose Of Texas" familiar today—thanks largely to Mitch Miller's 1955 bowdlerized sing-along version—bears scant resemblance to the original text(s) in the mid-nineteenth century. The first publication of just the lyrics was in a songster—a collection of songs' words without their melodies—*Christy's Plantation Melodies, No. 2* (Philadelphia: Fisher & Bro., 1853), and the first stand-alone sheet music of the song with its music was published by New York's Firth, Pond, and Co. in 1858, these two imprints arguing that the lyricist was a northerner. The latter publication is especially significant because of its statement filling most of the title page, "Composed and Arranged Expressly for Charles H. Brown by J. K." The identity of J. K. remains something of a mystery (see Dunn and Lutzweiler), but by most accounts Brown was a variety entertainer of the day, most probably a blackface solo and minstrel performer. In addition to the two published texts of "The Yellow Rose," there is a handwritten manuscript of the words in the University of Texas at Austin library. Long thought to be an early original of the piece, that manuscript turns out to be merely a transcription of the 1858 published lyric, as seen in its word choices, the spelling "Dearest May" rather than the "Mae" of the earlier 1853 *Christy's* text, and other evidence. So, ultimately, the Texas manuscript is apropos of nothing. The differences between the 1853 and 1858 lyrics are generally minor. From the top, the singer of "The Yellow Rose" identifies himself as a black man, the object of his affections a mulatto (1853 version): "There's a yellow girl in Texas / That I'm going down to see; / No other darkies know her, / No darkey, only me." One could argue that this song is moot since it's about a mulatto girl in Texas, a state beyond my perimeters for Dixie in this book. But there are other women in the tune than just the "Yellow Rose." In the refrain, the "darkey" defends his girl's beauty by singing (1858 text), "You may talk about your Dearest May, and sing of Rosa Lee, / But the Yellow Rose of Texas beats the belles of Tennessee." We can be absolutely certain the black singer isn't referring to white belles in Tennessee; they *had* to be black ones within his own frame of reference, social order, and experience.

So too, the three Alley songs in question are sung by a black, and each features a black or mixed-race heroine. Andrew B. Sterling (Harry Von Tilzer's frequent lyricist) wrote the earliest such song, "My Georgia Lady Love" (T. B. Harms, 1899), with music by Joseph E. Howard and Ida Emerson, the team best remembered for writing "Hello! Ma Baby [Hello, ma honey, / Hello, ma ragtime gal]." In a darky dialect the singer describes his "little brown eyed queen, / The nicest gal you ever seen, / With hair as black as night, / And skin that's almost white." Alley songs about Southern Belles almost never refer to a girl or woman directly as a "belle," so when Sterling has this singer say, "My Georgia lady-love, my Southern Queen," that's close enough for me. Lyricist Harry H. Williams (best known for "In The Shade Of The Old Apple Tree") and his usual composing partner Egbert Van Alstyne wrote "My Sweet Magnolia" (Shapiro, Bernstein, 1903), idealizing the natural beauty of an "octoroon in Alabama": "She don't wrestle with the curling iron problem, / 'Cause her jetty hair is kinky as can be, / And ev'ry single kink, just represents a link, / That binds that octoroon to me." Last, "Nell Of Tennessee," with heavy darky dialect lyrics by Wilson S. Mowry and music by Will Armstrong (C. L. Partee, 1914), is the rare darky Alley song that employs the word *belle:* "Oh, she works down in de cotton fiel' / An' tempts de honey bee / Her name is Nell an' she's a belle / Dis gal in Tennessee."

Pittsburgh's Stephen Foster wrote "Lou'siana Belle"; "The Yellow Rose Of Texas" was written for a white, northern, blackface performer, very likely *by* northern writers as well (though later sung with altered words by Confederate troops); and the three Alley songs about black or mixed-race belles came from northern urban songwriters. These facts all suggest that the social or ethnic type of the black or mixed-race Southern Belle never existed in reality, but only in the fancy of Yankee lyricists.

Yet the white Southern Belle was, and remains, a real social type in the South, as well as the featured subject in generations of Tin Pan Alley Dixie tunes, whether the lyrics call her a belle directly or not (usually not). Alleymen wrote such songs between 1899 and 1936, but most of the young ladies in them fell short of the beauty, charm, and grace of the legendary belles, and equally few of the Alley's top-shelf lyricists penned many of the twenty-one pieces describing or idealizing Southern Belles. Still, there were some standouts over the years, and others were well-intentioned attempts to describe this ethereal southern being right from the earliest Alley days, as when in

W. R. Williams's "My Southern Rose" (Chicago: Will Rossiter, 1899) the singer claims, "[I]n the Mississippi Valley . . . / There dwells Rose, a perfect Southern beauty . . . / Prettier than a picture, for she's nature's perfect flow'r . . . / No smile is sweeter, / No maiden neater, / Fairer than any wild-flower that grows," each line stressing Rose's *natural* beauty. Charles Horwitz (lyrics) and Frederick V. Bowers's (music) "She's The Flower Of Mississippi" (Shapiro, Bernstein & Von Tilzer, 1901) is almost a carbon copy of "My Southern Rose" in tone, imagery, and locale, as seen in just the chorus: "She's the flow'r of Mississippi, / Is my little southern Sue, / And her smile is sweet as roses / That are nourished by the dew; / And her voice is soft and gentle / As the music that is true, / She's the flow'r of Mississippi is my Sue."

Popular songs extolling the virtues of the Southern Belle in such sweetly sentimental ways quickly became passé. With one strange late exception, from the 'teens through the mid-1930s most such songs, and certainly the best of them, while no less sincere, were more lighthearted tributes to the Southern Belle, taking on a more playful air, perhaps in keeping with the belle's own legendary frivolity, whether in the song's overall conceit or in its lyrics' up-to-the-minute colloquial or even slangy diction. But to deal with the strange late exception first, New York's M. Witmark & Sons published a Dixie tune in 1935 titled "Darling Of L. S. U." In part the singer declares his love for this lovely coed at Louisiana State University, but he also extols her as the apotheosis of all Southern Belles in phrases like "darling of my dreams," "the world's in bloom for you," and so forth. But what's astonishing about this piece, with music by LSU bandmaster Castro Carazo, has little to do with its sentimentality as late as 1935, but with the fact that its lyricist was Louisiana's U.S. senator at the time, Huey P. Long.

Playfully putting the Southern Belle on a musical pedestal began in 1916, thanks to two very talented, prolific songwriters. Canadian émigré to the Alley Alfred (Al) Bryan wrote not only the words to nineteen Dixie tunes but also the lyrics for such hits as "Peg O' My Heart" and "Come Josephine In My Flying Machine." New Jersey's own Harry Tierney was the melody man for seven southern songs and composed the enormous smash of its day, "Alice Blue Gown." Together Bryan and Tierney wrote "She's Dixie All The Time" (Jerome H. Remick, 1916), in which the verse stating that a southern bride-to-be doesn't want to move north is only an excuse for the whimsical chorus defining a Southern Belle as a unique product of Dixie heredity and environment: "She was born in old Kentucky, She was raised in Tennessee / Went to school in Alabama, Where she learn'd her A. B. C. / Then she mov'd down to Georgia when she was sixteen / Spent vacation with her relation 'Bout a year or two in New Orleans. / She's been in ev'ry state in Dixie, 'cept the state of marriage bliss, / She takes a dip each morning in the Brandy-wine, / Hangs her clothes upon the Mason Dixon Line. / She was born and rais'd in Dixie, And she's Dixie all the time." All of which says you can take the belle out of Dixie but you can't take Dixie out of the belle! Lest anyone wonders what the Brandywine is, it's not the un-Dixie Brandywine River that flows through parts of Delaware and Pennsylvania. The reference is to Mississippi's Brandywine Spring, researched by my Cajun friend, Michelle Menard, originally from Lafayette, Louisiana. The American Quartet recorded this delightful tune for Edison in 1916, and it's on the Internet.

William Tracey is perhaps best known as one of the Alley's white lyricists who primarily worked with a black composer, in his case with Maceo Pinkard. The two wrote four Dixie tunes together, including the hugely successful "Mammy O' Mine" in 1919, as well as the non-Dixie smash of 1930, "Them There Eyes." On the other hand, Tracey must not have won many kudos for his Southern Belle tribute, the lyrics of which he wrote in collaboration with Lou Klein. "Oh! Southern City Send Us Some Beautiful Girls," with music by Nat Vincent (Shapiro, Bernstein, 1916), crosses the line from lightheartedness to preposterous would-be humor. The premise is that in Kankakee, Illinois, the unmarried boys outnumber the pretty unmarried girls by twenty to one, so an enterprising guy telephones someone in Tennessee, knowing that "I hear you've got a lot of girlies there, / We'd like to have a few if you have some to spare, / . . . Your girls are pretty, / So sweet and pretty, / Won't you send us out a few, / Lord knows we need 'em here." The song progresses from there, but, trust me, nothing more is worth quoting. It only strikes me as odd that the lyricists chose to call the piece "Oh! Southern City . . ." when the desperate boys of Kankakee are addressing the entire *state* of Tennessee to ship some Southern Belles up North.

In 1919, a song appeared with Bobby Jones's words and Will Donaldson and Rubey Cowan's music that was similar to, but not nearly so clever as, "She's Dixie All The Time," painting a picture of the Southern Belle as an amalgam of attributes of various states in Dixie and the South in general. The chorus of "Everybody's Crazy Over Dixie" (Broadway Music Corp., 1919) sums it all up: "Ev'rybody's crazy over Dixie. / All her charms remind you of the South. / Cheeks like Georgia peaches rare, / Southern sunbeams match her hair, / And her smile is bound to win yer, / She's the pride of old Virginia / Blue eyes like the blue grass of Kentucky. / Lips as sweet as sugar cane down there. / Where ev'ry boy throughout the land / Has tried to win her heart and hand / They're crazy over Dixie in dear old Dixieland." Vernon Dalhart, assuming, as he often did for Dixie tunes, a dreadful southern accent, recorded the song, which is on the Internet, on an Edison Blue Amberol cylinder in 1919.

Fast-forwarding to the 1930s, two songs illustrate how songs idealizing a Southern Belle—in each case a *particular* one—did so through the light-hearted colloquial diction, syntax, and imagery of the time in which they were written. In Alexander Hill's "Dixie Lee" (Joe Davis, 1933), the singer describes the eponymous belle thus: "Should you ever see, / Somebody full of T. N. T.— / And yet as sweet as she can be, — / That's DIXIE LEE; — / Should you ever meet, — Somebody lookin' cute and neat, / With dancin' eyes and happy feet, / That's DIXIE LEE." Glen Gray and the Casa Loma Orchestra, with a vocal by Pee Wee Hunt, recorded "Dixie Lee" for Brunswick in 1934, and it may be heard on the Internet. Between 1932 and 1935, the Alley's masterful wordsmith Mitchell Parish penned, sometimes with a co-author, six Dixie tunes, all but one with music by Frank Perkins. One of those was "Georgia's Gorgeous Gal," written with James Cavanaugh and with Perkins's melody (Mills Music, 1934). Parish and Cavanaugh scattered throughout the lyric current expressions in the service of idealizing this particular Southern Belle: "If you are looking for beauties who are easy on the eyes, / If you're looking for cuties, here is one who takes the prize, — ... She's an angel on exhibition, all arrayed for the beauty parade, — ... With the sunniest disposition, she's a wow with a capital 'ow.'"

Finally, back-pedaling to 1925, I have deliberately saved for last the apotheosis of Southern Belle tributes in the fancies of Alley songwriters and the public at large, considering how long she has endured in familiarity and popularity, even though this particular Dixie tune does not describe her in much detail at all. The number is the product of the prolific lyric-writing duo of Sam M. Lewis and Joe Young, who together wrote the words for eighteen Dixie tunes (as well as more individually, along with many other popular songs), and Harry Akst, composer of nine other Dixie tunes, who wrote the music. Even without lavish details describing this particular belle, the bare-bones opening words of Lewis and Young's chorus combined with Akst's catchy tune have immortalized "Dinah" (Henry Waterson, 1925) forever: "Dinah—is there anyone finer in the state of Carolina, — If there is and you know'er, — / Show'er to me?" Even before Eddie Cantor interpolated the tune into his long-running musical *Kid Boots,* thus popularizing it and making it a hit, the great black performer Ethel Waters introduced "Dinah" at New York's Plantation Club and also first cut it for Columbia in 1926, as heard on the Internet.

Good Old Boys and Hillbillies

Other than the Southern Gentleman, only two other kinds of white males from Daniel Hundley's 1860 catalogue of Dixie social types survived into twentieth-century Alley songs—and neither made the trip without changing its name on the way. (Hundley's final group, The Negro Slave, was obsolete by the end of the Civil War, so the prototypes for Tin Pan Alley's "happy darkies" and other southern blacks had to lie in other sources, as we shall soon see.)

One social type that survived from Hundley's list to the Alley did so in just one song, and then only in the Alley's waning days of turning out any Dixie tunes at all. Hundley named this man the Southern Yeoman and saw him as one of the pillars of the South, even more than his category of the Middle Classes (Hundley's plural, not mine). To Hundley, the Southern Yeoman was the true common man, usually a tiller of the soil, though often not much of it—just enough to raise crops for subsistence for him and his family plus a bit to sell for some little profit. The Yeoman might even own a slave, but if he did, when his fields needed plowing he would plow shoulder to shoulder with his slave, each stripped to the waist, sweating under the summer sun. In brief, the Southern Yeoman was a physical, honest, hard-working man, epitomizing, along with the Southern Gentleman (though on a different rung of the social ladder), all that was best about the South. In the twentieth century, according to John Shelton Reed, this type became known as the good old boy (or good ole boy, or good ol' boy) "among rural and working-class white Southerners," who admired him for his "reliability, independence, good-fellowship, some physical courage, and self-deprecating humor" (*1001 Things* Item #937).

When I first examined the song in question, Preston Miller's "Alabama Saturday Night" (Bob Miller, 1952), not being expert in the fine points distinguishing modern southern social types, I e-mailed a transcription of the lyrics to John for his best guess as to whether the piece was about rednecks or good old boys. He replied succinctly, "If I have to choose between redneck and g.o.b. I'd pick the latter—if you go with the old-timey view that the redneck is mean and the g.o.b. is easygoing and good natured" (Reed e-mail to the author, January 29, 2012). A quip by no less an authority than Billy Carter that the Reeds employ in their definition of the redneck villain in *1001 Things* Item #939 substantiates Reed's e-mailed distinction: "A good ole boy is somebody that rides around in a pickup truck . . . and drinks beer and puts 'em in a litter bag. A redneck rides around in a pickup truck and drinks beer and throws 'em out the window."

In Miller's song, it's clear that all the good old boys—and, by extension, their good old gals as well—are as good natured and easygoing as can be while having a grand old time: "We're gonna be dancin' when the rooster crows, / On Saturday night 'way down in Alabam' / . . . And we don't go in for fancy bars, / We get our kicks from old fruit jars, / . . . So come on boys, get on the run! / If you ain't got a gal just grab you one, / On Saturday night, 'way down in Alabam'." I can't account for there being no previous Alley songs about good old boys, yet it is significant that "Alabama Saturday Night" in 1952 holds the unique place of being the "last." In the years leading up to that date, in the 1940s and early '50s, the music business in Nashville was growing like a proverbial weed, spearheaded by Acuff-Rose Music, the venture of country music performer Roy Acuff and songwriter/publicist Fred Rose. Soon Nashville songwriters, performers, publishers, and record companies had shaped a multi-million-dollar industry out of songs specifically about, by, and for good old boys and girls, leaving the Alley as extinct as the mastodon in producing country music (see Epilogue).

Long before Hundley discussed the other social type to go on to Tin Pan Alley, Poor White Trash was already the appellation for Appalachian and other down-and-dirty hill and mountain folk. Hundley listed other regionalisms for this odd breed of southern humanity, but then noted that "every where [sic] Poor White Trash [is used], a name said to have originated with the slaves, who look upon themselves as much better off than all 'po' white folks' whatever" (Hundley 257). Hundley's portrait of the Poor White Trash male—along with his wife and kids—is vividly colorful, much of it lasting into the twentieth century and Alley songwriting. Only the name morphed into something new—hillbilly.

Hundley begins characterizing the Poor White male by meticulously describing his dwelling-place: "Each householder, or head of a family, builds him a little hut of round logs . . . builds at one end of the cabin a big wooden chimney with a tapering top . . . puts down a puncheon floor, and a loft of ordinary boards overhead; fills up the inside of the rude dwelling with a few rickety chairs, a long bench, a dirty bed or two, a spinning-wheel (the loom, if any, is outside under a shed), a skillet, an oven, a triangular cupboard in one corner, and a rack above the door for old Silver Heels, the family rifle" (260). Once his cabin is set up for housekeeping, the Poor White clears about five acres around it, and "pretends to cultivate, planting only corn, pumpkins, and a little garden truck of some kind or other" (260). He builds a kennel for his dog(s), a pen for his horse, one for his cow, and a henhouse for his chickens.

If Hundley graphically described the living space the Poor White Trash male created for himself and his family, he truly hit his stride and then some in describing the "chief characteristics" of this social type itself: "They are about the laziest two-legged animals that walk erect on the face of the Earth. Even their motions are slow, and their speech is a sickening drawl, worse a deal sight than the most down-eastern of the worst Down-Easters; while their thoughts and ideas seem likewise to creep at a snail's pace" (262). "All they seem to care for, is, to live from hand to mouth; to get drunk, provided they can do so without having to trudge too far after their liquor; to shoot for beef; to hunt; to attend gander pullings; to vote at elections; to eat and to sleep; to lounge in the sunshine of a bright summer's day, and to bask in the warmth of a roaring wood fire, when summer days are over" (262–63). As for physical appearance and demeanor, Hundley observed that the male Poor White was "lank, lean, angular, and bony, with flaming red, or flaxen, or sandy, or carroty-colored hair, sallow complexion, awkward manners, and a natural stupidity and dullness of intellect that almost surpasses belief" (264). As for female Poor Whites, "If any thing, after the first freshness of their youth is lost, the women are even more intolerable than the men—owing chiefly to their disgusting habit of snuff-dipping and even sometimes pipe-smoking . . . it is not at all strange that the female should so soon lose all trace of beauty and at thirty are [sic] about the color of yellow parchment" (264). Also according to Hundley, Poor White women grew old before their time because "every home is filled with its half-dozen of dirty, squalling, white-headed little brats, who are familiarly known as Tow-Heads—on account of the color of their hair, as well as its texture and generally unkempt and matted condition" (264–65). Hundley remarked that his vivid portraits of Poor Whites of both sexes and all ages "present in the main a very pitiable sight to the truly benevolent, as well as a ludicrous one to those who are mirthfully disposed" (264), "among whom I fear we must number Hundley," quipped John Shelton Reed (*Southern Folk* 44), along with, I must add, most Alleymen who wrote of the Poor Whites' lineal descendants, the hillbillies.

"Most," but not "all," since the first Alleyman to write about hillbillies, Halsey K. Mohr, was chiefly a composer but turned to lyric writing also for "At The End Of The Trail" (Shapiro, Bernstein, 1916). While not, in Hundley's words, "truly benevolent," Mohr still wrote a song that was sweetly sentimental, even though its subject, feuding, later became the stuff of songwriters' and audiences' comic delight. In this case Mohr creates a sort of reverse Romeo and Juliet tale in which the first-person singer tells of a long-standing feud between the family of "my own daddy" and that of "the daddy of my sweetheart Sue" on either side of a trail "in the mountains of Kentucky." These two peaceloving young people plan to end the feud by marrying, a scheme they actually pull off successfully, according to the chorus of the song: "On our wedding day, / Love will find a way, / It will show our daddies what they ought to do, / And the call to them all will not fail, / It will bring them from the mountain, hill and dale, / And the many rival clans / Will meet and all join hands / On the bend at the end of the trail."

After Mohr's 1916 rather idealistic piece on a way to end feuding among rival hill-country clans, the Alley was silent regarding hillbillies until the 1930s and early '40s, during which three songs about them were written, culminating in a final smash comic hit by two major songwriters, published in 1947. After that, hillbilly songs, like those about good old boys, found their way from New York to Nashville. In 1932 the three-way team of Arthur Lippmann, Manning Sherwin, and Harry Richman wrote both the words and music of the hilarious multi-stanza extravaganza "She Came Rollin' Down The Mountain" (De Sylva, Brown & Henderson, 1932), in which "Down in West Virginia / Lived a gal named Nancy Brown," who is pursued in successive verses by different men wanting to marry her. In each case, Nancy and the guy hike up the mountain until "he tried to get too pally," at which point, "She Came Rollin' Down The Mountain," rejecting that particular suitor out of hand. Until, in the third verse, that is, when "a city slicker / Who had hundred dollar bills / Came ridin' in his auto / To the West Virginia hills." That was enough for love at first sight for Nancy: "She stepped into his roadster and the rest is history!" except to observe that "her pappy chased poor Nancy out of sight." The final verse and chorus let us know Nancy couldn't care a hoot about that since she got a diamond bracelet on her wedding day, now lives an affluent life in the city, and sometimes recalls with glee how in times past "She Came Rollin' Down The Mountain by the stills." A highly amusing song, if without any redeeming social value. The tune was clearly popular, since the Internet refers to or plays recordings by various country or what were then called hillbilly artists well into the 1940s, some singing stanzas not in the sheet music of the song. Only the hillbilly Aarons Sisters trio cut an unaccompanied version in 1932, in which the lyrics are totally faithful to the published "sheet."

The year after the publication of "She Came Rollin' Down The Mountain," a hillbilly song emerged from the Alley that wasn't so much comic as simply fun and at the same time idealized a type of Dixie female who couldn't be categorized as a Southern Belle. With lyrics by Raymond Klages and music by two composers who often collaborated, Al Goodhart and Al Hoffman, the song's punning title is "Joan of Arkansaw" (Shapiro, Bernstein, 1933). The tune describes in lighthearted ways a girl who is "the biggest thrill in her own hillbilly town" in Arkansas: from her physical appearance, "She's the cutest thing when she wears a gingham gown"; to her effect on the local menfolk, "When she passes by, they all desert their stills," and the seemingly hyperbolic "Just a little smile from her can stop a feud" and "Nine thousand guys have asked her paw, / If he'll fix it up with Joan of Arkansaw." The title of Al Fish and Charles O'Flynn (lyrics) and Jack Betzner's (music) "There's A Blackout In My Blue Ridge Mountain Home" (Sprague-Coleman, 1940) capitalizes on the lingo of the world at war, even though the United States had not yet entered the conflict soon to be called World War II. The nightly "Blackout" started in Britain in September 1939, and even before America was in the war a few cities began practicing blackout drills, while others on both coasts tried full-scale blackouts from time to time. Once the United States was in the war, none ever engaged in nightly blackouts, but some, like New York City, had "dim-outs" to make their taller buildings and brightly lit areas like Times Square and Broadway less visible from the air. The singer-narrator's "Pappy" in this goofy five-chorus song "could not stand the strain no more" of incessant day-and-night feuding, and so declared nightly blackouts on the shooting for the rival parties "to figure out the score." Of course his plan backfired in a big way: ". . . you strike a match and zing! / You may hear the angels sing / And you'll be six feet beneath some apple tree." Ultimately Pappy, "never thinkin' lit his pipe," and was, as Hamlet said, hoist with his own petard, when a bullet got him between the eyes; it didn't kill him but it "flattened out against the bone," offering lyricists Fish and O'Flynn the chance to use one of the war years' favorite adjectives: "Now poor Pappy sure looks wacky / Chewin' on corn silk tobaccy / Since that Blackout in My Blue Ridge Mountain Home."

The last of the Alley's hillbilly songs is also unquestionably its most outrageously hilarious (if not by today's standards entirely politically correct) and all-around greatest, which is perhaps only to be expected since its writers, lyricist Al Dubin and composer Burton Lane, were outstanding in their fields, whether writing for the Broadway stage, Hollywood films, or stand-alone popular songs for Alley publishers. Dubin is most remembered for his classic 1930s songs with composer Harry Warren such as "42nd Street," "We're In The Money," and "Lullaby Of Broadway." Lane's biggest hit from the '30s was his collaboration with lyricist Harold Adamson on "Everything I Have Is Yours," but his biggest claim to fame came the same year the hillbilly song in question was published, when on January 10, 1947, *Finian's Rainbow* opened on Broadway with a score by Lane and lyricist E. Y. Harburg, including such songs destined for immortality as "Old Devil Moon," "If This Isn't Love," and "How Are Things In Glocca Morra." Dubin and Lane originally wrote "Feudin' And Fightin'" (Mara-Lane Music, 1947) for the short-lived 1944 Olsen and Johnson Broadway musical revue *Laffing Room Only,* in which Pat Brewster sang it. The piece attracted so little attention at the time that it wasn't even published then. Lane only decided to bring it out of mothballs and publish it two years after Dubin passed away in 1945. This circumstance no doubt accounts for the sheet music reading "Words by Al Dubin and Burton Lane," suggesting Lane tweaked the lyrics a bit after Dubin's death.

In any event, in 1947 singer Dorothy Shay, who billed herself as "The Park Avenue Hillbillie," performed "Feudin' and Fightin'" in nightclubs and on radio with great success and made a hit recording of it, with other records by Jo Stafford and Bing Crosby not far behind. Shay's classic 1947 recording of the complete tune for Columbia may be heard on the Internet. The verse justifies feuding by explaining it's a quicker way to settle quarrels than long, drawn-out litigations. Then the first of the two verses gets right down to business: "Don't like them ornery neighbors down by the creek, / We'll be plumb out of neighbors next week." Though the first chorus about "Poor ol' grandma" getting shot is the most familiar, the second about the youngest female of the family is possibly the funniest, except to animal rights and gun control advocates: "Daughter—Baby daughter, / Poisened [sic] all the neighbors [sic] chickens. / . . . Daughter hadn't oughter / . . . They hit her with a shovel! / Let's give our daughter a pistol now that she's four and go Feudin' and Fightin' some more." The next southern social, or here ethnic or racial, type portrayed in Alley songs was as benign as most hillbillies were belligerent, and it existed more in songwriters' imaginations than in the reality of Dixie.

The Alley's "Happy Darkies"

The best way to understand Tin Pan Alley's "happy darky" is as an idealized image of the southern African American and the total opposite of his demonization as the "black beast rapist" by many white southern men in the late nineteenth century (see Silber 153ff.). D. W. Griffith carried this demonization into the twentieth century in his epic 1915 silent film *The Birth of a Nation* at the very time the Alley's happy darky was gaining national currency in song. Of course, the Alley's "happy darkies" were not solely males as the previous sentences may have implied, but women and children as well, and together they were a fun-loving, carefree, yet most often hard-working socio-ethnic type in all the songs where they appeared. Only a few of these "portraiture" pieces are in this chapter; the rest are in other places with tunes about such Dixie activities as barbecues and spontaneous celebrations for nearly anything. Dixie tunes' happy darkies exhibit racial pride, are at ease with whites when they are together in songs, and must not be confused with the subservient "Uncle Toms" or "white man's niggas" of earlier literature.

There are few precedents or prototypes for the Alley's idealized happy darkies, and what ones exist, whether imaginative and fictional or actual and historical, are about as romanticized as those from the pens of popular songwriters. Previously mentioned in Chapter 1 were the portrayals in Currier & Ives lithographs between 1868 and 1870 of southern blacks in colorful garb always singing and dancing, whether loading cotton on or off riverboats, or entertaining themselves for their own enjoyment outside their cabin, or for that of a young white family in a barn. In the late nineteenth century, as documented by Nina Silber, northern travelers to Dixie observed numerous real southern blacks who in some ways resembled the Alley's happy darkies of just a decade or two later. In Silber's words, blacks "became . . . a 'picturesque' element on the southern scene. . . . [and] Many travelers chose to view African Americans as simply another feature of the landscape" (78). She quotes from a northern female visitor to Dixie who recorded in her journal not just seeing the beautiful plantations that lined the Mississippi River, but also hearing "the singing of the negroes as they discharged and took on cargo" (78). Southern blacks even became attractions hyped in tourist brochures, as in one aimed at train travelers: "The negro huts along the way, with a grinning, turbaned colored woman standing in each doorway, apprises [*sic*] the Northerner that he is certainly 'right smart down South.'" (78). Whether Alleymen read such descriptions of southern blacks on which to base their happy darkies isn't known, but seeds of the type existed before they began writing their idyllic musical portraits of these folks.

In 1910 Alley songwriters began painting musical pictures of southern happy darkies, and they continued doing so through 1928 in a total of nine Dixie tunes about evenly divided between those depicting them at work and in domestic situations—usually group portraits but one solo sketch as well. A common feature of these pieces—and there's no way this could have been by design—is that wherever the darkies are and whatever else they are doing, they are always singing, dancing, or both. The question asked in Earle C. Jones's lyric for "Cotton Time" with music by Charles N. Daniels (Jerome H. Remick, 1910), which uses the rarely used "coon" in a Dixie tune, but clearly not disparagingly, appears either naïve or rhetorical: "Why are those banjos ringing, honey, dear? / Why are those coons a prancing while they're dancing? / Oh, tell me why they're singing, honey dear?" To which the obvious reply is, "Don't say that you have forgotten that they are picking the cotton," indicating these musical and terpsichorean activities were normal parts of the darkies' workday in the cotton field. The popular recording artists baritone Arthur Collins and tenor Byron G. Harlan, noted for their duets in darky accents, recorded this ragtime happy darky Dixie tune for Edison Standard in 1910, and it's on the Internet. Similarly, the other song about cotton picking, written by the great three-way collaboration of B. G. ("Buddy") De Sylva, Lew Brown, and Ray Henderson eighteen years later, corroborated Earle C. Jones's impression of happy darkies' behavior while at such labors in "Pickin' Cotton" from *George White's Scandals, Ninth Edition* (De Sylva, Brown, and Henderson, 1928). According to the lyrics, "Cotton pickin' is a kind of a spree. . . . There's a beat, there's a measure. . . . They make work seem a pleasure / Dancing as they go / . . . Sing as you go right down the row / Pickin' cotton away."

The other two idealized musical pictures of happy darkies at work, separated in time by fourteen years, are also about cotton, but these focus on the stevedores loading bales of it on or off riverboats for transport to cotton mills. Both the words and music of the earliest of these, "Down On The Levee" (Chicago: Will Rossiter, 1914), were written by one of the great black Alleymen, Shelton Brooks—born in Canada, raised in Detroit, and best known for writing Sophie Tucker's signature tune throughout her career, "Some Of These Days." Almost in the manner of the southern visitors' brochures Nina Silber writes of, Brooks's lyric to "Down On The Levee" makes that district of Mobile, Alabama, sound like a veritable tourist attraction: "If you ever go to Mobile. . . . Go down to the Levee. . . . That's the only place to go when you're feeling blue, . . . Everybody's always feeling gay, . . . All day long the Darkies are singing, / While they wheel away the cotton, / No matter how heavy, / They keep singing just the same, This place is known in the Hall of Fame." From the tone of Brooks's description, the stevedores' songs are no low mournful chants, but upbeat, foot-tapping tunes. The title of Willard Robison's "Lazy Levee Loungers" (Irving Berlin, Inc., 1928) along with the first verse and the chorus are misleading, since they make it seem as if this song is only about a bunch of happy but lazy darkies who just lie around on the levee, croon a few languid tunes, dance a bit if they can muster up the energy, and shoot some craps now and again. But in the second verse, when a boat pulls in, these darky stevedores snap to life: "When they load the boats with cotton, weavin [sic] roun' between the bales / All the passengers and all the crew, gather roun' the rail / Boss man knows the folks are waitin' / Just to hear those darkies sing / When that startin' whistle starts to blow joyful voices ring." The common thread through the four Alley tunes depicting idealized happy darkies at their jobs is that these people didn't casually overlay song and dance on their work, but that the playfulness of singing and dancing was ingrained in their workaday tasks, no doubt to help relieve the strain and monotony of laboring in the cotton fields or on the levees.

L. Wolfe Gilbert wrote the lyrics for the first two songs depicting happy darkies in domestic situations, the first a solo portrait, "Mammy's Shufflin' Dance," with music by Melville J. Gideon (Chicago: Will Rossiter, 1911), the second more of a group photo, "Take Me To That Swanee Shore," with Lewis F. Muir's music from the Winter Garden revue *Broadway to Paris* (F. A. Mills, 1912). The mammy of the earlier song is "as gray as she can be" and "tho' Mammy's heavy, / There's none can dance as she." Mammy dances for her own amusement and the joy of it, with or without musical accompaniment, even though the preacher tells her she's "much too old" to behave that way. Though her steps are improvised, they outshine some of the fashionable dances of the day: "'Grizzly Bear,' 'Cubanola Glide' / None of them compare, / with ole mammy's slide." On September 26, 1911, the American Quartet featuring Billy Murray recorded "Mammy's Shufflin' Dance" for Victor, as may be heard on the Internet. In "Take Me To That Swanee Shore" Gilbert widens his lens to take in a whole group of happy darkies at play for no reason whatever, but at the end of the verse he zooms in on one of them: "See ... real colored folks, / Singing, dancing, laughing, telling old minstrel jokes; ... Led by Deacon Johnson who just turned ninety-six." This may be a bit of a stretch, but between Mammy's dance and Deacon Johnson, I detect in Wolfie a veneration for old age that he brought with him to America when a boy (emigration date uncertain). Born in 1886 in the tightly knit Jewish community in Odessa, Ukraine, as a child Gilbert would have been immersed in an Old World Jewish culture that venerated age, a culture in which the elderly, as in these songs, had a joyous lust for life ("L'Chaim"—to life!), often expressed through song or dance. That energy radiates through Collins and Harlan's rendering of "Take Me To That Swanee Shore," replete with interpolated comic dialogue, which they cut on September 27, 1912, and which is on the Internet.

"Cotton Blossom Time" (Leo Feist, 1914) is a slightly comic piece by lyricist Jack Mahoney and composer Percy Wenrich. It randomly describes a bit of work, but mostly the play of happy darkies "Way down Mobile town": "Uncle Eph' forgets his 'rheumatiz' and he does a 'buck and wing' for his; ... ev'ry day, /Their work is play. / Pickin' cotton blossoms, / huntin' possums / They don't need money, life is sunny, / ... Oh, Lordy! ev'ry body's swingin' and a-clingin',' / Banjos are a-ringin', / They're a-singin' all in rhyme, / In cotton blossom time." Collins and Harlan add their trademark darky accents plus a second verse not on the sheet music and some comic dialogue to their 1915 Edison Diamond Disc recording of the tune, which is on the Internet. Another happy darkies song which was a ragtime hit in its own day but decades later transmogrified into a perennially popular country tune was "Alabama Jubilee" (Jerome H. Remick, 1915), with lyrics by Jack Yellen and music by his frequent partner, ragtime composer George L. Cobb. The song's two verses establish that the town's darky band is tuning up to supply music for a dance celebrating nothing at all, after which the tune's famous chorus takes over: "You ought to see Deacon Jones when he rattles the bones, / Old Parson Brown foolin' 'roun like a clown / Aunt Jemima who is past eighty-three, / Shoutin' 'I'm full o' pep! Watch yo' step, watch yo' step!'" *ad infinitum.* Again Collins and Harlan cut hit recordings of the piece in 1915 on an Edison Blue Amberol cylinder, with their comic darky accents, and on Victor without them, as may be heard on the Internet. (The practice of recording artists cutting the same song for more than one label was not uncommon in the early years of recorded sound.) "Alabama Jubilee" found its way into country music many decades after its original success. All traces of its southern darky references in the chorus were anonymously bowdlerized out of it (as both verses had been entirely), until it became "You oughts see Mr. Jones when he rattles the bones / Old Colonel Brown jumpin' round like some clown / Ol' aged mama she done past eighty-three shoutin' out I'm full o' pep / Watch your step and help yourself," etc. To beat all, the tune no longer resembled ragtime one bit, the sung chorus merely an excuse for the virtuosic guitar-picking in later years by the likes of Red Foley (1951), Chet Atkins (1954), Roy Clark (1964), and Jerry Reed (1970). Finally, Charles A. Mason (lyrics) and Richard A. Whiting's (music) "Cotton Hollow Harmony" (Jerome H. Remick, 1918) sketches how song pervades all aspects of the lives of Dixie happy darkies: "Down in Cotton Hollow they just sort of wallow / In an atmosphere of melody and rhyme. / That hamlet harmonizes night and day / Singin' when they fight or when they pray—Hear those cotton pickers moan—Hear the deacon's baritone / The mammies sweep in rhythm / Their pickaninnies with 'em / . . . Darkies actin' like they just got free / That's Cotton Hollow Harmony." The last lines just may help explain the prevalence of song and dance among the happy darkies that the Alley idealized.

Southern Scamps and Vamps

Neither Daniel Hundley nor any later amateur or authentic ethnographer would recognize and accept scamps or vamps as legitimate social groups widespread throughout or with significant longevity in the South. But as scattered individual types these sexually irresponsible men and women lurked as much in Dixie as in the rest of the United States, and Alleymen richly, if often comically, celebrated—as in admired—them for their prowess at wholesale lovemaking, primarily in the 1920s. It's not even going too far to say that many such songs actually idealize the "love 'em and leave 'em" skills of these extraordinary ladies and gents, much in the southern tradition of telling tall tales, in which the "hero," scoundrel though he be, has to be admired and even idolized for his cleverness and trickery. To appreciate the Alley's scamps and vamps for who they are, the listener or reader must put moral judgments aside and just enjoy these characters' exploits on their own terms. It would be gentlemanly to begin with the ladies, but since songs about scamps started earlier, I will start with them.

The term "scamp" for a ladies' man goes back well before the Alley's songs about southern ones. Nor is the word used in any of the Dixie tunes themselves. Here I just employ it to rhyme with "vamp," which was very much in use not just by songwriters, but by the American public as early as 1911, according to the *Oxford English Dictionary*. As for "scamp" as used in Alley songs, my own earliest acquaintance with it is in Gilbert and Sullivan's 1875 *Trial by Jury,* in which the jurymen sing, "Oh, I was like that when a lad! / A shocking young scamp of a rover, / I behaved like a regular cad; / But that sort of thing is all over." Not so for any scamps in the nine Dixie tunes Alleymen wrote about them between 1921 and 1934. Each one is as promiscuous at the end of his song as at the beginning, women following him the way today's groupies follow rock stars. As we will also see with pieces about vamps, scamp songs are colorblind; four are about black scamps, four about white ones, and one about all southern scamps regardless of race. Also, for no reason except perhaps that such risqué songs would be fun to write and might have been very marketable during the Roaring Twenties, songs about Dixie ladies' men and designing women attracted some of the top songwriters of their time.

The first was Lew Brown (born Louis Brownstein in Odessa, Ukraine, in 1893), best known as the Brown of the songwriting trio of De Sylva, Brown, and Henderson starting in 1925, whose most famous Dixie tune together was "The Birth Of The Blues" (see Chapter 4). Earlier, Brown's frequent composer was Albert Von Tilzer (Harry's younger brother). The two wrote "Dapper Dan" (Broadway Music, 1921) about a Pullman car porter who "Had a girl in ev'ry town." The chorus, sung by Dan himself, isn't vintage Brown but is a serviceable "list song" of this black porter's conquests (all Pullman porters were black then) wherever the trains he rode carried him, in the following pattern—"If I lose my gal in Tennessee / That won't worry me / 'Cause I've got another honey lamb / Waitin' for me down in Alabam"—all around Dixie. Dan's secret for his success is simple: "Now I ain't handsome, I ain't sweet / But I've got a brand of lovin' that can't be beat." Though Brown's lyrics are fairly pedestrian, he ends the final chorus with a surprise punch line, "I won't let no gal run my life / 'Cause if I lose them all I still got my wife." Frank Crumit cut the song for Columbia in 1921, and it's on the Internet.

With Milton Ager's music, Jack Yellen wrote the words for "Lovin' Sam (The Sheik of Alabam')" (Ager, Yellen & Bornstein, 1922), as well as for two vamp songs. Together these make Yellen's lyrics in the 'teens look almost like apprentice work. The song was such a hit that other songwriters, as we'll see, refer to Sam in their own scamp and vamp tunes, assuming listeners would recognize the character they were alluding to. Sam's charisma was electrifying: "There ain't a high-brown gal in town / Who wouldn't throw her daddy down / To be the bride of this cullud Romeo." He knows all the moves for attracting the ladies: "Does he step? Does he strut? / That's what he doesn't do nothin' else but!" Like Dapper Dan, he's no flashy man-about-town; "tho' he's just a valet for horses / He's causing lots of divorces." Miss Patricola (vaudevillian Isabella Patricola's stage name) with The Virginians under Ross Gorman cut the most complete "Lovin' Sam" for Victor in 1922, with the first verse, the first and part of the second chorus, and a patter section not in the sheet music, all on the Internet.

On the other hand, the "hero" of "The Memphis Maybe Man" (Jerome H. Remick, 1923), with words and music by Haven Gillespie, Charles L. Cooke, and Billy Moll, is suave, cool, a classy dresser, slick to the point of being oily, vacillating—and seemingly white; in brief, the "most uncertainest he-vamp in the land." The names of the writers may not be terribly familiar, but Haven Gillespie is notable for being one of the few white Alleymen born in the South—in Covington, Kentucky, to be precise—and is best known not for any Dixie tunes but as the lyricist of "Santa Claus Is Coming To Town." But the Memphis Maybe Man is no Santa Claus; in fact he's more of a Grinch when it comes to stealing not only love but money from women: "Maybe he's fast Maybe he's slow / Call [sic] a grandma baby if she's got the dough." His whole technique is to make no commitment to anything or anyone, but say maybe yes, or maybe no and never get too close to any gal. This guy is truly unpleasant and the piece is the only scamp song not written in a comic or even lighthearted manner: "Maybe he wants you / Maybe he don't / If he gets a chance he'll break your heart / He's the Memphis Maybe Man." Humor returns in "Sweet Henry (The Pride Of Tennessee)" (Jack Mills, 1923) with Benny Davis's words and Harry Akst's music, the team that three years later wrote the hit "Baby Face," which proved a perennial standard ever since. Davis's humor is often subtle, sneaking up on the hearer from the start of the tune when we learn Henry was "all that a good man ought to be, / At grabbin' wimmen, say! He could trim'em all." Later Sweet Henry's love-making technique is encapsulated in a comparison to the heroes of two previous scamp songs: "Dapper Dan and Lovin' Sam can grab those highbrow [sic; should probably read "high brown"] maids, / Take my word, that this here bird / Can give 'em cards and spades (and beat 'em) / He's clever, he never wants for company / They envy Sweet Henry / The Pride of Tennessee." Performing rather than songwriting, the black team of Noble Sissle and Eubie Blake recorded the first verse and chorus of "Sweet Henry," along with some material not in the published sheet music, on January 1, 1924, for Victor, with Blake at the piano and Sissle singing, and it's on the Internet. "Mose (They Call Him Dark Town Mose)" (Breau & Tobias, 1925) had words by one Ed Gladstone, about whom I discovered nothing, and music by the equally mysterious Jimmie Counzelman and Charles Tobias, who was also a talented lyricist. The song's lyrics about "that struttin' man" who is driving "All the gals from miles around" Birmingham crazy could have used some help from Tobias the lyricist. The piece is about a *classy* black scamp: "Clothes tailor made / Hose any shade," but mostly, he's good at his avocation: "Love affair ev'rywhere / Calls it a joke / When he starts breakin' hearts / Boy they stay broke."

When scamp songs moved into the early 1930s, they continued to look much the same as in the '20s except for one big difference: The scamp featured in three of the four '30s tunes is white, and the fourth piece celebrates southern scamps of any color. "Sentimental Gentleman From Georgia"

(Mills Music, 1932) was one of the five Dixie tunes that lyricist Mitchell Parish wrote with composer Frank Perkins between 1932 and 1934. The verse says of the title's ladies' man that "he's hot," but his manner is sophisticated and debonair: "When he struts along and swings his cane, / Husbands tie up their wives with a ball and chain." His primary quality, stressed several times in the song, is that he's "Gentle to the ladies all the time," which pays off for him: "Oh, see those Georgia peaches hangin' around him now, / 'Cause what this baby teaches nobody else knows how." The original 1932 recording by Isham Jones and his Orchestra, with vocal of just the chorus by Eddie Stone, reveals the piece was an up-tempo foxtrot (prefiguring early swing), and "Sentimental Gentleman" also attracted the talents of three popular "girl groups" who made successful recordings of it, the Boswell Sisters and the Pickens Sisters, both in 1932, and the Dinning Sisters in 1945 (discography research by Al Pavlow). The Victor Isham Jones / Eddie Stone record is on the Internet. "Alabama Man" (De Sylva, Brown and Henderson, 1933) is by one of the Alley's most prolific lyricists, Mack Gordon (born Morris Gittler in Warsaw, Poland, in 1904), whose best-known Dixie tune is "Chattanooga Choo Choo." The music is by equally prolific English-born Harry Revel. The song begins by describing how the Alabama Man attracts crowds of screaming girls in public, and tells how hot he is. Like Lew Brown's "Dapper Dan," this isn't top-shelf Gordon, except for one silly line: "When he kisses you, you blister, / If he kissed a cow you'd have roast beef!"

Taking the final two '30s scamp songs out of chronological order because of their content, "He's A Colonel From Kentucky" (Leo Feist, 1934), with words by Charles Tobias and Jack Kroll and music by Abel Baer and Murray Mencher, shows Tobias's strength as a lyricist. The premise is preposterous and may be briefly summarized. The title "Kentucky Colonel" is an honorary one, granted by the governor of that state, not necessarily for military deeds but for any outstanding accomplishments. This tune is about a man "Who won his fame by making love / And just for that they made him a Colonel." Though the piece goes on for two verses and a chorus, that's all one really needs to know about it. Finally, the very makeup of the team that wrote "He's A Son Of The South" (Joe Davis Inc., 1933) gives a clue to what the song is about. The great black lyricist Andy Razaf coauthored the words with white publisher/lyricist Joe Davis, and British-born black composer Reginald Foresythe wrote the music. The piece offers tips on how to spot if a particular ladies' man, white or black, is from Dixie: "If he's dressed up to kill / And his feet won't keep still, / You can bet HE'S A SON OF THE SOUTH, / ... He's so polite, / If he's right on the spot, / When the music gets hot, / You can bet HE'S A SON OF THE SOUTH." Louis Armstrong recorded the chorus on January 26, 1933, for Victor, and it is on the Internet. Overall, except for "The Memphis Maybe Man," the attitudes expressed toward the protagonists of scamp songs and their exploits are those of awe, admiration, and even idolization, suggesting Alleymen managed to fit even these dubious types into their idealizing of Dixie unto its most unlikely parts, as will be seen in vamp songs as well.

Call her what you will—gold digger, Jezebel, red hot mama, femme fatale, designing woman—but this lady who intentionally and sequentially attracts, exploits, and unceremoniously dumps men is by any other name a vamp. According to the seven Dixie tunes about her, the southern variety is the finest flowering of the species, as first revealed in Jack Yellen's lyrics for "Louisville Lou (The Vampin' Lady)" (Ager, Yellen & Bornstein, 1923), with Milton Ager's music. The verse says Lou is plain dangerous in her vamping: "Cullud gals, ... / If you've got a man you're crazy about, / ... if he meets this high brown doll / Then you haven't got a chance at all." And to beat everything, Lou's passionate lovemaking is matched by her lack of morality: "Hot lips / That are pips / And no more conscience than a snake has hips!" Many early recordings were instrumentals by the likes of Ted Lewis and His Band and other dance orchestras, but Arthur Fields sang "Louisville Lou," which is on the Internet, for the ironically named Puritan records in 1923. Close to Yellen's humor was black lyricist Henry Creamer's in "Vamping Sal The Sheba Of Georgia" (M. Witmark, 1923), with white Lew Pollack's music. Like most vamp tunes, this describes Sal's lovemaking and lists her suitors, but Creamer sneaks in two topical references, the first to a scamp song: "When Sal heard about that lovin' Sam, / She just vamped him out of Alabam'." The second spun off from French psychologist Émile Coué's self-help mantra popular in the '20s, "Every day in every way, I'm getting better and better": "As a vamp she's the champ, you can't forget her, / Ev'ry day, ev'ry way she's getting better."

As the jive expression from the '30s went, Jack Yellen was really cookin' with gas when he teamed with Bob Bigelow and Charley Bates on the words for "Hard Hearted Hannah (The Vamp Of Savannah)" (Ager, Yellen & Bornstein, 1924), with music by Milton Ager, front-to-back the funniest vamp song of them all. Hannah, who is white by the way, is the most peculiar of the vamps. She's no red hot mama, but cold as ice, not quite sadistic but definitely a tormentor of the male sex, as the famous lines about her at the beach pouring water on a drowning man indicate. But more than that, Hannah is frigid, as neatly summarized by the ending of the second chorus: "An evening spent with Hannah sitting on your knees / Is like trav'ling thru Alaska in your B. V. D's; She' Hard hearted Hannah, The Vamp of Savannah G. A." "Hannah" was a big hit for Belle Baker the year it was published, when she recorded the complete tune for Victor on August 28, 1924, even though she changed the hilarious final lines quoted above, as may be heard on the Internet. The song continued to be performed and recorded in later decades by the likes of Ella Fitzgerald, Ray Charles, and Frank Sinatra. Another hit vamp song came from the Alley the following year in the form of "Sweet Georgia Brown" (Jerome H. Remick, 1925), with words by almost unknown white lyricist Ken Casey and music by black Maceo Pinkard and, supposedly, white bandleader Ben Bernie, whose band introduced the piece and "who, for plugging purposes cut himself in on the song as cocomposer although he did no writing" (Jasen 310). Black Georgia is just as sweet as white Hannah is poisonous, and her sweetness pays off: "Fellers she can't get are fellers she ain't met / Georgia claimed her / Georgia named her / Sweet Georgia Brown." Ethel Waters cut the first verse and chorus in 1925 for Columbia, as may be heard on the Internet. *Billboard* charted her record at #6 for two weeks in September of that year. Decades later, Anita O'Day sang the tune at the 1958 Newport Jazz Festival, Ella Fitzgerald made many recordings of it, and the number is the Harlem Globe Trotters' theme song.

The remaining vamp songs never made the splash that the ones about Hannah and Georgia Brown did. Henry Creamer wrote the words for the final two; although not at the top of his game in either one, he penned some amusing lines in each. Prior to those appeared "Sadie Green The Vamp Of New Orleans" (Chicago: Milton Weil Music, 1926), with words and music by Gilbert Wells and Johnny Dunn. This is a prosaic piece about an apparently white vamp ("Ev'rybody talks about this pretty little belle") which still on occasion manages to unload a clever line or two: "When she walks by, the Mothers cry, Firemen save my child"; and "She makes bald men tear their hair." But for the most part the lines are what by then had become clichés about driving men wild and the like. In "She's The Hottest Gal In Tennessee" (Shapiro, Bernstein, 1926), with Jimmy Johnson's music, wordsmith Henry Creamer idealizes the title character through outrageous hyperbole based on the notion of "she's so hot that. . . ." Apparently white, "This gal is so fev'rish / Her face is always red / Ev'ry morning her old man / Fries pancakes on her head." As far as her vamping goes, "when she starts to loving on the porch / All the furniture begins to scorch." Creamer's "Clementine (From New Orleans)" (Shapiro, Bernstein, 1927), with music by white composer Harry Warren, was the last southern vamp song. Judging from Creamer's calling New Orleans "that Creole town," it is as likely as not that Clementine herself is Creole, but nothing specifies that in the lyric, which is generally undistinguished except for some lines in the patter section to be sung between choruses: "Talk about Tobasco [sic] mamas, / Lulu Belles and other charmers / She's the baby that made the farmers / Raise a lot of cane." On that preposterous pun, so end the Alley's portraits of the scamps and vamps and indeed of all the southern social types, as we move forward to examine how Tin Pan Alley viewed (and of course idealized) Dixie's legendary hospitality and its leisure-time activities.

4

"Y'ALL COME"
Southern Hospitality, Conviviality, and Leisure-Time Fun

Okay, the song title I filched to head this chapter isn't from a Dixie tune but from Texas singer-songwriter Arlie Duff's 1952 country classic. Still, it resonates with the welcoming spirit of the southern activities northern Alleymen wrote about for decades prior to Duff's song, and which shaped so much of Dixie life and culture, whether or not those Yankee songsmiths ever traveled in the South to witness or partake of them themselves. Many of the activities Alleymen wrote about kept to the South—celebrations from the spontaneous to the more formal, including a small subset on barbecues and other food-fests, some about the spectator and participatory pastimes of horse races and riverboat cruises, and those on southern hospitality itself. But the Alley also produced songs whose subjects began as leisure-time activities in Dixie, but spread to the North to become pastimes not regional but national: Dixie music and dance crazes.

"That Southern Hospitality"

This song with Charles McCarron's lyrics and Raymond Walker's music (Broadway Music, 1915), more than any other of the thirteen Alley songs on the subject between 1909 and 1937, caught precisely what southern hospitality was, which the Reeds in *1001 Things* Item #926 labeled "legendary and mostly real." Just the chorus gives an idea of the warmth and sincerity embodied in the term "southern hospitality": "When you're down in Dixie, In a town in Dixie / With its Southern ways, Its 'Home and Mother' days / In their arms they take you, Right at home they make you. / Oh, oh, oh, you're always pickin' on a chicken / When you're down in Dixie in a town in Dixie / You're welcome, you're welcome to all you see, / And the population's at the station there / When your train pulls in from 'Anywhere' / They're always glad to see you, take it from me, / It's That Southern Hospitality." The Peerless Quartet cut the song for Victor on February 24, 1915, and it's on the Internet.

No other southern hospitality songs get so specific about what it is. Instead, all but one or two follow the pattern of a singer who has just visited up North now inviting the friends he met up there to come visit him down South, most often in his own home. Songs with this scenario range from those by the Alley's lesser lights to two by Irving Berlin written in the space of two years, "Down in Chattanooga" (Waterson, Berlin & Snyder, 1913) and "When You're Down in Louisville (Call On Me)" (Waterson, Berlin & Snyder, 1915). The first is on a 1913 Victor recording by Collins and Harlan, and the second by the same duo on a 1916 Victor record, both on the Internet. The sameness of these songs' lyrics doesn't bear quoting, but the titles of other ones show how some writers understood the essence of southern hospitality: "Everybody's Welcome in Dixie," with words by William Tracey and music by Halsey K. Mohr (M. Witmark, 1921); "Let My Home Be Your Home (When You're Down in Dixieland)," with words by Al Bernard (who was born in New Orleans) and music by Russel [*sic*] Robinson (Henry Waterson, 1924); and "You're Living Right Next Door To Heaven When You Live In Dixieland," with words by Alfred Bryan and music by Jean Schwartz (Jerome H. Remick, 1919). This unusual piece has lyrics that go past describing southern hospitality to idealizing it as part of an idyllic South: "Dixie hospitality / Good old Southern chivalry / From each heart it flows like the Swanee River / Just as easy and free / Honest folks that are sincere / Simple manners that endear / If you stay awhile you will learn to love them / Live among 'em and see."

Polar opposite to this was the sentiment expressed in the first southern hospitality song back in 1909, or one should more correctly say southern inhospitality song. The amusing product of three of the most talented black lyricists and composers of the day, J. Tim Brymn, Jim Burris, and Chris Smith, "Come After Breakfast (Bring 'Long Your Lunch and Leave 'Fore Supper Time)" (Jos. W. Stern, 1909) became popular in vaudeville as well as sheet music and on phonograph recordings. It tells of cranky Aunt Mandy Lou in South Carolina, who in the first verse devises a scheme to keep Deacon Jasper Green from calling on her at meal times, and in the second applies the same device to keeping the "women's Christian temp'rance union," which she just joined, from having meetings at suppertime at her place as well. The chorus explains her solution: "Come after breakfast, bring 'long your lunch and leave 'fore supper time. / If you do that I'm positive that I will treat you fine; / For ev'ry body's welcome at my house whether in rain or shine, / If they come after breakfast bring 'long their lunch and leave 'fore supper time." No model of southern hospitality but one for a comic novelty song, which Arthur Collins took advantage of on his 1910 Columbia record, which is on the Internet.

Celebrating Celebrations

From 1911 through 1955 Alleymen wrote thirty-one songs about southerners white and black—mostly black—celebrating all manner of things: the arrival of something special in town, personal rites of passage like birthdays and weddings, community events, or absolutely nothing at all—just plain ol' spontaneous celebratin' for the heck of it. The two smash-hits were the second from the beginning, "Waiting For The Robert E. Lee," with lyrics by L. Wolfe Gilbert and music by Lewis F. Muir (F. A. Mills, 1912), introduced by Al Jolson at the Winter Garden in New York City in 1912, though he didn't record it until 1946, and the second from the last, Paul Mason Howard and Paul Weston's "Shrimp Boats" (Walt Disney Music, 1951), which Jo Stafford cut a million-seller of with the Norman Luboff Choir and Paul Weston's Orchestra. Most of the other songs celebrating celebrations weren't as much to write home about, but some captured the flavor of jamborees, jubilees, and other good times in Dixie.

For sheer vitality, none filled the bill more than the aforementioned "Waiting For The Robert E. Lee," as it depicts in ragtime a whole unnamed town turning out on the levee to greet the arrival of the famed sidewheeler riverboat. Who cares that in Wolfie's imagination the levee is in "Alabamy," nowhere near the Mississippi River, or that this very present-tense song is about a historic steamboat that burned almost to its decks back in 1882? After all, what's a nice Russian-Jewish boy turned Alley lyricist supposed to know about such things—or his up-to-date New York audiences supposed to know or care for that matter! All that mattered were the vigorous, simple, direct words of Gilbert's chorus, a perfect match for Muir's exuberant, virtually archetypal ragtime tune: "Watch them shufflin' along / See them shufflin' along / Go take your best gal, real pal, / Go down to the levee, / I said to the levee and / Join that shufflin' throng, / Hear that music and song. / It's simply great, mate, / Waitin' on the levee, / Waitin' for the Robert E. Lee." The popular singing group with a name like a classical musical ensemble, the Heidelberg Quintette, Billy Murray taking the second tenor part, recorded the complete "Robert E. Lee" for Victor on July 11, 1912, as may be heard on the Internet. The song charted at #1 in September 1912 and was an instantaneous hit not only in the States but in England too. In a 1913 *Variety* article on American ragtime in England, Fred Day of the London music publishing firm of Francis, Day & Hunter noted that "Waiting For the Robert E. Lee" was the third most popular American rag in England, preceded by Gilbert and Muir's own "Hitchy Koo" (not a Dixie tune), which in turn was preceded by Irving Berlin's "Alexander's Ragtime Band" (which is in fact a march, not a rag—see the Music section below). Day noted Brits enjoyed "Robert E. Lee" though they had no idea what it was about: "English people had trouble deciphering the 'Lee' song, said Mr. Day. Almost any Englishman would inquire, 'Why all the fuss over this Lee person and why were they waiting at the dock for him,' but they liked the tune" (*Variety* June 27, 1913: 6). Clearly, folks across the pond didn't listen closely to Wolfie's lyrics.

"Waiting For The Robert E. Lee" falls into the group of songs celebrating the arrival of something special in town. Four others were also about riverboats, but all pale by comparison to the Gilbert/Muir tune, even though one, "When The Henry Clay Comes Steaming Into Mobile Bay" (Jerome & Schwartz Pub. Co., 1912), was the work of three fine Alleymen, lyricists William Jerome and Grant Clarke and composer Jean Schwartz. Perhaps because the song was written for the musical *My Best Girl* and the lyrics had to fit the needs of the show, they lack the vibrancy of Gilbert's for "Robert E. Lee," although the scenarios of the two songs are nearly identical. As for the name of the riverboat, though the song is written in the present tense, both historical *Henry Clay* sidewheelers were long gone: the most famous crashed in a fiery conflagration on the Hudson River near Riverdale in 1852, and the other was a casualty of the Civil War at Vicksburg in 1863 (see *Riverboat Dave's Paddlewheel Site* online, which also indicates by their absence that the steamboats to follow were fictional). "Loading Up The Mandy Lee" with Stanley Murphy's words and Henry I. Marshall's music (Jerome H. Remick, 1915) is about darkies in Natchez celebrating after getting their pay for loading cotton on a steamboat of that name. The American Quartet, with solos by the inimitable Billy Murray, recorded the whole number on January 1, 1916, for Victor, as may be heard on the Internet. And, rather late for such songs, "The Jefferson Davis," with Walter Donaldson's lyrics and Pete Wendling's music (Jerome H. Remick, 1924), returns to the motif of a whole town celebrating the arrival of a paddlewheel riverboat, again in the present. In an even later song, "Welcome Home" (M. Witmark, 1929), an entire town—seemingly all white this time—turns out for the arrival of a hometown boy on a sidewheeler. To Harry Akst's music, the usually meticulous Grant Clarke wrote a lyric that is bafflingly contradictory: we first learn that "our wandrin' boy is comin' home / Now our hearts will never no more be heavy / If he'll stay and promise not to roam"; after which the mayor says, "Gorry lad, we're glad you're home on vacation"; then, reunited with his sweetheart, "He'll soon be off on his honeymoon." Whether the boy is coming or going, the townsfolk are thrilled to see him, even with a band to greet him, and all in the here and now. What's charming about these tunes is that their writers wrote them as present-day events decades after the era of steamboatin' had passed, so there's no sense the songs are nostalgia pieces at all.

One of the other songs celebrating something special arriving in a Dixie town could take place in any time period at all. "Circus Day In Dixie," with Jack Yellen's words and Albert Gumble's music (Jerome H. Remick, 1915), spends most of the time describing the circus parade itself, but also such lines as "Circus day in Dixie, / Always is a holiday" make it clear this once-a-year one-day event is a time for the town to celebrate. The American Quartet recorded the tune, full of various "animal noises," for Victor on July 26, 1915, and it's on the Internet. The remaining song in the group, by the same lyricist and composer, is as specific to the year it was published as "Circus Day" is generic. Though the lyric doesn't mention the Great War, it is implicit as the backstory to "Alexander's Band Is Back In Dixieland" (Jerome H. Remick, 1919), since after Irving Berlin's hit at least one song was written about Alexander taking his band "over there" to play for the troops during World War I. Yellen and Gumble celebrate Dixie's celebrating the band's return home, with no mention of the war. The American Quartet as the Premiere Quartet, its name when recording for Edison rather than Victor, cut this ragtime rouser on an Edison Blue Amberol cylinder in 1920, which is on the Internet.

Alleymen wrote only six songs about personal celebrations among the denizens of Dixie—one birthday and five weddings. Of those, the first and last became popular successes of some magnitude, not just in sheet music sales, but as phonograph records too. Starting things off was "Mammy Jinny's Jubilee" (F. A. Mills, 1913) by the intrepid duo of L. Wolfe Gilbert writing the words and Lewis F. Muir composing the tune—not a rag this time, but a one-step. The number joyously celebrates all of a town's darkies turning out to congratulate their matriarch because "Mammy Jinny's eighty-two today." Arthur Collins and Byron G. Harlan made a successful Victor recording of the piece on July 24, 1913, which one may hear on the Internet. Four of the five wedding songs are fairly pedestrian, and all but one are about white weddings in both senses of the word. The exception is an amusing number, with Lew Brown's lyrics and Jack Glogau's music and the slightly ironic title "Celebratin' Day In Tennessee" (Leo Feist, 1914). The singer is a darky girl who can't quite grasp a celebration she's watching until she finally wonders, "Who's that girl dressed up as a bride, / Is that my honey, There by her side?" Again Collins and Harlan gave it the comic treatment it deserved when they recorded it for Victor on March 16, 1914, as may be heard on the Internet. Even this comic song notes what an idyllic spot Dixie or a part of it is for a wedding, as do other less distinguished wedding tunes. The theme also appears in the widely popular "Mandy 'N' Me" (Shapiro, Bernstein, 1921), recorded by Billy Murray and the American Quartet on Victor in 1921 and charted #12 in February 1922, which is on the Internet. The tune had Bert Kalmar's words and Con Conrad and Otto Motzan's music, and is not to be confused with Irving Berlin's "Mandy," also a wedding song, but not a Dixie tune. The focus is on the bride and groom's joy, but the opening of the second verse makes clear that much of their happiness is due to their marrying "In that sunny milk and honey Southern atmosphere," which the first verse identified as "Caroline."

The ten Alley pieces between 1911 and 1955 depicting celebrations of community events divide between five that vibrantly catch their spirit and five so lifeless we can only hope the events were livelier than the songs about them. To dismiss the second group first, within three years three dull songs came out about happy darkies rejoicing after picking cotton: Harry Tobias's "When It's Cotton Pickin' Time in Alabam'" (Harry Tobias Music Pub., 1915); "Cotton Pickin' Time in Alabam'," with Harold Cool's words and Arthur J. Daly's music (William Jerome, 1916); and "At The Cotton Pickers Ball," with lyrics by Alex Gerber and music by Maurice Abrahams (Puck & Abrahams, 1917). Dave Ringle's "Melon Time In Dixieland" (Leo Feist, 1921) is like the cotton songs in the key of watermelon, but now with all of Dixie, white and black, celebrating the melon's harvest. "Christmas Time In New Orleans," with words and music by Dick Sherman and Joe Van Winkle (Regent Music, 1955), is an embarrassment, with such phrases as "Fields of cotton look wintry white" and "Mississippi folks gather there" (both in NOLA?). The only specific Big Easy reference is to Santa leading a Creole band "Down on Basin Street." Otherwise, the song could be about Christmas in Milwaukee.

But the other five songs celebrating local events are something to celebrate about. The first is also the first Dixie celebration song of any kind, "At The Levee On Revival Day" (Jos. W. Stern, 1911). The tune is one of the white/black Alley collaborations, with lyrics by white Charles R. McCarron and Ferd E. Mierisch and music by black Chris Smith, writing a rollicking two-step that sets the tempo for the more than lively darky revival meeting that is the subject of the song. McCarron and Mierisch's lyrics are energetic and fully descriptive of the revival experience, and, while laced with humor, in no way do they parody or demean the enthusiastic brand of worship the darkies display at the revival on the levee, as can be seen from the chorus after each verse: "You can hear them moanin' / You can hear them groanin' / You can hear them cantin' / You can hear them chantin' / You can hear them prayin' / With their bodies swayin' / You can hear them screechin' / While the preacher's preachin' / In their wild elation, / Yellin' for salvation, / When the organ starts to play, / Glory glory halleluja, (splash) / Overboard goes Sister Julia, / Boats will be capsizin' / Folks will be baptizin' at the levee on Revival Day." Chris Smith comically set "Glory glory halleluja (splash)" and the following line about drenched Sister Julia to the familiar "Battle Hymn Of The Republic" refrain. On November 5, 1912, Collins and Harlan cut a spirited Victor recording of the song that may be heard on the Internet.

In 1914 a less-well-known Alleyman, Andrew K. Allison, wrote the words and Alleywoman Verna Wilkens composed the music for an equally rousing tune about a secular black Dixie celebration. Though its lyrics employ the less-used word "moke" for the song's title character, there is nothing derogatory in its usage here. The opening lines make it plain that in "Down At Jasper Johnson's Jamboree" (F. B. Haviland, 1914), this huge happy party celebrates something near and dear to the hearts of all southern blacks: "Old Jasper Johnson, a Kentucky colored moke, / Said 'I'm goin' to give a picnic to the colored folk, / It's just fifty years ago we were set free, / So I'm goin' to celebrate it with an old time Jamboree.'" And Jasper does, as does the rest of this song full of details about darkies coming from as far as Baltimore to dance the latest "Tango swing" and eat possum pie, a good time had by all. Ballard MacDonald wrote the words and Harry Carroll the music for "At The Dixie Military Ball" (Shapiro, Bernstein, 1918), describing a gala for the officers and men of a southern black regiment before shipping out "over there" during the Great War. It's one of the jazziest military balls on record, with "Drum Major Jones / Pulling dark blue music from the saxophones." The officers are models of bravado, "Each dressed to kill old Kaiser Bill," but they and the enlistees are one in purpose: "They're goin' to Walk the Dog and Ball the Jack / All the way to Berlin and then shimme back." Popular singer Marion Harris cut the piece for Victor in 1918 but it isn't on the Internet.

Once you get past the preposterous images of cotton fields on the banks of the Swanee River where swampland should be, and sidewheelers plying its sluggish waters to dock at levees for darky stevedores to load them with cotton bales, "Sunday On The Swanee" (Southern Music, 1936), with words and music by Walter G. Samuels, Leonard Whitcup, and big band leader Teddy Powell, turns out to be a song about a local, regularly repeated celebration. Far from the upbeat razz-ma-tazz rhythms of the previous numbers, this one is much more mellow, befitting the words of the cotton pickers and stevedores celebrating Sunday, the one restful weekly day off from their labors: "Bring out that rockin' chair, / Put it by that Swanee River shore. / Light up my pipe, / Sing me a song, / And let me watch that Ole Man River go 'long." Also frequent, though not weekly, are the community celebrations sung about in the hit "Shrimp Boats" (Walt Disney Music, 1951), with words and music by Paul Mason Howard and Paul Weston. The only local celebration song *not* about darkies, "Shrimp Boats" concerns the lives of shrimpers, at the time of the song mostly Cajuns of French Canadian descent living on the bayous of southern Louisiana. Sung from the point of view of the shrimpers' womenfolk, the tune alternates between its joyous upbeat refrains of "SHRIMP BOATS is a-comin' / Their sails are in sight. / SHRIMP BOATS is a-comin', / There's dancin' tonight" and the almost lugubrious verses in which the lonely women await their men's indefinite return from the dangerous sea. The masterful musical construction directly conveys the song's alternating moods, as may be heard on Jo Stafford's million-selling 1951 Columbia recording on the Internet. Stafford's "Shrimp Boats" was on the *Billboard* charts for seventeen weeks, peaking in the #2 spot.

The remaining eight celebration songs described Dixie folk celebrating for no particular reason. Four are worth saying something about, one deserves passing mention for its peculiarity, and the other three we can pretend never happened. "Dixie Jamboree," with words and music by Howard Johnson and Joe Davis (Triangle Music, 1929), is peculiar since the first verse and chorus describe a darky barbecue and the second, using many of the same phrases, a prayer meeting. I presume singers could take their pick of which to sing depending on their present degree of hunger or spirituality. Between 1909 and 1919 composer Albert Gumble seems to have made a career out of writing the music for nineteen Dixie tunes with words by ten different lyricists—Jack Yellen for six of the nineteen. But in 1914, Gumble's lyricist wasn't Yellen but A. Seymour Brown for "At The Mississippi Cabaret" (Jerome H. Remick, 1914), a happy collaboration in which "Most ev'ry one in the town" somewhere in Tennessee, white folks and darkies alike, turn out "Most any night" on the levee to dance and sing at a free outdoor cabaret, whose spirit was caught by the American Quartet in its 1914 Victor recording that is on the Internet. A town's levee seems to have been a popular place for outdoor celebrations of nothing at all, at least in the imaginations of Alley songwriters, since such a place is also the setting for lyricist Jack Yellen and composer Melville Morris's "Down Around The River At the Dixie Jubilee" (Leo Feist, 1919). This is strictly a darky event and a special one, not a near-nightly occurrence, since "Tickets cost a dime, the wardrobe's free. / The Jazzbo band will be there, / You mustn't miss this swell affair." This jubilee gets quite lively and, at one point, risqué: "I declare! There goes the parson's daughter, / Looky there she's with a Pullman porter, what a time he'll give her, / Down around the river, / At the Dixie Jubilee." To continue songs about celebratin' for the helluvit, black lyricist Henry Creamer and Jewish composer Maurice Abrahams teamed up to express in "Jubilee Blues" (Maurice Abrahams, 1923) the antics of much too happy darkies preparing for a camp meeting, as in the lines "There's moonshine on the hill / There's moonshine in the dell / But the moonshine in the still / Is the best moonshine they sell / Just one sip makes you see / This whole Jubilee." On the Internet one may hear Belle Baker with the Virginians' 1923 Victor recording capturing the flavor of these celebratin' Dixie darkies. Later Ray Bauduc and Bob Haggart wrote the instrumental "South Rampart Street Parade" (Leo Feist, 1938), an exemplar of authentic Dixieland jazz. Bob Crosby and His Orchestra cut the major recording for Decca in 1939 and it's on the Internet. In 1952 Steve

Allen wrote lyrics to the tune (Leo Feist, copyright renewed), making it a piece about folks in New Orleans—most probably white, black, and Creole all together—celebrating just because some band is playing and marching on South Rampart Street. That year Bing Crosby and the Andrews Sisters recorded it on a 45 rpm disc, also for Decca, which too is on the Internet.

Playing with Food

Considering southerners' love of good cooking generally and barbecue in particular, it's surprising that aside from casual references in pieces about hospitality, celebrations, and other things, the Alley turned out only four songs focusing specifically on a Dixie shindig where food was the main event. I'm even stretching my criteria for the Alley to include one tune I couldn't leave out since it happens to be the best of the bunch and is the only one of the four that *isn't* about a barbecue. That's country singer/songwriter Hank Williams's exuberant tribute to Louisiana Cajun cooking (and a lot of other things) in "Jambalaya" (Nashville: Acuff-Rose Publications, 1952). Considering its lyricist/composer and publisher, the tune could be classified as a country, not an Alley Dixie, tune but since Jo Stafford, an artist strictly associated with the Alley, cut its biggest-selling record for Columbia, with its long history of ties to the Alley, "Jambalaya" may be counted a product of both the Alley in its waning days and Nashville in its nascent ones. Stafford's disc, charting at #3 on *Billboard*'s pop music chart, outstripped Williams's record on the country chart. Her 1952 Columbia recording is on the Internet. The lyrics are more specific about some delights of Cajun cookin' than are any Alley barbecue songs, right in the opening of the chorus: "Jambalaya and a crawfish pie and fillet [*sic,* for filé] gumbo."

The three barbecue songs are much earlier, two dating back to 1914, the third to 1936, and a curious bunch they are. About all the barbecuing going on in any of them is in the songs' titles. In "Down At The Barbecue," with words and music by Roger Lewis and Ernie Erdman (Chicago: Will Rossiter, 1914), the culinary hit of the event called a "barbecue" in a small Dixie town—white or black not specified—never saw a pit or grill: "Oh! Oh! You 'Possum stew, what we won't do to you; / There won't be any left at all, when we get thro.'" At least that tune mentions *something* to eat, unlike Dave Reed's

"The Mississippi Barbecue" (M. Witmark, 1914), which mostly sings of dark-ies coming by boat from Tennessee to Kentucky for a grand barbecue on the bank of the Mississippi with no word about the food except to say, "Smell the grand aroma of that cookin' sweet," hinting there might be a pig in a pit some-where in the vicinity. In "Alabama Barbecue," which Benny Davis (words) and J. Fred Coots (music) (Mills Music, 1936) wrote for *Cotton Club Parade of 1936*, more singing and dancing than eating's going on, and the gath-ered darkies are feasting not on barbecue but "cornbread an' fried chicken." The paucity of southern food songs and the lack of details about barbecue and other fare in the few culinary songs Alleymen wrote may be attributed to their relative unfamiliarity with such things. Whatever the reason, the result was mighty slim pickin's in Dixie food tunes.

Kickin' Back in Dixie

Item #928 of *1001 Things* proclaims, "A taste for leisure (laziness, if you dis-approve) has also [along with manners, discussed in Item #927] been a part of the image of the South since before there was a South. This was an equal-opportunity image: the gentry had leisure, poor whites and slaves were lazy—nobody worked any harder than he had to." To document this, the Reeds go back to the writings of seventeenth-century author and landowner Virginian William Byrd II's view of people moving to North Carolina, "where plenty and a warm sun confirm them in their disposition to laziness for their whole lives." For a more positive outlook, the Reeds turn to Edward King's *The Great South* (1875): "This is the South, slumberous, voluptuous, round and graceful. Here beauty peeps from every door-yard. Mere existence is plea-sure; exertion is a bore." Small wonder the leisure-time activities in Dixie tunes required minimal effort from spectators or participants—horse races and riverboat rides.

The two horse-racing songs appeared three decades apart, in 1918 and 1948. "Derby Day In Dixie" (Jerome H. Remick, 1918) had words by Ray-mond Egan and music by Richard A. Whiting, who wrote many hits together, some Dixie tunes, some not. Elaine Gordon's sprightly 1918 Edison record-ing, replete with horse-hoof effects, is on the Internet. The tune depicts a horse race (*not* the Kentucky Derby), showing the good time being had by all even if they lose money, as the singer does by taking Old Parson Lee's advice to bet on a horse named "Remorse," that leads till the final lap when "Sun Briar" passes him and wins. Still, "the throng so happy" is made more so since "A Dixie band makes you understand that it's Derby Day in Dixieland." The second horse race song, "Blue Grass" (Chappell, 1948), *is* about the Kentucky Derby and debuted in the revue *Inside U. S. A.*, with Howard Dietz's lyrics and Arthur Schwartz's music, which opened on April 30, 1948. It's a comic lament by a woman who loses her lover to his love of the ponies at Churchill Downs. Dietz laced his lyrics with lines like "Hard to compete / With gallopin' feet" and "He can't keep me warm with a Racing Form."

A 1922 song with both words and music by L. Wolfe Gilbert unintentionally bridged the Alley's few songs about horse races and its equally skimpy output of pieces about riverboat cruises. Seemingly, sometime during the ten years following Wolfie's writing the words of the anachronistic 1912 "Waiting For The Robert E. Lee," this Alleyman brushed up on the history of that storied boat. The result was his historically accurate tune about the famous 1870 race between "The Natchez And The Robert E. Lee" (L. Wolfe Gilbert, 1922). Here riverboat racing is a spectator sport. The first verse begins, "Listen to your Grand-Daddy / He's got a story to tell," a proper introduction for this narrative piece in the past tense. The song stresses the size of the crowds, white and black, gathered along the banks of the Mississippi to see the two boats race between St. Louis and New Orleans: "Standing on boxes and pails / They come to see the race between the old side wheelers." The *Robert E. Lee* won with a time of 3 days, 18 hours, and 14 minutes, the *Natchez* behind at 3 days, 21 hours, 58 minutes.

A cruise on a riverboat was far more leisurely than racing one, or even getting one's adrenalin pumped up watching such a race, and the three Alley songs about twilight cruises embody moods from relaxation to romance. With Roger Lewis's words and James White's music, the long title "Floating Down The River ('Cause It's Moonlight Now In Dixieland)" (Chicago: Will Rossiter, 1913) is so explicitly romantic that quotations from the text hardly seem necessary. Yet curiously the melody isn't dreamy and legato, but jolly and up-tempo, as one can hear on the September 9, 1913, Victor recording by the American Quartet on the Internet. Quite differently, the folks who spend an evening "On The Good Ship Whippoorwill" (Shapiro, Bernstein 1915), with words by Coleman Goetz and music by the prolific Walter Donaldson, have a grand time not just lounging on the decks but singing and dancing to the band on board, yet Donaldson's melody is comparatively mellow, as may be heard on the Internet on the 1915 Columbia record by Arthur Collins and Byron G. Harlan. The last of the riverboat cruise songs came comparatively late and had both words and music by Mildred C. Ewald. "Can't You Hear The Whistle" (Jerome H. Remick, 1924) is about a young darky's efforts to hustle his girl along so they don't miss the boat (literally) for an evening's cruise: "Come on Mandy Johnson don't be slow / Can't you hear the whistle? / Don't you hear the whistle? / . . . get your hat get your coat / The calliope has started playing / And all the folks—just see them swaying. . . . Come on let's catch that river boat." The piece never states if they catch it or not, but the boy's urgency makes it clear that such a ride is the kind of romantic evening he wants with his girl.

"Those Dixie Melodies"

Five Alley songs embodied myths or legends about the origins of the kinds or components of Dixie music, from the famous "Birth Of The Blues" (1926) to one in which music helped create a town, "Mobile" (1953). I'll say no more about these now, but save them for their proper place later with Dixie tunes about southern myths. Here instead is a picture of some of the Alley's nineteen other songs about Dixie music or Dixie musicians, with the overriding theme that whatever sort of music was being played, it sounded better by southern musicians.

The earliest Alley tune about music in Dixie was also the biggest hit in this group—Irving Berlin's "Alexander's Ragtime Band" (Ted Snyder, 1911). Yet there isn't much in either Berlin's music or lyrics that has "Dixie" written all over it: The line "And if you care to hear the Swanee River played in ragtime" refers to northerner Stephen Foster's song, and only the bandleader's name, Alexander, was a clue that this was a darky band, since among whites at the time "Alexander" was a common buzzword first name for darkies. As for the piece being a rag, it absolutely is not; it's a march. This can be clearly heard on the Internet in the very four-square, regular beat in the record Collins and Harlan cut for Victor on May 23, 1911. Still, for Berlin this number almost singlehandedly made his name and a whole lot of money. Not as popular as

Berlin's song, but more authentically in a southern vein was "Listen To That Dixie Band," with words by Jack Yellen and music by George L. Cobb (Jerome H. Remick, 1915). Yellen's lyrics capture a town's enthusiasm for the arrival of "that Dixie band / From my home in Dixieland," and the music by consummate ragtime composer Cobb is filled with all the syncopation absent from "Alexander's Ragtime Band," as is clear on the Internet on the September 1, 1915, Collins and Harlan recording for Victor. Between these numbers were two, both in 1914, boasting that anything played by a band in Dixie was played better than anywhere else. With words by L. Wolfe Gilbert and music by Lewis F. Muir, "Camp Meeting Band" (F. A. Mills, 1914) declared of the darky band at an old-fashioned camp meeting, "Then hear them darkies play / The tune of the old Stars and Stripes, just like new, / If Sousa could hear them play it, he'd say so too." Adding some comic dialogue after the second verse, Collins and Harlan recorded "Camp Meeting Band" for Victor on January 22, 1914, and it's on the Internet. In "That Bandana Band (Way Down In Dixie Land)," with Robert G. Irby's words and William Warner's music (W. T. Pierson, 1914), white folks giving a ball "Way down in Tennessee" find the white band they hired "sounded tame," and so send for darky "Johnson's band, / A truly band what am" to liven things up: "They don't need no notes, it's in their throats / Out to their feet and hands."

The significance of these four songs and the six similar ones to follow is that they form a microcosm of idealizing the South in all its aspects by showing that any music played by Dixie musicians sounds better than music played elsewhere. But before turning to the other six songs of this type, it would only be fair to show that Alleymen also wrote some songs about Dixie music from other perspectives, mainly humorous. In the early decades of the twentieth century, an epidemic of Hawaiian melodies swept across the United States, and the South wasn't immune from the disease, to the extent that Bernie Grossman, Billy Winkle, and Arthur Lange teamed on the words and music of the wonderfully silly "Since They're Playin' Hawaiian Tunes in Dixie" (Joe Morris, 1917). The singer bemoans how traditional Dixie tunes are being replaced by Hawaiian music: "Old uncle Joe sold his old banjo, / Plays the Ukalele [sic] soft and low / Deacon Brewster taught his rooster to / Ya-ka-hu-la-hi-cky doo-la cock-a-doo-dle-do." Given the date of the song, by the second verse things get downright scandalous: "The girls wear skirts made of hay, / They cut them shorter each day." When Jack Strouse wrote the words and music of "They Called It The Dixie Blues" (Joe Morris, 1919), he may not have intended the song to be funny, but it turned out that way. In the verse, some musicians, led by "Ragtime Joe," decide the way to write "a song about the south" is to "steal those southern melodies / Like all the composers do." The verse contains snatches, in order, of Stephen Foster's "Old Black Joe," "Massa's In De Cold, Cold Ground," "Old Folks At Home [Swanee River]," "The Old Kentucky Home," and Dan Emmett's "Dixie." What's amusing about their choices is that all the "southern melodies" they chose are by *northerners,* Foster born in Pittsburgh, Emmett in Mount Vernon, Ohio. There are no genuine southern melodies in the bunch, as can be heard on the Internet in Bert Harvey's 1920 Edison recording. With Clarence Gaskill's words and music, "That Swanee River Melody" (Harms, 1922) is more wry than funny as a fable of how George Gershwin came to write and publish his first hit, "Swanee" (though George's lyricist Irving Caesar is not in sight). The piece exists for the punch line when the publisher is talking to young Gershwin: "He said 'You must be a Southern Lad / You'll make your Mammy and your Dad feel glad, / And you'll be going home, when you get your royalty,' / But he lives in New York town that's between you and me," which could apply to nearly *all* Alleymen writing Dixie tunes.

A black man who *was* a southern composer, musician, and publisher and in almost no time became an Alley composer, musician, and song publisher was W. C. Handy. An early instrumental tune he wrote in 1912, "The Memphis Blues," within a year had words written to it by white lyricist George A. Norton (most famed for "My Melancholy Baby"), words in part a tribute to Handy himself and his music. The version with Norton's lyrics was first published by Theron G. Bennett in New York in 1913 but transferred to the more going concern of Joe Morris Music by at least 1916, the date on most copies of the sheet music. Though he titled it a blues, Handy himself described the upbeat tune as a "Southern rag" (which it is, unlike Handy's more famous "St. Louis Blues," a true blues in its form). In the song, a visitor to Memphis rhapsodizes over the city's hospitality, but soon switches his feelings to an actual band there, its leader and composer a real-life case of music sounding better in Dixie: "I went out a-dancin' with a Tennessee dear, / they had a fellow there named Handy with a band you should hear— / and while the whi' folks gently swayed / All dem darkies played real Harmony / I never will forget the tune that Handy called the Memphis Blues." On October 2, 1914,

Morton Harvey, the first singer to record a blues song, cut the first verse and chorus for Victor, and it's on the Internet.

It's been said that the word "jazz," although spelled "jas" in the piece, first appeared in the early Gus Kahn lyric to "That Funny Jas Band From Dixieland" (Jerome H. Remick, 1916) with Henry I. Marshall's music, another number extolling music south of the Mason-Dixon Line. The tune is a rousing one about a darky jazz band somewhere in Dixie so proficient that "When you listen to mad musicians playin' rhythm / So you can't help swaying with them." Such early Kahn rhyming reveals a glimmer of his later cleverness in songs like "Carolina In The Morning," and the music of lesser-known Marshall is what today we'd call authentic Dixieland Jazz, as can be heard on the Internet on the 1916 Edison Diamond Disc recording by Collins and Harlan, especially during the instrumental breaks by the Edison House Band. "Those Dixie Melodies" (Jerome H. Remick, 1919) was by two long-time Alley stalwarts, lyricist Alfred Bryan and composer Jean Schwartz. They wrote it for the musical extravaganza *Hello, Alexander,* a vehicle for the blackface vaudeville team of McIntyre and Heath (see Bordman 342). Not only does the piece acclaim Dixie music as the best anywhere, but it also shows something about how Bryan and Schwartz collaborated on this song. Most popular songs get written with the composer writing a melody and then the lyricist setting words to it (or vice versa). But here in the verse lyricist Bryan and composer Schwartz had to work absolutely in tandem through every note and word to make the thing come out right. The premise is that the singer likes Dixie tunes better than grand opera arias, "Like O Pagliacci what a wonderful theme," which Schwartz set to the familiar melody from that opera, as he did similarly with bits from *La Traviata* and *Il Trovatore* to accompany Bryan's lines, "A tune like Traviata Flowing like a beautiful dream / Don't sing that song from Trovator, a famous one called Leonora," climaxing with "Never mind that dreamy La Boheme" which Schwartz set to "Musetta's Waltz" from Puccini's opera. All this prefaced a ragtime chorus in which the singer declared, "I love those Dixie melodies / Old fashioned Dixie harmonies. . . . Take me back to old Virginny / Carve that possum please / O there ain't no music can compare with those Dixie melodies."

The remaining three "music sounds better in Dixie" tunes may be briefly mentioned since they are so straightforward in what they sing about. With words and music by Grant Clarke, Edgar Leslie, and Pete Wendling, the title of "Maxie Jones King Of The Saxiephones" (Stark & Cowan, 1923) says most anything one needs to know about the song, except that Maxie is a "member of the colored race" who leads "the Dixie Five down in a Dixie Dive" "upon the Swanee Shore . . . a little 'two by four' / Where ev'rything is second hand / All except a first class band," and that when Maxie blows his sax he "Annihilates his instrument." In "Nashville Nightingale" (Harms, 1923), Irving Caesar (lyrics) and George Gershwin (music) extolled a black lady blues singer there with a voice so seductive that "All the darktown preachers and the bible teachers say they're losing all their trade, / For the good church people all desert the steeple / When she starts to serenade." The lyricist Gershwin, brother Ira, wrote the words and Philip Charig the music of "Blowin' The Blues Away" (Harms, 1926), about the seeming paradox of a Dixie band playing the blues to chase one's blues away: "There's an aggregation down South, / Playing syncopation down South. / It will never snow there, / When the blues they blow there."

Dixie Dancing

Between 1910 and 1949, the Alley turned out more songs about recreational dances that supposedly originated in Dixie than it did about music in the South. The bulk of these twenty-six dance-tunes were mediocre at best, but among them were three of the biggest Dixie tune hits the Alley ever produced. Yet there were also a few atrocities like the last in the bunch, "The Dixieland Rhumba" (Life Music, 1949). One line, "Then I wish I was in Dixie O-lay, o-lay," says you need hear no more of this abomination to ignore it. The remaining tunes can be divided into pre-"Charleston" and post-"Charleston." (The tune with Cecil Mack's words and Jimmy Johnson's music, along with its dance, was titled just "Charleston," not "The Charleston.")

Ten Alley Dixie dance-songs preceded "Charleston." "Old Fashioned Cake Walk" (1922) was a nostalgia piece about the dance in the title. Other mediocre ones about alleged new dances titled "The Georgia Grind" (1910), "Mississippi Splash" (1911), "That Alabama Bear" (1912), "That Dixie Glide" (1912), and "The Palm Beach Dip" (1917) aren't worth saying much about except that they are variations of ragtime dances, and all but the Palm Beach one are expressly darky dances. The other four are of more interest. With semi-tongue-twisty words by Ballard MacDonald and a sprightly melody by W. Raymond Walker, "The Mississippi Dippy Dip" (Jos. W. Stern, 1911) is a darky ragtime dance, as one can hear on the Internet from Collins and Harlan's April 5, 1911, Victor record. What also can be heard is how Walker wove not just a snatch of "Dixie" into his melody, but also the musical phrase set to the lyric "Johnny, get your gun, get your gun, get your gun," in its original appearance in "Johnny Get Your Gun," with words and music by F. Belasco, one of Monroe H. Rosenfeld's pseudonyms (Harms, 1886). Six years after "Dippy Dip," George M. Cohan snitched the "Johnny" melody, with Rosenfeld's bellicose words intact, for the verse of his World War I smash "Over There" (Leo Feist, 1917).

The date of the song and the quality of the writing suggest that both Henry S. Creamer's lyrics and Will H. Vodery's music for "West Virginia Dance" (The Rogers Bros., 1911) were pretty much apprenticeship work for each of them, though Creamer went on to be one of the Alley's most talented and prolific black lyricists, and Vodery an African American composer of considerable note, best known for his choral and orchestral arrangements for the original 1927 production of the musical *Show Boat*. Still, despite its youthful flaws, "West Virginia Dance" may be more authentic than many of the made-up Dixie dances by white Alleymen since it was the product of two black songwriters, one—Creamer—even a southerner from Virginia. The piece is a bold, openly seductive one to be sung and danced by a woman: "Oh my Joe, oh my Joe / Come and dance here with your Flo; / Oh my honey baby. / Glide up with that pretty motion while your mind is in the notion / . . . Oh Lovie hear that band, let us prance, come on, honey, take a chance, / I'm wild about that West Virginia Dance." Ferd E. Mierisch's lyrics and John B. Lowitz's music are laced with humor to make "The Swanee River Bend" (F. B. Haviland, 1912) not just an energetic darky ragtime dance but an amusing one too, as is heard on Arthur Collins's June 3, 1912, Victor recording on the Internet. Lowitz embeds within his own tricky dance tune what by now seem obligatory snatches from "Dixie" and, for good measure, a fairly substantial hunk of Foster's "The Old Kentucky Home," which lyricist Mierisch has some fun with by setting its tune to "You forget about your Ole Kentucky home, when you're doin' that Swanee River Bend, in Georgia—when you do— / When you do—That Swanee River Bend." The last pre-"Charleston" dance-song is worth noting only for who wrote it, showing how far the Dixie dance craze went in the 'teens of the twentieth century. One thinks of Rudolf Friml as the composer of operettas like *The Firefly* (1912), *Rose-Marie* (1924), and *The Vagabond King* (1925). But for a trivial musical called *High Jinks,* Friml and his librettist Otto Hauerbach (later changed to Harbach) wrote a Dixie dancing ditty called "The Dixiana Rise" (G. Schirmer, 1913).

Which brings us to 1923 and "Charleston," a watershed year for purported Dixie dances and the Alley songs that in most cases created them. Cecil Mack and Jimmy Johnson wrote "Charleston" itself for their score of the all-black Broadway musical *Runnin' Wild.* One phrase of Mack's lyric was almost prophetic: "Buck dance, / Wing dance, / Will be a back number, / But the Charleston the new Charleston / That dance is surely a comer." It proved not just the smash-hit of the show, but also a huge seller in the instrumental recording on the 1923 Victor disc by Arthur Gibbs and his Gang, which is on the Internet. In no time, the tune launched a national dance craze, appealing to young and old, black and white, and it remained the country's most popular dance until supplanted by another supposed Dixie dance a good three years later. But to mention that one now would get ahead of the story, since other Alley attempts at Dixie dance-tunes trying to best "Charleston" came along in the meantime. For the musical *Big Boy,* B. G. De Sylva wrote the words and Joseph Meyer and James F. Hanley the music of "The Dance From Down Yonder" (Harms, 1925). The premise is that since "Ev'rything that's wonderful comes from my Southland," and since the South is "the home of many a brand new dance," then "That syncopated swaying back and forth / Has got most ev'rybody way up North / Doing the dance from Down Yonder / Chasing away the blues." The tune wasn't a success as a song *or* dance. "Go South" with Owen Murphy's words and Richard Myers's music (Harms, 1925) advised folks who used to go to San Francisco to learn new dances, to "Go South, young men, go South, old men, / That's where they dance it today; . . . Don't tell me those Western dances are new, / Hush up your mouth— / Don't talk, go South, — South where a dance is a dance." A third 1925 piece doesn't challenge "Charleston." "That South Car'lina Jazz Dance," with words and music by Noble Sissle and Eubie Blake (Jerome H. Remick, 1925), encourages folks to Charleston "To chase those blues away": "do that South Car'lina jazz dance. . . . It's called the Charleston—some fun / Ev'ryone's learning how / To do the cut out it's a wow."

In 1926 one song bragged it had taken over from "Charleston" in popularity, whereas in fact about two months earlier another piece had quietly begun to accomplish that feat without overtly making such a claim. The braggart was "Alabama Stomp" (Robbins-Engel, 1926), which had music by the same composer as "Charleston" itself, Jimmy Johnson, and lyrics by Henry Creamer. The song premiered on Broadway on August 24, 1926, in the Fifth Edition of *Earl Carroll's Vanities,* and the opening words bemoaned in mock sympathy, "Good-bye, Charleston, gee I hate to see you die / But you've had your day / So be on your way / For the newest dance from Dixie has reached Broadway." The dance may have been in Carroll's splashy revue, but it never took off. The only clever thing about the tune is one phrase in the chorus: "'Cause your Mammy and Pappy / Don't give a yam." Nor did the dancing public. Meanwhile, a little over two months earlier, without fanfare, braggadocio, or mock sympathy for the death of "Charleston," another pseudo-Dixie dance-song debuted in another big Broadway revue, the Eighth Edition of *George White's Scandals,* on June 14, 1926. With words by B. G. De Sylva and Lew Brown and music by Ray Henderson, "Black Bottom" (Harms, 1926) and the dance that went with it (a kind of supercharged "Charleston") quickly took the country by storm and *did* surpass "Charleston" as the #1 dance craze demographically, regionally, and even nationally. The verse explains that the dance was supposedly conceived by darkies living by the Swanee, imitating the shaking of the muddy river bottom. But few cared about that, and they wanted to get to the familiar chorus for dancing: "Black Bottom / A new twister; / It's sure got 'em, / And oh, Sister: they clap their hands and do a raggedy trot, / Hot! / Old fellows with lumbago / And high yellows, / Away they go: / They jump right in and give it all that they've got!"—all set to Ray Henderson's jazzy tune. Howard Lanin and His Orchestra's 1926 Victor disc with Frank Harris's vocal is one of the only records that was not just instrumental, and it's on the Internet.

Not long after the success of "Black Bottom," Harry Barris wrote the words and music of "Mississippi Mud" (Shapiro, Bernstein, 1927), apparently thinking there was money to be made off dances based on the oozy goo of river bottoms. He was right. Though never quite the smash-hit song or dance that "Black Bottom" became, it had great success as each, largely due to several renditions, recorded in 1927 and 1928, by Paul Whiteman's Orchestra with vocals by The Rhythm Boys, of which Barris himself was one, along with Bing Crosby. The song began with the familiar lines, "When the sun goes down, the tide goes out / The darkies gather 'round and they all begin to shout / 'Hey! Hey! Uncle Dud / It's a treat to beat your feet on the

Mississippi Mud." One of Whiteman's recordings combined the talents of the Rhythm Boys with those of Irene Taylor and was cut for Victor on February 18, 1928, as may be heard on the Internet. Also in 1927, Harms published two inconsequential dance tunes, which are mere curiosities. "Palm Beach Walk" and "Savannah Stomp" had music by Walter G. Samuels and inane lyrics by Morrie Ryskind, better known as a playwright than a lyricist for his work with George S. Kaufman on *Of Thee I Sing* and his scripts of Marx Brothers comedies. Ryskind and Samuels's two "southern" songs were just frames for intricate dance steps that prominent choreographer Ned Wayburn created for them, the instructions printed in the sheet music.

In 1929 Irving Berlin created the lyrics and music for a fictional Dixie dance called "Swanee Shuffle" (Irving Berlin, Inc., 1929), written to be sung and danced by the then-unknown sixteen-year-old Nina Mae McKinney in the all-black MGM film *Hallelujah!* directed by King Vidor. The dance is supposed to imitate the walk of flat-footed darky waiters in Dixie and is replete with lines like "Against the beat, you make your feet / Swanee Shuffle along— / If they're flat just make em flatter like a pancake on a platter" and "Come with me where Dixie marches, marches on its fallen arches." It's questionable whether Berlin intended the tune to become a recreational public dance craze. Personally, I doubt it.

The last Dixie dancing number (other than that dreadful "Rhumba" thing mentioned at the top of this section) wasn't about a new dance, but was a tribute to a very real dance hall in Birmingham, Alabama—"Tuxedo Junction" (Lewis Music, 1940), with words by Buddy Feyne and music by Erskine Hawkins, William Johnson, and Julian Dash. Feyne's simple lyric declares that when "Feelin' low!" then "Where people go to dance the night away" is the eponymous dance hall. Indeed, there "In their tux they greet you," so clearly Tuxedo Junction was some classy place and not your average roadhouse. The Andrews Sisters recorded the version with Feyne's lyrics in 1940, and it is on the Internet. That same year, Glenn Miller and his Orchestra immortalized the tune in all its instrumental glory on Bluebird, also on the Internet.

5

DIXIE IS FOR LOVERS

Pardon me, Virginia, for tinkering with your official travel and tourism slogan to head this chapter, but long before you coined it, over the course of sixty years Tin Pan Alley songwriters viewed not just the Commonwealth of Virginia, but the whole of Dixie from Miami to Little Rock as a romantic land for lovers. They wrote a whopping lot of love songs (80) and even more about Dixie romance or romantic Dixie (108). This only makes sense since love and romance have been songsmiths' most popular topics since time immemorial, so why should Alley writers of Dixie tunes have been an exception? Yet the quantity of these songs poses a problem (as it will again later with even greater quantities of songs about homesickness, going home, and idealizing Dixie): With so many songs, do I write excessively long chapters or confine myself to being *very* selective in the number I discuss in each one? For the sake of economy in the book's length, I was compelled to make the latter choice, only hoping not to omit too many significant Dixie tunes by doing so. In this chapter the problem takes care of itself since only comparative handfuls of Dixie love songs and songs about romantic Dixie are either significant—or were popular—enough to warrant discussion or even a brief mention. What I classify as Dixie love songs—those in the chapter's first part—are songs sung by a singer in Dixie directly to the object of his or her love, usually in that person's presence, but sometimes begging a lover to return to Dixie from somewhere else. Also here are those pieces, often labeled "torch songs," sung by either a man or a woman, about the end of a Dixie love affair, in which the singer bemoans how his or her lover "done her wrong." Unlike the direct address in Dixie love songs I discuss first in this chapter, narrative or descriptive writing is typical of songs of Dixie romance in the second part. Some of these view a romantic southern relationship over time, while others paint pictures of how romantic certain spots in Dixie are for lovers.

"Pardon My Southern Accent"

In that playful Dixie love song with Johnny Mercer's words and Matt Malneck's music (Irving Berlin, Inc., 1934), the singer tells the object of his affection, "It may sound funny, ah, but honey! I love y'all," and to reply to "'Do you love me' / All you gotta say is 'Sho 'nuff.'" Paul Whiteman and His Orchestra with Mercer and Peggy Healy on the vocal cut the tune for Victor in 1934, and it's on the Internet. Behind Mercer's fun is some truth since many Dixie love songs were written in a southern accent or dialect, or, more properly, in an Alleyman's idea of one, mostly, but not always, when a "darky troubadour" serenaded his "dusky lady love."

A few Dixie love songs showed promise, but mostly there was a numbing sameness about them that no doubt accounts for none becoming substantial hits in their own day, let alone standards down through the annals of Dixie tunes. The scenario repeated ad nauseam in dozens of these songs is of an eager or impatient southern boy wooing—to come out in the evening to "spoon" or, more seriously, to marry—an equally hesitant or downright recalcitrant young woman or girl. Tunes with this "plot" began as early as 1905 and didn't let up until the '20s with almost no variation in content or quality. One of the earliest, "My Southern Belle" (T. B. Harms, 1905), contained the clumsy lines "My Louisiana Anna / How I'd like to hold you in my arms in loving clasp; / I see your image / In the smoke of my Havana / And then you flit away / Just when your hand I grasp." The music was by Max C. Eugene and those banal words by Jerome Kern. We can be thankful Kern found he could write music, quit writing lyrics, and went on to become arguably the greatest all-time melodist of American popular, film, and theatre music.

I selected a small group of pieces to illustrate the sameness and mediocrity of this eager boy/hesitant girl type of Dixie love song, beginning with one of the better ones, "Hannah Won't You Smile A While On Me" (Theodore Morse Music, 1911), written by two fairly notable Alleymen—Jack Mahoney (lyrics) and Theodore Morse (music). The number is straightforward in the boy's pleading with the girl, although the sense of the lyric gets a bit muddled in the 1911 Columbia recording by the male-female duet of Walter Van Brunt and Elise Stevenson, but it at least helps one get the flavor of the tune, as may be heard on the Internet. Not only the same scenario but specific imagery repeats in two 1912 songs and a third from 1918—not enough to cry plagiarism, but to suggest this motif was so much in the air that lyricists grabbed pieces of it from places they may not have even been aware of. In "'Neath The Mississippi Moon" (Geo. W. Meyer, 1912), with Robert F. Roden's words and George W. Meyer's music, the verse's opening proclaims, "I can hear the Mississippi flowing, / As I'm standing by your cabin door." That same year, Otis L. Knight's "Tildy Lee" (Chicago: Will Rossiter, 1912) opens with "Outside your cabin door I'm waiting, waiting for you Tildy Lee." And in 1918 the black team of lyricist Henry Creamer and composer Turner Layton wrote "I'm Waiting For You Liza Jane" (Broadway Music, 1918), which begins with a "dusky troubadour . . . leaning up against the cabin door."

To return briefly to "Tildy Lee," Otis L. Knight's first-verse lyrics read like a textbook example of the eager boy/hesitant girl Dixie love song: "Outside your cabin door I'm waiting, waiting for you Tildy Lee, / Now don't you dare to keep me waiting, cause I'm anxious as can be / And wedding bells will soon be ringing folks are gath'ring 'round, / They're all so curious to see, your brand new gingham gown / So don't be hesitating when you know I'm out here waiting, / My pretty little Tildy Lee." Similarly, to return to "I'm Waiting For You Liza Jane," it's remarkable how Layton turned Creamer's plaintive words into a sprightly number, as may be heard on Vernon Dalhart's January 3, 1919, recording for Victor, which is on the Internet. Even Irving Berlin wrote an eager boy/hesitant girl love song, "Lindy" (Irving Berlin, Inc., 1920). The Harmonizers' 1920 Brunswick disc is on the Internet.

The eager boy/hesitant girl motif wasn't the only long-running cliché among Dixie love songs. There were others, some less palatable, some more so. One that became shopworn pretty fast was naming the singer's sweetheart for the region or state she lived in, including "Come Back, Dixie!" (Leo Feist, 1915), with Jack Mahoney's words and Percy Wenrich's music, in which a boy asks his girl Dixie to come back to Dixie; "Come Back Virginia" (Jos. W. Stern, 1911), with lyrics by Ballard MacDonald and music by Robert Engel, in which the singer begs Virginia, a girl, to return to Virginia, the state; and similarly with "Virginia Lee" (Joe Morris Music, 1915), with Jeff Branen's lyrics and Arthur Lange's music, and "Wait For Me Virginia" (Joe Morris Music, 1918), with Arthur J. Lamb's words and Alex Marr's tune. Other Dixie tunes sang of Georgia in Georgia and Caroline in Carolina. The best one can say is that the South is the only section of the country about which such pieces could have been written.

A lover's immutable adoration for his beloved has been a stock-in-trade of songwriting since songwriting began, perhaps best epitomized by the late 1930s and early '40s hit "Yours," with music by Gonzalo Roig and English lyrics by Jack Sherr. Dinah Shore recorded it in 1939 and Jimmy Dorsey's orchestra with vocal by Bob Eberly and Helen O'Connell in 1941, with its famous opening, "Yours till the stars have no glory!" Well, Dixie tunes singing of love's immutability didn't have such celestial images to compare a lover's feelings to, so they relied on more earthly things below the Mason-Dixon Line, two of them coming up with the same image for eternal love eight years apart: "Just As Long As The Swanee Flows" (Jerome H. Remick, 1911), with words by Alfred Bryan and music by Henriette H. Blanke-Belcher, and Jack Mahoney's "Till The Swanee River Runs Dry" (Geo. A. Friedman, 1919).

In a few Dixie love songs the singer not only lets his sweetheart know how much he loves her but idealizes her in the process. The singer in "Rose Of Virginia" (McCarthy and Fisher, Inc., 1920), with words and music by Jack Caddigan and Chick Story, is a bold young man. Upon first meeting a young woman he walks straight up and kisses her before expostulating on his feelings and telling her what an ideal creature she is, as one can hear on the Internet on the 1920 Columbia record by Henry Burr. For the *Ziegfeld Follies of 1931,* lyricist Mack Gordon and composer Harry Revel wrote "Your Sunny Southern Smile" (Miller Music, 1931), in which a man idealizes his sweetheart's smile by listing all it contains: "The breath of the springtime, the bloom of the rose; / The spell of the moonlight, the stars they disclose— / I see them all for they always repose / In your sunny southern smile," with more bits of the South in later stanzas.

A few Dixie love songs were lighthearted, frivolous, or downright humorous. In two of them, the frivolity or humor, respectively, of the words, may have been influenced by the typically lighthearted melodies that were a signature quality of the single tunesmith of both songs, the great popular composer and vaudevillian Gus Edwards. In 1902 Edwards teamed with lyricist Andrew B. Sterling to write "Louisiana Louise" (F. A. Mills, 1902), in which Sterling's words scarcely resemble the usual even-tempered romantic or weepy lyrics in his work with his more frequent composing partner Harry Von Tilzer. No, nothing even-tempered here at all. The boy's mere sighting of the girl he falls for brings, out of nowhere, exclamations that sound like he's having the happiest sort of manic attack: "I was seated in a garden where the roses bloom, oh! my, —oh! me, oh! my, / When I heard somebody humming a familiar tune—oh! my, —oh! me, oh! my, . . . But one glance at the singer drove away my pain— / I yelled oh! my, oh! me, oh! my." Later he calms down enough to sing the refrain to Louise fairly coherently. By 1912 lyricist Edward Madden and Gus Edwards were no strangers to one another. In 1909, together they had written the enormous hit and perpetual standard "By The Light Of The Silvery Moon," and, in the same year, in the field of frivolous (though not Dixie) love songs, "Up, Up, Up In My Aeroplane," first performed by Lillian Lorraine in a mockup plane flying above the audience's heads during the *Ziegfeld Follies of 1909*. In 1912 Madden and Edwards jointly wrote a semi-comic Dixie love song, "Levee Lou" (Jerome H. Remick, 1912). The piece begins like any eager boy/hesitant girl courting song, but at the top of the second verse, Madden's lyric takes a decidedly comic turn: "Where's your ma—where's your pa? / I got such a creepy kind of feeling— / If they see you with me / They'll be chasing me for chicken stealing." Simply lighthearted were Louis Herscher's words and music of "There Are Just Two I's In Dixie (Two Blue Eyes That Mean The World To Me)" (Philadelphia: Emmett J. Welch, 1919). The singer of this charming spelling bee to his sweetie shows he can spell the names of southern states, although he misplaces the Swanee River: "You'll find four S's in Mississippi, / Where the Swanee River flows. / There's a pair of G's in Georgia, / Where the sweet peach blossom grows. / While there are four A's in Alabama, / And four E's in Tennessee, / There are just two I's in Dixie, — / TWO BLUE EYES that mean the world to me." A cute, fun Dixie love song.

Nothing like cute or fun, let alone lighthearted, frivolous, or comic characterizes the final group of Dixie love songs worth looking at, yet it's one of the most important for their quantity, longevity, and success when measured against the other kinds of Dixie love songs, even though these pieces aren't even *cheerful*. These are the Dixie torch songs, sung after love or a lover has gone. Broadly speaking, torch songs know no geographical boundaries, so the only thing that defines the Dixie torch song is that the singer is singing somewhere below the Mason-Dixon Line, or, in one case, is planning to go there after a failed love affair up North. As for their longevity, Dixie torch songs ran from 1913 to 1958, or almost as long as the Alley was publishing Dixie tunes of any kind. Six of them will be examined here.

Gus Kahn wrote the words to the first Dixie torch song, "Moonlight On The Mississippi" (Jerome H. Remick, 1913), and his soon-to-be wife Grace

Le Boy composed the music. The singer, who could be male or female, bemoans a lover's departure in two verses and a refrain, as in the first verse: "Moonlight sets me dreaming, honey, / Bright stars softly gleaming, honey, / Start my poor heart beating for the dear dead days gone by. /When you were my only only, / Then you left me, oh, so lonely! / It's moonlight on the Mississippi, / That's the reason why / I sit alone, here tonight, / Sighing with all my might." A year later, these mournful words were followed by others just about as doleful from A. Seymour Brown, for the torch song "Way Down On Tampa Bay" (Jerome H. Remick, 1914), with music by Egbert Van Alstyne. The feelings of what again seems to be a unisex singer are almost identical to those in "Moonlight On The Mississippi"; only the setting shifts from the banks of that river to the shore of Tampa Bay: "Twilight is falling, I'm so lonesome and blue, / Twilight is calling back sweet mem'ries of you. / And as the night-breeze sighs in the palm trees / Somehow it seems to say: My heart is yearning for your returning, / Way down on Tampa Bay." Unusual for a Dixie tune, Van Alstyne wrote a tango, as heard on the Peerless Quartet's December 12, 1914, Victor record on the Internet.

It's not that the next two Dixie torch songs from 1923 don't have intrinsic merit as songs on their own, but their popularity was also greatly assisted by both being recorded that year by Bessie Smith, and a few other fine blues singers as well. Clarence Williams not only wrote the words and music of "Gulf Coast Blues" but also published it in 1923 through his Alley publishing firm of Clarence Williams Music Pub. Co. This is definitely a female torch song, sung by a woman up North whose "man's gone away . . . and if it keeps on snowing, I will be Gulf Coast bound," making the number ultimately a Dixie torch song. It is also a true blues song in the format of its music and lyrics, as can be heard on the Internet in Bessie Smith's 1923 Columbia record with Williams himself at the piano. That same year, Smith recorded "Beale Street Mamma" (Waterson, Berlin & Snyder, 1923), with words and music by Roy Turk and J. Russel Robinson. The spelling "Mamma" is only on the sheet music; it's "Mama" on all recordings. This is a torch song that seems designed for a male singer, as the first lines reveal: "Mamie Neal, / Down in Beale, Gave her papa the air. / Left him cold, / Got him told / That she didn't care." But in the hands (or voice) of Bessie, the number sounds tailor-made for a skilled female blues artist as heard on the Internet on her 1923 Columbia recording. Ten years after these two Dixie torch songs, another appeared whose popularity is indicated by the number of major big bands that recorded it, despite how truly grim the song's content is. "Louisville Lady" (Shapiro, Bernstein, 1933) has words by Billy Hill and music by Peter De Rose, and is the only torch song—Dixie or otherwise—that I'm aware of in which the singer takes the blame for the end of the affair. What's more, it appears that whatever he did to cause the breakup led to the lady's suicide by drowning in the Ohio River, which flows past Louisville. The verse isn't on any of the recordings, but it contains the line, "She left me for the River / That flows down to the sea." Yet quite explicitly in the chorus that *is* on many of the recordings are the words "Out of the River comes a melancholy wail, . . . Louisville Lady, moanin' as she drifts along, / I was her man, / Why did I do her wrong? / Oh! Louisville Lady, forgive me for being untrue / Now that you're gone, / How can I live without you?" Some of the lead recordings, all in 1933, were by Isham Jones's orchestra with Eddie Stone's vocal (Victor), Paul Ash's orchestra (Columbia), Dick Robertson's orchestra with Robertson himself on vocal (Crown Records), and the popular Anson Weeks and his orchestra with vocal by Carl Ravazza at the ballroom of San Francisco's Mark Hopkins Hotel. The last of these may be heard on their 1933 Brunswick record on the Internet. Last, the multi-Oscar Best Song Award team of lyricist Paul Francis Webster and composer Sammy Fain wrote "Bourbon Street Blues" (Leo Feist, 1958) for the 20th Century-Fox Picture *Mardi Gras.* This Dixie torch song sung by a man won absolutely nothing, and deservedly so, as shown by just the horribly stretched metaphor of the first line: "I could float an ocean liner on the tears I've shed for you—oo—oo—oo!" 'Nuff said.

"Oh You South"

Irving Caesar, whose lyrics in 1919 expostulated to George Gershwin's tune, "How I love you, my dear old Swanee," hyped all of Dixie in 1927 with a song of that title to Maurice Abrahams's music (Jerome H. Remick, 1927). The singer has fallen so in love with the South that "From now on I will go there twice a year / Spend six months ev'ry time." Caesar's words sum up many songs about Dixie romance—that the South is the most romantic part of the United States not just for vacations, but to live in. Other pieces are about love affairs being *in* Dixie or about how their being there helps foster happy outcomes of relationships, as if the South interacted positively on the hearts of people in love.

Unlike Dixie love songs that mostly divide into the two large groups of those with the eager boy/reluctant girl scenario and torch songs, songs of Dixie romances have only one dominant category of pieces, with the motif of a boy going away for a considerable time but returning to marry his faithful sweetheart. There are also a few small groups of minor types, plus one large bunch of songs worth mentioning for their oddity. I begin with the thirteen songs based in the wandering boy motif, twelve between 1899 and 1914, and the thirteenth belatedly in 1931. In 1899 the vaudeville team of Howard & Emerson (Joseph E. and Ida, respectively) wrote and performed the ragtime classic "Hello! Ma Honey," and that same year penned the words and music of the earliest Dixie wandering boy song, "My Pretty Southern Girl" (T. B. Harms, 1899). In it, a poor boy and girl promise eternal love to one another "'Neath an old pine tree down in Tennessee," though he tells her he must go away for a number of years for reasons unspecified. When he returns in the second verse it's to marry his girl, with whom he exchanged that vow years before. That's the motif in its straightforward form, which five other songs follow exactly: "I Lost My Heart Way Down In Alabama" (Jos. W. Stern, 1905), with Rene Bronner's words and H. W. Petrie's music; Don Valentine Harwood's "In Tennessee, The Land Where I Was Born" (The Modern Music Pub. Co., 1905); Robert Levenson's "I Want To Be In Georgia When The Roses Bloom Again" (Boston: Garton Bros., 1905); "Lady Love" (Jerome H. Remick, 1909), with William M. McKenna's words and Albert Gumble's music; and Halsey K. Mohr's "In That Blue Ridge Vale of Love" (F. B. Haviland, 1914).

The seven remaining songs ring various changes on the fundamental motif, the earliest two looking like mirror images. In Charles K. Harris's "My Virginia" (Chicago: Chas. K. Harris, 1907), people try to persuade a Dixie girl that her lover, who has gone up North, is unfaithful and won't return. Yet in the end he writes her, "I am coming home to wed you, let all the folks know, / Don't you listen to the tales they tell you, don't you weep or sigh / For I love you, my Virginia, love you till I die." In "You'll Not Be Forgotten, Lady Lou" (Jos. W. Stern, 1907), with Alfred Bryan's words and George W. Meyer's music, it's the girl who travels to the North, leaving her "Southern lad" "by the Swanee river." Up North, "Another sought her hand, /As at her feet his love he told," but she spurns him and returns to the South to marry her faithful Dixie boy. This song wasn't the only one with the girl going away. It happened also in "Dinah (From Carolina)" (York Music, 1909), with Junie McCree's words and Albert Von Tilzer's music, but the boy and girl's separation poses no threat to their love since she's just leaving wherever they are in Dixie to visit her folks in Carolina. The boy is so sure of their love that he writes to Dinah, "When you're leaving Carolina, / Come back to me I mean, with your mama on the chu-chu car, / There'll be a parson waiting, / Gee: but it's nice in a shower of rice with you, Dinah Green."

The year 1913 was a big one for variants on the wandering boy motif, and major Alleymen wrote two of the three songs. Each variant on the motif makes for a different tone or mood in the number in which it occurs. With Jack Yellen's words and George L. Cobb's music, "Bring Me Back My Lovin' Honey Boy" (Chicago: Will Rossiter, 1913) could hardly escape being a lively ragtime number, and that's exactly what it is, even though the whole lyric consists of instructions from a young lady on a levee somewhere to the captain of the steamboat *Henry Clay* to bring back her "honey boy"—seemingly a crew member, though it's not specified—safe and sound to her after the boat's impending voyage up or down the Mississippi. The overall feeling of the song is "cute," a rare quality among wandering boy tunes. Also out of a Chicago publisher but by lesser-known songsmiths came "Along The Lane That Leads To Lexington" (Chicago: Harold Rossiter, 1913), with words by Will J. Harris and music by Hampton Durand. In this variant of the motif, the singer meets "darling Sue" in Lexington, Kentucky, and they fall in love, but he's just passing through and must continue on his way. Yet not being able to get her out of his mind (or heart), he turns back along the lane that leads to Lexington, hoping to find Sue again and propose to her. The number is a cliffhanger, never stating whether the singer finds Sue again, or, if he does, whether she accepts his proposal or not. By far the wandering boy hit of 1913 was "The Trail Of The Lonesome Pine" (Shapiro Music, 1913), with Ballard MacDonald's words and Harry Carroll's music, the piece suggested by John Fox Jr.'s best-selling 1908 novel of the same name. MacDonald's lyric varies the motif insofar as it is severely truncated, the singer singing when he is almost home after an absence of unspecified duration. The song met with considerable success both as sheet music and as a recording, as can be heard on the Internet from Manuel Romain's 1913 Edison Blue Amberol cylinder. "Lonesome Pine" was given a second life decades later when it became something of a signature tune for radio and TV personality Arthur Godfrey.

The 1931 latecomer was Jeannette Conrad's "When The Leaves Are Turning Brown In Carolina" (Harms, 1931). Among songs that spun off of the wandering boy motif, this one was odd since the couple sets a timetable for their period of separation, with the man leaving Carolina one autumn but promising to return in the fall of the following year, and both the man and woman vowing fidelity to one another during the intervening months.

The remaining Alley tunes about either romance in Dixie or romantic Dixie fall into five rather loose categories, some with as few as two songs in them, others with considerably more. Viewing them by these groupings helps bring some order to this fairly large, unwieldy body of songs written over a long period of time. One group contains songs whose premise is either that Dixie is the only place for true romantic love or that it's possible to fall in love (or lose it) anywhere in Dixie—songs that vary greatly from one another. One of the earliest is the already mentioned "My Lady of Kentucky" (Jerome H. Remick, 1905) by lyricist William Jerome and composer Jean Schwartz. The song is masterfully simple, as can be seen in part of Jerome's lyric for the first stanza: "My sweet lady of Kentucky I love you / Other boys are not so lucky that's quite true / Happy only when you're near me your blue eyes they always cheer me / My sweet lady of Kentucky, old Kentucky I love you." The mere fact that Jerome opted to set his lyric in Kentucky rather than, say, Rhode Island (which, for songwriting, has the same number of syllables accented identically) suggests the writer, born and raised in Cornwall-on-Hudson, New York, felt in touch with the romantic aura of the southern state he chose, which is absent from Little Rhody. The year prior to Jerome and Schwartz's minor masterpiece, lyricist Edgar Smith and composer Maurice Levi wrote for Weber and Ziegfeld's *Higgledy-Piggledy* a piece titled "For You, Honey" (Chas. K. Harris, 1904), in which a boy makes a more inflated claim to a girl that while *words* of love are spoken the world over, she will never fully understand its *meaning* except in the South: "But you'll never know its melody, / Or the meaning true will understand, / Till I've sung to you, beneath the bayou tree, / In my fair Dixie land." (According to my research, a bayou tree is any tree, but usually a cypress, that grows right up out of the water in the bayous of Louisiana and other Gulf Coast states, so the boy must have been soaking wet up to his waist as he serenaded his lady about true love in Dixie.)

The singer in Irving Berlin's "I Lost My Heart In Dixieland" (Irving Berlin, Inc., 1919), "while trav'ling below the Mason Dixon line," falls in love with both "a Tennessee Kid" (female) and the South itself, and so returns to marry the former and settle down in the latter, captivated by the romance of Dixie and one of its delightful denizens. A 1933 song said there was romantic love to be found all over Dixie, and it must be labeled country or hillbilly music. But since it would be more than a decade before Nashville became the hub for publishers of such tunes, the Alley was home to country music publisher Peer International, which published "Peach Picking Time Down In Georgia," with words and music by country singer/songwriter Jimmie Rodgers and country fiddler Clayton McMichen. The lyrics of the first verse are those of a "list song" in which the singer declares, "When it's PEACH PICKIN' TIME IN GEORGIA, / Apple pickin' time in Tennessee, / Cotton pickin' time in Mississippi, / Everybody picks on me; When it's round-up time in Texas, / The cowboys make "whoopee," / And 'way down in old Alabamy, / It's gal pickin' time for me." In his last recording session before his early death, Rodgers cut a successful record of the song for Victor in 1932, which is on the Internet.

One song never had such success but is a charming piece saying not just that love can be found in any corner of Dixie, but that love found there can last a lifetime. "As We Sat On A Rock In Little Rock, Arkansaw" (Harry Tobias, 1916), with words and music by Harry Tobias and William J. Hart, is a reminiscence in which a husband of some years sings to his wife about shared childhood and teenage memories, activities, and scenes as once again they sit on the same rock in Little Rock where they fell in love and he proposed to her years ago. Three other songs, two that became enormous hits, one fairly obscure, proclaimed one could find (or lose) love just about anywhere in Dixie, and the two hits shared parentage between the Alley and Nashville. The purely Alley number was a cute tune with Edgar Leslie's words and Joe Burke's music, which could be sung with equal sense by someone of either sex, titled "At A Dixie Roadside Diner" (Miller Music, 1940). In the verse we find the singer did *not* meet his or her love "by the Alamo," or in Borneo, or any "place of mystery with a bamboo tree." No, it was "At a Dixie Roadside Diner down in Caroline" where the singer and the object of his or her love meet each night to dance to the jukebox, which makes the singer happy "In the heart of Caroline." The chorus is sung on Charlie Barnet and His Orchestra's record, with a vocal by Harriet Clark, cut for Bluebird records in 1940, as may be heard on the Internet.

It's not made specific where the action takes place in "Bonaparte's Retreat" (Nashville: Acuff-Rose Publications, 1949). With words and music by country singer/songwriter Peewee King (born Julius Frank Anthony Kuczynski in Milwaukee), the lyric only states, "Met the girl I love / In a town way down in Dixie." While it may have been written by a country singer and published by a Nashville publisher, the song's success, which only began a year after its sheet music publication, strictly resulted from mainstream Alley-allied performers recording it on mainstream labels. The biggest seller of "Bonaparte's Retreat" (the title referring to the tune the couple was dancing to as they fell in love) was Kay Starr's 1950 Capitol recording, which is on the Internet. The cut on RCA Victor by Gene Krupa and his Orchestra followed closely, Krupa seemingly on the vocal, with both artists about as far from country as possible. The same is true for Patti Page's recording of Redd Stewart and Peewee King's "Tennessee Waltz" (Nashville: Acuff-Rose Publications, 1948). The tune attracted little notice in country circles for nearly two years after its publication and RCA Victor's record by King with Redd Stewart on vocal in 1948. Then Patti Page cut it on Mercury in 1950, and the song took off with mainstream listeners, topping the charts for thirteen weeks and selling three million copies. The lyric doesn't state where in Dixie the singer's friend steals her lover, and Tennessee is pretty tangential except as the waltz the singer is dancing to when the "friend" swipes her sweetie, as heard on the Internet.

In two songs written over forty years apart, displaced southerners either discover or rediscover one another up North and return to Dixie together, much happier than before. In "Take Me Back To My Louisiana Home" (Shapiro, Remick, 1904) with words by prolific Alleyman Will D. Cobb and music by Gus Edwards, a southern boy "far from home and friendless" in an unnamed northern city hears through an open window a girl's voice singing "Dixie" and discovers that she is his own "Dixie sweetheart" Jessie, "For there's no girl north of Mobile, / Can sing like Jessie can." The two are reunited, return south, and "today's our wedding day." We must stretch our parameters of Dixie to accept the boy's home in "A Boy From Texas—A Girl From Tennessee" (Shapiro, Bernstein, 1948), with words and music by Joe McCarthy Jr., Jack Segal, and John Benson Brooks. The lyric is about two lonely strangers in New York: "The boy said 'Howdy' / The girl said 'Hi you-all' / He could have kissed her when he heard that Southern drawl. / They walked up Broadway / As though they owned the town / . . . The home folks smile to see / The boy from Texas with his bride from Tennessee." Nat "King"

Cole and his trio had the leading disc of the song for Capitol in 1948, which is on the Internet.

Two songs can only be labeled what the popular music trade called them—novelty tunes. One, to be looked at second, is a comedy song; the other's title makes it sound as if it should be, but in fact it's deadly serious. With words by L. Wolfe Gilbert and music by Lewis F. Muir, in "Buy A Bale Of Cotton For Me" (F. A. Mills, 1914) a socially and economically conscious young woman is distressed by the condition of the South while visiting there with her fiancé and asks him *not* to buy her "diamond rings, other fancy things, . . . I hate to lose those presents, so, but please hear my plea, / I must murmur nixie, just to save old Dixie, / Buy a bale of cotton for me." He's a bit slow to grasp what her request is all about, saying, "Ev'ryone buys cotton bales," but in the end comes to understand her wanting to bring economic aid to Dixie, saying, "Sweetheart the bargain is sealed, / I'll buy a whole cotton field." Going from this song's nobility of thought and deed to the silliness of the next is truly a case of moving from the sublime to the ridiculous, but this was a master's ridiculousness. The great Scottish songwriter and performer Harry Lauder (Sir Henry after he was made a knight of the British Empire in 1919) wrote the words of "Trixie From Dixie (A Scotch American Romance)" (T. B. Harms & Francis, Day & Hunter, 1913); Lauder's son, John, who was killed in action in France in 1916, wrote the music. The lyric tells of a Scotsman visiting the States and falling for a Dixie girl and she for him, to the jealous fury of the local Dixie boys in the second verse. The first verse only is on the Internet just as Harry Lauder sang it on a January 18, 1913, Victor record.

In the aggregate, all Alley lyricists who wrote Dixie tunes—and especially those about the South as the land of romance—would have made dreadful astronomers and rotten meteorologists to boot. This isn't immediately apparent when reading the words to only one song like, for example, "Moon Over Miami" (Irving Berlin, Inc., 1935), Edgar Leslie's 1935 hit with music by Joe Burke. But when there are lyrics about the silvery lunar orb—invariably full or nearly so, considering its brightness in all the songs—shining down from a cloudless sky on lovers strolling, canoeing, or sitting and spooning in a bare *minimum* of thirty songs about romance in Dixie, and in more Dixie tunes in other categories, it makes it seem as if the moon is working overtime, shining 365 nights a year to cast its light on so many romantic couples out for the evening in the South. The continual lunar activity and coincidental cloudless nights become simultaneously an astronomical absurdity and a songwriting cliché. Some tunes using this moonlight conceit sneak it in regardless of the song's title, but a good many give the listener or reader fair warning it will be coming. The nineteen moon-titled tunes just from the Dixie romance class of songs with only their publication dates are: "Dixie Moon" (1908), "Moon-time" (1909), "Underneath The Mississippi Moon" (1910), "Dixie Moon" (1911), "Tennessee Moon" (1912), "Under The Swanee Moon" (1913), "Under The Cotton Moon" (1913), "Georgia Moon" (1914), "Alabama Moon" (1917), "Southern Moon" (1918), "Dixie Moon" (1919), "Moonlight Down In Dixie" (1919), "Florida Moon" (1920), "Lazy Lou'siana Moon" (1930), "Blue Kentucky Moon" (1931), "Roll Along Kentucky Moon" (1932), "With My Sweetie In The Moonlight Under Dreamy Southern Skies" (1932), "Moon Over Miami" (1935), and "Miami, The Moonlight And You" (1939). Aside from "Moon Over Miami," about which I will say a bit when I return to it in the group of songs to which it belongs—those about romantic places in Dixie—only one "moon" song is of any real interest because it's a twist on the usual boy wanting the moon to shine to help sustain a romantic atmosphere. In "Tennessee Moon" (Wenrich-Howard, 1912), with Jack Mahoney's words and Percy Wenrich's music, the boy asks the moon to take a hike so he and his girl can have some dark and privacy: "Mister Moon I've introduced you to my turtle dove, / Now why don't you move along while we are making love, / Don't you linger longer, / Two is company, / My love's growing stronger / Leave my gal and me, / Shine on Dixie but please stay away from Tennessee / . . . I want to spoon, Hide behind a cloud while I am humming love's sweet tune." The Heidelberg Quintette featuring Billy Murray recorded this tune for Victor on July 26, 1912, and it's on the Internet.

Till now, the core of pieces about romance in Dixie was the romantic couples in the South. But the final group's focus is not on people in love but the settings themselves, or what I call the Dixiescapes that make Dixie so romantic. Six such songs are worth remarking upon; three became hits in their own day and two of those all-time standards. Of the songs that didn't achieve such status, "Sunny South" (Harms, 1922) by Louis A. Hirsch, Gene Buck, and Dave Stamper for the *Ziegfeld Follies of 1922* paints a conventional picture of the "Paradise in Florida" but doesn't come close to the detail of Edgar Leslie and Joe Burke's "Moon Over Miami" with its lines like "Hark to the song of the smiling troubadours, / Hark to the throbbing guitars. / Hear how the waves offer thunderous applause, / After each song to the stars." Connie (a.k.a. Connee) Boswell's 1935 hit record on Decca is on the Internet.

Two songs in the early 1930s sketched very different—and very lovely—Dixiescapes but never won much recognition. "(When It's) Darkness On The Delta" (Santly Bros., 1932), with words by Marty Symes and Al J. Neiburg and music by Jerry Levinson, details the romantic Dixiescape in the song's title: "When it's Darkness on the Delta, / Let me linger in the shelter of the night. / Fields of Cotton all around me, / Darkies singin' sweet and low, / Lord I'm lucky that you found me, / Where the muddy Mississippi waters flow. / Lounging on the Levee, / List'nin' to the Nightingales 'way up above, / Laughter on the Levee, / No one's heart is heavy, / All God's children got someone to love." Isham Jones and His Orchestra with Eddie Stone's vocal of the chorus cut a Victor recording of the piece on December 16, 1932, and it's on the Internet. With Arthur Swanstrom's words and J. Fred Coots's tune, "My Carolina Hide-A-Way" (Harms, 1934) sings of a man showing his fiancée where they will honeymoon and make a home: "The road may wind, / The house is hard to find, / But once you're there the world is left behind / And right before your eyes / You'll see a paradise, / My Carolina hide-a-way."

In 1922 Henry Creamer wrote the words and Turner Layton the music for a Dixiescape song that wasn't just a hit in its own day but has become a perennial standard (especially with Dixieland bands)—the classic number describing and idealizing the Big Easy, "'Way Down Yonder In New Orleans" (Shapiro, Bernstein, 1922). The hit record the year the piece was published was the instrumental by Paul Whiteman and his Orchestra on Victor, but for the tune with its lyrics, one needs to hear on the Internet the recording made in 1927 on Columbia by the song's composer Turner Layton and his performing partner Clarence (Tandy) Johnstone.

Perhaps because it's believed he was born in Shreveport, Louisiana, an Alley myth has been around for years that lyricist Mitchell Parish was a born and bred southerner. Nothing could be further from the truth. Michael Hyman Pashelinsky was born to his Jewish parents in Lithuania (then a part of the Russian Empire) on July 10, 1900, and arrived with them at Shreveport, where his paternal grandmother had relatives, on February 3, 1901, when he was not yet seven months old. He moved with his family to the Lower East Side of New York City, most likely before he was four, which hardly qualifies him as a southerner. The young immigrant went through the New York public schools and then received a B.A. from New York University, after which he lived in Manhattan for all ninety-two years of his productive and creative life. "He planned to study medicine but changed careers after a doctor gave some of his verses to a music publisher" (*New York Times* obituary, April 2, 1993). After that, as they say, the rest is history, with Parish writing the words to such standards as "Stardust," "Deep Purple," and "Sleighride." Though decidedly a New Yorker, Parish had an affinity for Dixie tunes, his first hit having been "Carolina Rolling Stone" in 1921. In the mid-'30s Parish and another non-southerner, composer Frank Perkins from Salem, Massachusetts, collaborated on a cluster of five Dixie tunes, each one different from the others. In the chapter on southern social types we already saw their wryly comic "Sentimental Gentleman From Georgia"— a far cry from the song under present consideration, which transcends such frivolity and whimsy, and in its transcendence has become a lasting classic and standard of the American popular music and jazz repertoire. The song is, of course, "Stars Fell On Alabama" (Mills, 1934), in which Parish's elegantly brief, descriptive Dixiescape of a romantic night in Alabama is fully in sync with Perkins's equally simple yet evocative melody, as can be heard on the Internet in Jack Teagarden's 1934 Capitol recording. In a word, the whole sounds as if it came from one mind and one voice, making—for me, at least—"Stars Fell On Alabama" arguably the single most gorgeous song about idyllic, romantic Dixie ever created.

6

UNDERCUTTING THE IDYLLIC
Realism, Satire, and Parody

Most Alley Dixie tunes in the earlier chapters either idealized the South and its people or created idyllic pictures of the South, reaching their zenith with "Stars Fell On Alabama." So too, idealizing Dixie is the core of the huge body of songs in the following chapters since these are the pieces about homesickness, going home, and mammy, and after that those on Dixie pride, Dixie myths, and the direct glorification or romanticization of the South. This chapter, on the other hand, looks at a small group of songs that cut through those proclivities to idealize Dixie, instead offering realistic views of it, or, in a few cases, satiric looks at the way the South really is. These fewer than twenty realistic or satiric tunes are a not-so-still-small voice sounding a wake-up call about what lay beneath idyllic imaginings of Dixie. The songs fall into two natural groups, those about Dixie's land and those about its people.

Wind and Water

For most of his career, Kansas-born Carson J. Robison was a country singer/songwriter of both words and music, who "may have had only a grade school education," yet by the 1920s he had earned a well-deserved reputation as a "master at writing topical songs about natural disasters and news events" (Birchfield 682), many of which ended with a moral lesson. During World War II, Robison shifted the content and manner of his songs to write a series of sophisticated, scathingly satiric, and wildly funny "Axis-Bashing" pieces about Hitler, Tojo, and Mussolini (see Jones 137–40). Two of Robison's '20s natural disaster songs were Dixie tunes. He wrote and published the first, "The Miami Storm" (Triangle Music, 1926), in the wake of the death and destruction left behind by what became known as The Great Miami Storm of September 18, 1926, a category 4 hurricane that virtually decimated the fledgling city and, by all accounts, put an end for a time to the Florida land boom that till then had been rushing forward headlong for years. Robison's hurricane song, like many of his, is a narrative ballad, starting with a stanza on Miami's beauty and the happiness of its residents before the storm, then getting darker with the impending hurricane, and concluding with the storm's aftermath and the small lesson to be learned: "And then when the gray dawn came stealing, / The toll of the storm was known; / And sad were the cries of the injured, / The streets with dead were strewn; / We cannot explain this disaster, / We know not what fate may befall; / And we should be ready each hour, / To answer the master's call." Vernon Dalhart cut the song in 1926 on an Edison Blue Amberol cylinder, which is on the Internet.

Less than six months after the Great Miami Storm, the most destructive flood the United States had known, the Great Mississippi Flood of 1927, began slowly as torrential rains swelled the banks of the river and its tributaries in the late winter of 1926 and early spring of 1927, climaxing on Good Friday, April 15, 1927, when the river broke out of its levee system in 145 places from Cairo, Illinois to New Orleans, the rank waters lingering until June. The flood caused $400 million (in 1927 dollars) in damages, killed about 246 people in seven states, and left another 600,000 homeless. It moved four Alley publishers to release songs about it, one by Carson J. Robison again, two by seemingly less-known writers, and one by two major songwriters whom we have encountered before.

Robison's "The Mississippi Flood" (Jack Mills, 1927) is, like his "The Miami Storm," a narrative ballad, but this time in five stanzas and spending less time with happy precatastrophe days than the prior song. Yet as in the earlier tune, Robison ends with some quasi-religious musings on the meaning of it all: "We can't explain the reason these great disasters come, / But we should all remember to say 'Thy will be done'; / And tho the good may suffer for other people's sins, / There is a crown awaiting where eternal life begins." Using Al Craver, one of his pseudonyms, Vernon Dalhart cut the piece, which is also on the Internet, for Columbia in 1927. Robison's ballad with its stoically religious ending is doleful enough, yet even more mournful—largely since it's sung in the first person by a man from whom the flood has taken all his friends, his home, his parents, and his sweetheart in successive stanzas of another ballad-like song—is "The Mississippi Flood Song (On The Old Mississippi Shore)" (Ager, Yellen & Bornstein, 1927), with Jed Hopkins's words and Sarah A. Westcott's music. The only respite from the incrementally more and more depressing stanzas comes during the final one when "All is quiet and peaceful tonight / While the world sheds a tear for the victims / Of the wrath of the great river's might / Thankful hearts breathe a pray'r for the heroes / Of the Red Cross so true and so brave / And the women and children they rescued / From the fate of a watery grave." This song may mention the work of the Red Cross, but only the final two flood songs are proactive in soliciting contributions to the relief agency. "Hoover's Mississippi Flood Song" (Shapiro, Bernstein, 1927), with words and music by Joe Hoover (which may have been a pseudonym for Alleyman J. Russel Robinson, something hard to confirm or deny), is another song in ballad format, but one mostly focusing on the destruction the flood left behind: "There were gray headed couples, / Who'd spent their lifetime in toil, / Bringing up good fam'lies, / Down there on Dixie's soil, / Their savings and work taken from them, / Homes ruin'd with water and mud, / So let us pray for the victims of / The cruel Mississippi flood." But prayer isn't enough in this ballad: "Countless poor little children, / Whose Mothers and Dads were drowned, / Are living without shelter, For beds, the cold, wet ground, / Good people, the Red Cross needs money, / Give like 'twas your flesh and blood, And help to relieve those suff'rers of / That cruel Mississippi flood." In a song published by his own publishing firm, The House of William Jerome, in 1927, that Alley lyricist with his frequent composing partner Jean Schwartz wrote "You'll Never Miss What You Give Mississippi." The most extraordinary thing about the piece is nothing in Jerome's lyric, but what's in a notice on the cover of the sheet music: "Jerome and Schwartz are donating their entire Song and Mechanical Royalties to the Red Cross Fund." Of all the Mississippi flood songs, Jerome and Schwartz's is the only one not in the form of a folk ballad. It's a typical Alley song with two verses and a refrain, the gist of all of them being that the affluent North should help the South in its time of terrible need. Jerome's refrain sums it all up: "Oh, you'll never miss what you give Mississippi, / 'Twill help to sunny up the sunny south, / No greater pedigree than hospitality / Let's nourish up each hungry Dixie mouth, / Let's show we are still their loving brothers, / Let's prove to all the world it's in our blood, / You'll never miss what you give Mississippi, / Let's dry her tears and still the cruel flood." Such songs never became popular or were even long remembered after what had occasioned their writing, but they stand as grim reminders that the South, the imagined

Dixie of moonlight and magnolias, is as fragile as anyplace else against the forces of nature, as later southern generations learned battling disasters like Hurricane Katrina in 2005 and the Mississippi Flood of 2010.

Authentic Southerners, White and Black

The chapter on southern social types shows how the Alley's Dixie tunes portrayed hillbillies and happy darkies more like cartoon characters than any real folk who ever walked the earth below the Mason-Dixon Line. Not so for a handful of songs portraying realistic poor whites and southern blacks with clarity and specificity. Though few in number, some of these songs had considerable success.

One of them was written to be sung as if by a southern poor white male and a second by a poor white or black of either gender, though the drawing on the original sheet music cover shows an elderly black man standing outside his cabin. (But sheet music art is notoriously misleading about what's behind it.) The song realistically depicting the life of a poor white was "Along Tobacco Road" (Edward B. Marks, 1935), with Tina Glenn's words and Jesse Greer's music. It was inspired by Jack Kirkland's long-running Broadway hit *Tobacco Road,* based on Erskine Caldwell's novel. The original sheet music cover featured a photo of James Barton as Jeeter Lester, who in 1934 succeeded Henry Hull as the dirt-scratching, foul-mouthed, Georgia tobacco sharecropper. "Along Tobacco Road" is a homesickness song that begins, "Homesick, Lonely, Tired of all that I see," but the home the singer longs for is a far cry from the idyllic spots in the next chapter's songs. It's a place where "life means plantin', where life means slavin', / Where life gives what you've sowed. / . . . / Tho' you're hungry and worn, clothing shabby and torn, / You smile but never complain. / So you plough and you plough, . . . / 'Til your body is doubled with pain, / Yet you ask no reward, in your pray'r to the Lord, / But forever here to remain."

The sheet music cover aside, there's nothing in Mort Dixon's lyric for "River, Stay 'Way From My Door," with Harry Woods's music (Shapiro, Bernstein, 1931), to indicate whether the singer is a poor white or a black, or even male or female; indeed the top-selling recording was Kate Smith's with Guy Lombardo and His Royal Canadians on Columbia in 1931. Her beautifully sung and moving rendition can be heard on the Internet. Other popular 1931 records of the song were made by Phil Harris on Victor and the Boswell Sisters on Brunswick, all of them white, and the great black singer/actor Paul Robeson on Victor. Arguing that the persona in the piece was intended to be a poor white is that, unlike the following songs to be sung by southern blacks, this first-person lyric employs no ethnic accent or dialect, or substandard English. Entirely in the first person, a poor elderly southerner apostrophizes to what he calls "just a lonely little river," making it clear he doesn't live on the banks of the Mississippi. Nor does the song reflect the Great Flood of 1927. Still, the singer knows rivers can overflow their banks, so he begs, "I don't bother you / Don't you bother me." That's in the verse, before the more familiar chorus's lines of "I just got a cabin / You don't need my cabin / River, stay 'way from my door— / Don't come up any higher, / I'm so all alone / leave my bed and my fire / That's all I own / I ain't breakin' your heart, / Don't start breakin' my heart / River, stay 'way from my door." A more pathetic tone than that of the sweating, slaving Georgia sharecropper, but that's more realistic than all poor whites reacting the same.

Except for the final two songs in this section, which deal with lynchings, the other realistic pieces about the lives of southern blacks and for the most part sung by them too all focus on stevedores. Two of them, written fourteen years apart, were by black Alley lyricists and composers of note, and these writers took the position that a realistic southern black can be portrayed as happy, at least some of the time. Not only were the lyricist and composer of "Roll Them Cotton Bales" (Jos. W. Stern, 1914), James W[eldon] Johnson and J. Rosamond Johnson, black; they were also brothers and southerners, born in Jacksonville, Florida, with writer James educated at Atlanta University. So it's pretty clear they knew whereof they wrote, though it's unlikely that the steamboat *Robert E. Lee* ever navigated the waters of the Savannah River "Chuck full of cotton from Tennessee" as the song's lyric purports it did. But the focal point isn't a boat, it's the black stevedores who "roll them cotton bales" for a living. The lyric divides between third person narrative and first person direct address, yet even the third person sections employ a southern black dialect, as in "That's where the cotton am a-growing." The stevedore singing the first-person portions does not complain about his backbreaking labor but knows he works with a purpose in mind: "I'm working hard along the levee, / So I can say to Lindy Lou, / Do, honey, tell me if you want me, /

Cause I'm working gal for you / . . . That means a dollar a day for me Lindy Lou it's all for you / That I roll them cotton bales." The Premier Quartet (the American Quartet when recording for Victor) with Billy Murray's solos cut the song on a 1914 Edison Blue Amberol cylinder, and it's on the Internet. Although each was black, neither lyricist Andy Razaf nor composer J. C. (born Jay Cee) Johnson was a southerner. Still, both recognized that in Dixie a "Dusky Stevedore" (Triangle Music, 1928) could be a person of several moods. In the song's two verses, the stevedore is portrayed as a cheerful guy, singing while he works: "See his ragtime shuffalin' gait, / Happy 'cause he's handlin' freight, / The levee's heaven for, / The Dusky Stevedore." Yet in the patter between the verses, the stevedore shows a different, darker, side of his life: "Chops fo' mammy, / Shoes fo' Sammy, / Move dem bales away, / Broke de stitches, / Needs new britches, / Move dem bales away, / Lan'lord says he's comin' back, / Wants de rent or wants his shack, / Dat ain't funny, I needs money, / Move dem bales away." Of the several recordings only the 1928 Victor one by The Revelers includes even part of the darker patter section, as found on the Internet.

On December 19, 1927, Broadway premiered the groundbreaking musical based on Edna Ferber's novel of the same name, *Show Boat,* written and composed by two giants of both Tin Pan Alley and musical theatre, Oscar Hammerstein II and Jerome Kern. Unlike typical shows of the time, *Show Boat* much more realistically viewed its characters, situations, and race relations, among other things. In presenting whites' perspectives on southern blacks during the late nineteenth century, when most of the action takes place, Hammerstein pulled no punches; after the overture, the first words audiences heard from a black chorus in what the complete vocal score calls only "Opening Act I" was, "Niggers all work on de Mississippi, / Niggers all work while de white folks play" (Harms, 1928: 12–13). Later productions softened the blatant racism of "Nigger" to "Colored folks." Yet even with that no-nonsense opening to the show, Hammerstein portrayed the only two named black characters, Queenie and her stevedore husband Joe, with sympathy and dignity. Joe, first played by Jules Bledsoe (not Paul Robeson as many think; Robeson first played Joe in the 1932 revival), sang one of the show's major hits then and a lasting classic ever since, "Ol' Man River" (T. B. Harms, 1927). It's a stevedore's lament about his hard life compared to the river which "jes keeps rollin' along": "You an' me, we sweat and strain, body all achin' an' racked wid pain. / 'Tote dat barge!' / 'Lift dat bale,' / Git a little drunk an' you'll land in jail." Robeson was unavailable to play the role Hammerstein and Kern had written specifically for him, but he recorded "Ol' Man River" minus the verse in 1928 for Victor with Paul Whiteman's Orchestra, and it's on the Internet.

Yet these troubles are nothing compared to those of the southern blacks sung about in the final two pieces in this small collection of realistic Alley numbers about them. Two songs, both in the 1930s, were about lynchings. The first was written, uncharacteristically, by Irving Berlin for a Broadway musical revue. The second was by a Jewish high school teacher from the Bronx, yet the recording of his song became a million-seller. With all the material somewhat topical in nature, Berlin wrote the songs and playwright Moss Hart the dialogue sketches for *As Thousands Cheer,* a revue that opened on September 30, 1933, ran for four hundred performances, and made a profit, even in the depths of the Great Depression. A blowup of a newspaper headline introduced the topic of each song and sketch. Whereas the majority of Berlin's numbers were his usual upbeat or light romantic types, including "Heat Wave" and "Easter Parade," when the audience saw the headline "Unknown Negro Lynched by Frenzied Mob" they would have known that whatever was coming next would not be lighthearted, let alone comic. What it turned out to be was the stellar black performer Ethel Waters singing "Supper Time" (Irving Berlin, Inc., 1933), which begins, "SUPPER TIME, / I should set the table, / 'Cause it's SUPPER TIME, / Somehow I'm not able, / 'Cause that man o' mine, / Ain't comin' home no more." She goes on to wonder what she'll tell her kids "when they ask me where he's gone," and continues in a similar vein throughout the remainder of the piece without ever explicitly mentioning that her husband had been lynched. Unusual for Berlin, it's a brilliant piece of indirection in lyric writing. Quite different are the graphic, detailed images of lynching in "Strange Fruit" (Edward B. Marks, 1940) by Lewis Allan (pseudonym of Abel Meeropol), who first wrote the words as a poem and later set them to music. Before the sheet music was published, in 1939 the piece found its way to Billie Holiday, who performed it to acclaim at the Café Society in Greenwich Village. Her usual recording company, Columbia, wouldn't touch the song for fear of racist reprisals but did give Holiday permission to record it with the jazz label Commodore, which she did. The Commodore record of "Strange Fruit," grim and hard to take as it is, sold a million copies. The power of Holiday's performance is heard on the 1939 Commodore disc on the Internet.

Dixie Satire and Parody

Three satires and a parody make up the final batch of songs that undermine an idealistic vision of Dixie as paradise on earth, and they mostly fulfill what they set out to accomplish. Three of the four take random comic potshots at just about everything southern. Only the first, and extremely silly, satire had one specific target. Sam Coslow, who in his songwriting maturity in the '30s wrote the lyrics for such hits as "Sing You Sinners," "Cocktails For Two," and romantic tunes for Bing Crosby, including "Down The Old Ox Road" and "Learn To Croon," wrote the words and music of this 1921 spoof. Coslow's "There's A Bunch Of Klucks In The Ku Klux Klan" (Robert Norton, 1921) doesn't go after the Klan's vicious practices of cross-burnings and lynchings, but focuses comically on the outward trappings and mindset of the Klan: "There's a bunch of klucks in the Ku Klux Klan / And they're all kuckoo, that's true, / With their awful hoke they're an awful joke / When you watch the things they do. / We ought to pile 'em in some asylum / And never let them out, / 'Cause we don't know and they don't know / What the deuce it's all about. / There's the grand high punk / With his grand high bunk / And his grand high palace, too, / But I've just found out how he got that palace, And I'll tell you." He got it by charging each "Kluck" a buck to join, implying the KKK was a con game to enrich "the grand high punk."

Perennial *Ziegfeld Follies* lyricist Gene Buck and composers Louis A. Hirsch and Dave Stamper wrote for the 1922 Follies "I Don't Want To Be In Dixie" (Harms, 1922), the singer's reason being simply, "Dixie isn't Dixie any more." To support his claim in this rather weak satiric piece he cites such things as "I don't want to be in Dixie, / My Tucky home in Dixie, / I'm satisfied to stay right here; / I haven't got a 'Mammy' / 'Way down in Alabammy / To sigh for and to die for ev'ry year. / My heart is never heavy / For moonlight on the levee, / Or picking cotton on the Swanee Shore; / It's really aggravating, / There's no one there a-waiting, / So Dixie isn't Dixie isn't Dixie any more." Much more pinpoint specific are the lyrics of Edward Eliscu, whose name isn't a household word, but who, as here in "It's The Same Old South"

(Mills Music, 1940) with music by Jay Gorney, was the writer of many satiric and ironic songs for sophisticated New York revues such as *Meet The People*, in which the present song appeared in late 1940 and '41. The song's premise is that if the singer's Grandpa, who died in 1884, came back today, he'd find Dixie unchanged: "It's a regular children's heaven / Where they don't start to work 'till they're seven / . . . With those old fashioned 'get togethers' / Colonel, pass me the tar and the feathers, / . . . / Let the Northerners keep Niagra [*sic*] / We will stick to our Southern pellagra / . . . / Why, the blood hounds that once chased Liza / Chase the poor C. I. O. organizer / IT'S THE SAME OLD SOUTH." And much more. It's striking that Eliscu picked up on some Dixie things Tom Lehrer missed in his great parody of homesickness songs thirteen years later.

I call Tom Lehrer's still-remembered "I Wanna Go Back to Dixie" (Tom Lehrer, 1953 and 1954) a parody because its form is a send-up of homesickness songs, qualifying it as such, at the same time its content satirizes aspects of the excesses of southern living. Its entirety is on the Internet in a studio recording by Lehrer, with the lyrics on a screen. An ironic and inevitable segue to the next chapter on home and homesickness are Lehrer's classic lines, "I wanna go back to Alabammy, / Back to the arms of my dear ol' Mammy, / Her cookin's lousy and her hands are clammy, / But what the hell, it's home."

7

"ALL ABOARD FOR DIXIE LAND"
Homesickness, Traveling Home, and "Mammy Songs"

"Redundancy is sometimes emphasis," jokingly said the arts editor of a newspaper I was second-string drama critic of years ago when he found I wrote the same thing twice in a theatre review. Still, repeating the same point *can* be useful, especially if the two instances are separated by some distance, so I'm opening this chapter with something I already included in the Prologue—a part of Stephen Foster biographer Ken Emerson's remarks on homesickness and my brief elaboration on his point. Emerson made his observation about homesickness in reference to "Old Folks At Home," which Foster wrote in 1851: "One reviewer called the 'homely tune' a 'catching, melodic *itch* of the time' . . . and nearly everyone scratched, be they Irish or German immigrants feeling homesick for the old country, frontiersmen or forty-niners pining for the folks they had left behind in the East or African Americans forcibly separated from their birthplaces and families. 'Old Folks at Home' was all things to all people" (Emerson 182). So too, for over sixty years, songs like "Swanee" (1919), "Carolina In The Morning" (1922), "Alabamy Bound" (1925), "Georgia On My Mind" (1930), and "Chattanooga Choo Choo" (1941) evoked feelings of homesickness in Americans, regardless of where they were born, where they were when they heard the song, or where they wanted to get back to, even though all the songs were about Dixie. This appeal to homesickness in people no longer living where they were born and raised and would love to return to helps account for the huge number of Dixie tunes about homesickness, traveling home, or a desire to be back with one's mammy (whether biological mother or black nursemaid as a human embodiment of the warmth and comfort of home). Songs embracing one or more of these themes number 491 of the 1,079, or 45.5 percent, of all archived Dixie tunes.

It should be obvious that I won't be discussing each of the nearly five hundred songs related to home in Dixie, so I'll explain how I chose those for inclusion before jumping into writing about their substance and significance.

A good number of tunes fell by the wayside simply by what might be called self-selection because of such factors as how perfectly dreadful their lyrics were, or—barring that—how clichéd these pieces were, or how repetitious of so many others, while lacking any ingenious images or flashes of brilliance to make them worth considering for inclusion. I further greatly pruned the massive number of songs by eliminating—except for a few classics on the subject—the large body of tunes in which the sole reason for the singer's homesickness or motive for traveling home is to see his sweetheart. Unlike wanting to see his mammy and daddy, relatively fixed figures connected to home and Dixie, to quote the Gershwins' *Porgy and Bess,* "a woman is a sometime thing," and the longed-for sweethearts in these songs could as easily have lived in Montana as Mississippi for all the absence of local color in this particular batch of Dixie tunes. So out they went, and while I didn't count them, they easily numbered in the hundreds. I also eliminated a fairly substantial clutch of songs about traveling home that, to me, embodied the wrong point of view. Rather than focusing on his elation to be home in Dixie again, the singer carries on about how everyone in town—friends, family, and even a band meeting him at the railroad station—will be so glad to see the local boy returning. This egocentric viewpoint isn't the vision of Dixie as idealized through the image of home that the core songs, and the most significant ones, are all about. Even after culling and pruning, I was left with a large number of viable songs, and it came down to my own subjective picking and choosing the ones I wanted to single out for full discussion, which for a mere mention or to briefly illustrate a point, and which to eliminate. My final choices didn't just boil down to songs that were most popular in their day or have remained standards (although plenty of both are represented here). Many lesser-known Dixie tunes about home and mammy appear here for what they say about home and family as central to the myth of an idyllic South.

That said, and before turning to the main categories of those pieces known as "mammy songs," those about homesickness, and those about traveling home to Dixie, attention must be paid to a small yet historically significant group of songs about displaced southern blacks feeling homesick or traveling home. Black lyricists (and a few composers) wrote several of these, along with white, some of the black ones having come north to the Alley from the South themselves.

Displaced Darkies

In *The Romance of Reunion,* Nina Silber observes that in the postbellum nine-teenth century, and specifically during and after Reconstruction, among all immigrants to the North, including those from Europe, "More than other migrant groups, southern blacks seemed to be bound to their homelands, regardless of the compulsions that may have taken them away" (Silber 130). This attachment to their Dixie homes, despite what they may have suffered under slavery and later, was echoed, Silber notes, in songs sung by both white blackface "delineators" in minstrel shows and black minstrel performers too. Typical lines from lyrics were: "We've been to see our birthplace / We couldn't stay away" and "We belong away down South, / Down in Alabama . . . / Nebber mind whar you be, / On this great wide earth, / A darkie's heart can never lose / The spot that gave him birth." (qtd. in Silber 130). Silber surmises that, hearing such sentiments, "Working-class [white] audiences, already confronting cramped and competitive conditions, must have derived some comfort from this message that one less ethnic group would be competing with them for jobs and dwellings in the industrial cities of the North" (130).

Charles Hamm, in *Irving Berlin: Songs from the Melting Pot,* applied this notion to later Alley songs that Hamm claims were about darkies traveling from North to South (which, in fact, most of them were *not;* it was whites who were traveling, as will be seen later). He made these Dixie tunes appear as if they were insidiously political around the time of the presidential election of 1912, when

> Theodore Roosevelt, running as a third-party candidate, was popular among New York City's Jews because of his "progressive rhetoric and philo-Semitism" and because he was less supportive of the country's growing nativist backlash against the recently arrived immigrant pop-ulation than were the other two candidates, Woodrow Wilson and Wil-liam Howard Taft. An important subtext of this election, particularly in northern cities, was the intensifying competition between immigrants and northward-migrant African Americans for unskilled jobs. If blacks stayed in the South, there would be more jobs for immigrants and for their fami-lies and friends still in Europe who were waiting for the chance to come

over. . . . It could hardly be a coincidence that Tin Pan Alley and vaudeville, with so many immigrants and first-generation people among the leading songwriters, producers, and performers, turned out a rash of back-to-Dixie songs at just this time. . . . Taken as a group, these pieces were hegemonic in making it appear commonsensical that blacks should stay in or return to the South. (Hamm 98–99)

All well and good, except that Hamm's theory doesn't stand up to the test of evidence. He never shows that these back-to-Dixie songs he writes of featured a black protagonist (almost none did), and doesn't even mention a group of such songs that *do* have a black either yearning to return to Dixie or actually going there.

Silber's observation that "southern blacks seemed to be bound to their homelands" even when they had deliberately moved to the North to find more rewarding or lucrative work is validated for a period much later than the postbellum nineteenth century she writes of. In the first third of the twentieth century the unusually noncommercial lyrics of black Alleymen and some of their white compatriots clearly demonstrate a sympathy with and for these displaced darkies. The earliest such song written and composed by blacks was "In My Old Home (In Dixie Land)" with words by "Mord" Allen and music by Tom Lemonier, published in 1908 by Gotham-Attucks Music Co., the firm created by Will Marion Cook and Richard C. McPherson to provide a publisher for the creative efforts of African American Alleymen. Allen's lyric states why true darkies consider Dixie their home, despite the hardships they must bear there: "You ask a real darkey whats [*sic*] the dearest place on earth, / What's nearest to perfection in his mind, / . . . You ask him what of comfort can the South hold out to him, / With all the things that go to vex him there, / . . . I can't help what you think of it, / There's no place on earth so fit, / As my old home in Dixie land." Two years earlier, in the mode of sentimental songs popular at the time, white lyricist Earle C. Jones and composer Max S. Witt wrote "My Mississippi Missus Misses Me" (Jos. W. Stern, 1906). In it a "darky, old and feeble" is standing by a river, presumably the Mississippi, and having reveries of "dear old Dixie before the war," dear to him even though he and his bride were then both slaves. His thoughts turn to returning home from the North, where apparently he had gone long ago to work, sending money to his wife in Mississippi: "'I'm gwine to go back home' he said, 'and see my Caroline / De packet now, is coming round de bend. / My Mississippi Missus ain't so much but she's all mine, / An' when I'm dar I'll know I've found a friend.'" That last line suggests, as do other songs, that the North is a cold, friendless place for displaced southern blacks who want to be in the community of others of their race.

A black songwriter who repeatedly made that point up front in his pieces about southbound darkies wanting to leave the impersonal North for congenial Dixie was the great bluesman and, for a time, Alley music publisher, Spencer Williams. Williams was a southerner who was born in New Orleans in 1889, and after the death of his prostitute mother, stayed there with an aunt who was "a noted madam" for a while, before moving to live with other relatives in Birmingham, Alabama in his teens (Jasen 430). By 1907 Williams had migrated north to Chicago, where he played jazz piano and began writing songs, and then on to New York in 1916, to continue these careers, both of which he did handsomely, his biggest Dixie tune hit being "Basin Street Blues." It's evident from some of Williams's lyrics about blacks wanting to be back in the South that regardless of the persona singing the words, many of the feelings about wishing to be again in Dixie or never to have left it were patently Williams's own. "Tishomingo Blues" (1917) and "I Never Had The Blues (Until I Left Old Dixieland)" (1919) show this best, whereas "Arkansas Blues" (1921) is just a conventional back-to-Dixie tune of the type that was proliferating like bunnies by that time. Williams wrote both the words and music of "Tishomingo Blues" (Jos. W. Stern, 1917), and while a jazz piece and not a traditional blues at all, there is a powerful sense of the singer's agony in both the text and melody. No contemporary vocal recordings, only instrumentals, appear on the Internet, but "Tishomingo Blues" can be heard with both verses and the chorus, in a modern performance by blues singer Marilyn Keller with the St. Louis Rivermen at the Central Illinois Jazz Fest in 2010. The most telling lines of Williams's lyric revealing the authenticity of its feelings are "Oh my weary heart cries out in pain, / Oh how I wish I was back again, / With a race, in a place, / Where they make you welcome all the time, / Way down in Mississippi," Tishomingo being a small town in the northeast corner of that state, near the Alabama line. Considering Williams's own dicey childhood, the youthful surroundings and upbringing described by the singer of "I Never Had The Blues (Until I Left Old Dixieland)," with music by white Charley Straight (Pace & Handy Music Co., 1919), are of a fictional nature. But the song's title and many of the sentiments expressed in the lyrics make it equally evident that Williams poured a lot of himself and his feelings into the tune. In the two verses, the singer—presumably up North—listens and reacts to a song sung and played by a piano man in a cabaret, a song "That took me back again, / To my old home sweet home so grand, / My heart began to throb, / And that is why I sob." In the chorus, the singer declares that, though black, "I never had the blues until I left old Dixieland / I never knew a moment's toil or care, because down there / Every one treats you so nice, they'll make you think of Paradise / . . . I miss the gentle shaking of the hand (you understand) / And when I left old Dixieland (I left behind) / A dear old mother's love so sweet and kind / I never had the blues until I left old Dixieland." Pieces such as these with lyrics *by* blacks confirm Silber's idea of African Americans being bound to their southern homelands, with "home" meaning a place of comfort for them—a far cry from Charles Hamm's thesis that only politically motivated whites wrote songs of southbound darkies to abet movements for sending blacks to Dixie where they belonged.

That in blacks' minds Dixie was their natural and desired home carried into the 1920s through a song, "Bandana Days" (M. Witmark & Sons, 1921), by the black team of musical comedy writers, composer Eubie Blake and lyricist Noble Sissle, from their hit *Shuffle Along*. Neither Sissle nor Blake was a southerner, but Sissle's lyrics reveal his grasp of blacks' affinity for the South, a feeling that didn't gloss over their hardships there: "Why the dearest days of my life / Were Bandana days, / Bandana days though filled with turmoil, trouble, and strife."

After "Bandana Days" twelve years elapsed before any more Alley songs appeared about blacks pulling up their temporary roots in the North and heading back to the South to replant them permanently and more satisfyingly in congenial Dixie soil. All but one of the four songs on that theme, which bunched up in the mid-'30s, were by white lyricists and composers, but ones who, judging from their lyrics, were very much attuned and sympathetic to blacks' states of mind. The one piece by a black team was "Mississippi Basin" (Joe Davis, 1933), with words by Andy Razaf and music by black British-born jazz pianist and composer Reginald Foresythe. The persona created by Razaf is tired of being a "rolling stone" and wants to return to the South, despite knowing, in the song's most telling lines, "Even though the work was heavy,

/ I was happy on the levee, / Wanna take my rightful place in that MISSIS-SIPPI BASIN back home, / (Why did I roam?)" Although he made his career mostly as a composer, Jimmy Van Heusen was the lyricist and Jerry Arlen (younger brother of Harold) the tunesmith for "There's A House In Harlem For Sale" (Santly Bros., 1934), their collaboration having begun when they attended Syracuse University together. In Van Heusen's lyric, a formerly southern black living in Harlem has gotten fed up with city life and is preparing for his personal reverse migration to the South: "Harlem town I used to love ya, / Now I'm oh, so tired of ya. / All your 'high life' just isn't meant for my life, / . . . I won't miss Harlem's 'Hi-De-Ho' / When I start singing 'Old Black Joe,' / There's a HOUSE IN HARLEM FOR SALE, / 'Cause there's a cottage in Caroline, / That's gonna belong to me." That same year another song expressing almost identical sentiments came out, "Fare-Thee-Well To Harlem" (Southern Music, 1934), with lyrics by Savannah-born white lyricist Johnny Mercer and music by Bernie Hanighen. The song's words include some of Mercer's wacky off-the-wall rhyming and also show a real sense of his being in touch with the feelings of southern blacks displaced in the North and planning to return to the familiarity and comfort of their Dixie homes: "Fare-thee-well to Harlem! / Fare-thee-well to night life! / Goin' back where I can lead the right life, . . . / Things is tight in Harlem. / I know how to fix it. / Step aside, I'm gonna Mason-Dix it / Fare-thee-well to Harlem! / . . . All this sin is 'fright-eous,' / Goin' back where everybody's righteous." The piece is a dialogue and the leading recording on Bluebird in 1934, by Paul Whiteman and his Orchestra with Mercer himself and Jack Teagarden singing the entire lyric plus some ad libs not in the published sheet music, is on the Internet. Songs about southbound blacks ended with lyricist Ted Koehler and composer Rube Bloom's "Cotton" (Mills Music, 1935), which appeared in *Cotton Club Parade* in 1935 at the famed Harlem nightclub so named. It's a heartbreaking lament by a realistic displaced southern black about what he or she would do to return to Dixie, as seen in such lines as "I'm out of place here in Harlem, / That's why I want to go home," and "I'd gladly pick all the Cotton, / Just to get back to that old log cabin shack / Among my kind of folks once more." The chorus as sung by Ivie Anderson with Duke Ellington and His Orchestra on a 1935 Brunswick disc is on the Internet.

"I'd walk a million miles for one of your smiles"

It could be argued that since most "mammy singers" like Eddie Leonard, Al Jolson, and Eddie Cantor performed in blackface in the early decades of the twentieth century when they sang their mammy songs about prodigals yearning to return to Dixie and the knees, arms, or breasts of their biological mothers or childhood nursemaids, these songs were extensions of the southbound darky tunes discussed in the previous section. This argument may have limited merit, but the homesickness in mammy songs reaches out more widely and affectively to people of any race and whether from Dixie or not; or, as Ken Emerson said of Stephen Foster's "Old Folks At Home," such mammy songs were "all things to all people." This type of mammy song was most preponderant among thirty written between 1910 and 1933, after which the genre ceased entirely. Aside from two pieces that can't be categorized, there was just one other sort of mammy song, that depicting a Dixie mother—usually black, but once possibly not—comforting her young child or infant or just singing it a bedtime lullaby. Although blackface mammy singers usually performed the more familiar type of mammy songs, ten others were of this Dixie mother and child variety. (I don't discuss or even mention all thirty mammy songs here; instead I have chosen a group of about twelve based on their artistry, significance, and/or popularity.)   Mammy songs began in 1910 with a southern lullaby of unusual parentage, although this managed to escape Karen L. Cox in *Dreaming of Dixie* (2011) despite the fact she reproduces the sheet music cover of the 1910 edition and writes a few platitudes about the song and the cover photo of "the young white man who wrote the music" (see Cox 20, 19). It's amazing Cox doesn't remark that the "young man" is wearing a jersey with "Chicago White Sox" on it. It was not fan gear, but his uniform, for the composer of "Little Puff Of Smoke, Good Night: A Southern Croon" (Chicago: Victor Kremer, 1910) was G. Harris ("Doc") White, who pitched for the White Sox for 11 years, winning 159 games, with a 2.30 ERA. More surprising, Cox doesn't note that the lyricist was Ring W. Lardner (just R. W. on the 1910 edition, but his first name was spelled out when the song was transferred to the larger Chicago publisher Harold Rossiter in 1916). One might forgive Cox for not following early baseball, but not to recognize Lardner, the cigar-chomping short story and sportswriter, seems a serious lapse in scholarly research, even though his early lyric is more sentimental than his usual work. Lardner's lyric is as affecting as White's music: "Go to sleep and rest, / On your mammy's breast, / While the angels watch will keep; / Sweetest dreams will come / To my sugarplum / To my little heart's delight, / Cuddle down and shut your eyes, / Waking with the bright sunrise, / Little Puff of Smoke, Good-night."

Whereas most of the mother/child mammy songs have a sameness about them that all pedestrian, generic songs do, three are notable, each for a different reason. "Sleepy-Time Rag," with Florence M. Cooke's words and Alma Sanders's music (M. Witmark, 1914), capitalized on the ragtime music of the day embodied in the tune's title and the song itself. It's an odd musical form for a lullaby but somehow it works. The two verses are purely descriptive of the black mammy soothing her young child's fear of the dark before bedtime, with the ragtime, syncopated chorus reserved for the lullaby itself: "Don't you cry my little bit of sugar cane, / Just as sweet as honey from the bee. / It's time for little pickanninny [sic] boy to be drifting off to slumber sweet; / . . . Jest hide yo' little kinky head, / I'll tuck yo' in your trundle bed, / And sing to you that sleepy-time Rag." A child in need of more serious comforting is the subject of "Mammy's Little Coal Black Rose" (Jerome H. Remick, 1916) by the eminent writers of many popular Alley tunes, Dixie and otherwise, lyricist Raymond Egan and composer Richard A. Whiting. The scenario has an omniscient narrator hearing a little black boy in Tennessee crying his heart out because he isn't white, whereupon his mother kisses him and sings him a lullaby that soothes the child with all the right reasons why he should feel good about being black. The Orpheus Quartet's 1916 Victor recording of the first verse and the lullaby chorus is on the Internet. Eight years later, Charles J. Cordray's "Georgia Lullaby" (Chicago: Forster Music, 1924) presented a strange case of what might be called "un-whitewashing" between the published sheet music and the chorus of this song containing a lovely melody, which is on a 1924 Victor record by The Troubadours (actually the Victor house orchestra conducted by Nathaniel Shilkret) with a vocal by contralto Marcia Freer; it's on the Internet. Perhaps for marketing, there are no references to the mother and child's blackness in the published lyrics, and the cover art makes it seem as if both are white. Yet in the recorded version of the song—which may have had wider sales than the sheet music in 1924— Freer turns Cordray's fairly generic "Go to sleep, my pretty baby" into "Go to sleep, my pickaninny" and "Pretty baby, don't you cry" into "Colored baby, don't you cry." The only Dixie reference in the published and recorded song is in the last phrase: "The sandman's coming, / Your mammy's humming, / A Georgia lullaby."

Mammy songs about a prodigal son yearning for the comfort of home and mammy began relatively late, starting only in 1917 with Irving Berlin's "There Are Two Eyes In Dixie" (Waterson, Berlin & Snyder, 1917). Here the wanderer doesn't so much want to return to his mammy (and daddy) as to be reassured that wherever he roams, their eyes are watching over him and keeping him morally straight: "There are two I's in Dixie, / D-I-X-I-E, / Two eyes in Dixie, / Always watching me; / And while I'm straying, / By day and night, / They keep on saying, / 'Turn to the right.'" Of two variations on the theme, better than the generic average, but neither a hit, one was "In Miami (Where Mammy Is Waiting For Me)" (Leo Feist, 1919), with words and music by Sidney D. Mitchell, Arthur Fields, and Archie Gottler. It's most likely the mammy figure here was the singer's childhood nursemaid rather than mother since he seems to be returning more for her food than for maternal nurturing. Beyond one brief remark that "Soon I'll hold her, to my shoulder / Just as tight as can be," everything turns culinary, with the singer even inviting the hearer to come along with him for some really great feeds: "I'll soon be looking, / At Mammy cookin' chicken fries, / In Southern style, / Her Dixie dishes, / Are so delicious, / Just for one, / I'd walk a mile; . . . / So come with me a flyin', / 'Cause 'taint no use denyin', / I know you'll soon be sighin', / For the meals my Mammy's fryin', / When you're pickin', / On that chicken, / What a glutton you'll be." The other, more spiritual, was "My Mammy Knows" (Waterson, Berlin, & Snyder, 1921), with words and music by Harry De Costa and M. K. Jerome. Here mammy functions entirely as the emotional comfort and support system for the returned prodigal disillusioned with his (mis)adventures in the world beyond Dixie. As he sings in the verse, "I need a word of cheer / And Mammy dear, / Will know just what to do," elaborating on this at several points in the chorus with "My mammy knows, / Just how to cheer and comfort me, / My mammy knows, / Just how to show real sympathy, / . . . In her arms I'll creep and cry myself to sleep, / I know I'll wake up with a smile. / . . . My poor heart is achin', how to keep it from breakin', / My mammy knows, / My mammy knows." Sentimental, yes, but the number richly embodies the mammy figure as the human emblem of home as comfort zone in idyllic Dixie. Thanks to research by discography expert Al

Pavlow, I learned that Charles Hart and Elliott Shaw made a vocal recording of "My Mammy Knows" on a 1922 Columbia record (not on the Internet) as the "B" side of Al Jolson's "Give Me My Mammy" (Sunshine Music, 1921), with words by B. G. De Sylva and music by Walter Donaldson. Jolson's piece was a hit, but though a mammy song, it does not refer to the South and is not further considered here. The one "My Mammy Knows" that had any success was a jazzy instrumental rendition for Victor in 1922 by the Benson Orchestra of Chicago directed by Roy Bargy, which *is* on the Internet.

Pieces such as these are representative, but perhaps most remarkable about the eighteen mammy songs on the theme of the prodigal wanting to be back with his mammy or at least get word to her is that five became hits in their day, some remaining perennial standards in the annals of popular song, a high number of tunes in any limited category. Several factors account for the success of these songs: the artistry with which most of them were written; the charisma of the singer (usually in blackface), who either introduced a song on stage or with whom it became associated (and who often also recorded it) after someone else first performed it; and, perhaps most importantly, the universality of the message and depth of the feeling about home with mother or nursemaid as a far better place to be than friendless in a cold, impersonal world—all regardless of whether the hearers of the songs had any ties to the South. A mammy song with all three things going for it was almost a guaranteed hit.

The first blockbuster prodigal son mammy song was one indeed, from the moment Al Jolson debuted "Rock-A-Bye Your Baby With a Dixie Melody" (Waterson, Berlin & Snyder, 1918) in *Sinbad,* which opened at the Winter Garden on February 14, 1918, through Jolson's first recording of it on Victor in 1918, complete with the verse, which is on the Internet. Lyricists Sam M. Lewis and Joe Young and composer Jean Schwartz wrote a mammy song that was melodically infectious, and one in which images were fresh, original, and memorable. These begin in a little-known verse. It was a cliché for the singer of such songs to call himself a rolling stone, but Lewis and Young have fun with this in lines like "Your little rollin' stone that rolled away" and "Your rollin' stone is rollin' home to stay." Their images become yet more fanciful in the chorus, spinning off of the song's title, "Rock-a-Bye Your Baby With A Dixie Melody": "Just hang my cradle, / Mammy mine, / Right on the Mason Dixon Line / And swing it from Virginia, / To Tennessee with all the love that's in yer." Yet for all the cleverness, the singer's feelings for his mammy are genuine: "A million baby kisses I'll deliver / The minute that you sing the 'Swanee River.'" Between the three songwriters' craftsmanship and Jolson's charismatic rendition, small wonder "Rock-A-Bye Your Baby" became the perennial classic that it is.

The year after the success of "Rock-A-Bye," and without the advantage of a stage performance by an entertainer like Jolson to launch it, "Mammy O' Mine" (Shapiro, Bernstein, 1919) became, says David A. Jasen, the first of several million-selling hits for black composer Maceo Pinkard, his mammy song with words by white lyricist William Tracey (see Jasen 310). Jasen doesn't specify whether the song sold a million copies of the sheet music, the phonograph record, or a combination of the two, but this hardly matters, since in 1919 a million copies of a tune in any form was impressive, and enough to rank it as one of the most popular songs of its day, although it has not had the same staying power as some other mammy songs. The piece is a homesick song, not one of the prodigal actually returning to his mammy. Both the verse and chorus are very short, to the point, and poignant, including such phrases as "Oh! Lordy, how I'd like to be with you / When I'm alone, / My thoughts go wandering home, / . . . Daddy used to say, the good Lord bless'd us, / When he gave us you, 'cause you're the bestes', / Angel divine, / You wonderful Mammy O' Mine." Soprano and actress Adele Rowland popularized "Mammy O' Mine" and cut it for Victor in 1919, including the first verse and chorus, and also a long patter section not in the sheet music, as is heard on the Internet. That Shapiro, Bernstein & Co. had high hopes for the song is seen in how much space they gave it in ads in *Billboard* and *Variety,* such as the blurb in their ad on page 30 of *Variety* on May 2, 1919: "We announce with pleasure the most beautiful syncopated Southern ballad to the artists of this country, 'Mammy O' Mine' By Billy Tracey & Maceo Pinkard." Given the song's sales, their ads paid off and then some.

The same two lyricists who scored big with "Rock-A-Bye Your Baby" in 1918, Sam Lewis and Joe Young, scored even bigger in 1921 in "My Mammy," this time with composer Walter Donaldson (Irving Berlin, Inc., 1921), although to look at various sources online and in print one might wonder just when the song first appeared. In its entry for the musical *Sinbad,* the often unreliable "Wikipedia" makes it seem as if "My Mammy" and other interpolated songs entered the show the year it opened in 1918, and such generally trustworthy reference works on popular music as those by Robert Lissauer and Roger D. Kinkle (see Bibliography) also give that date for the tune's debut in the show. Yet this is patently absurd since the copyright date on the sheet music is 1921, and a smart publisher like Berlin wouldn't have withheld such a smash stage hit from publication for three years from its premiere. Well, of course he didn't. The confusion in dates is clarified, though with some discrepancies in details, by Jolson biographers Herbert F. Goldman and Michael Freedland, although neither's book documents its sources of information. It's widely known Jolson didn't introduce "My Mammy" on stage. It was first sung in vaudeville at an uncertain date by William Frawley (the same William Frawley better known years later for playing Fred Mertz on TV's *I Love Lucy*). During one of the times Jolson closed *Sinbad* for about four weeks for some much needed R&R, he either heard the song or was shown a prepublication copy of the sheet music by Saul Bornstein, general manager of Irving Berlin's publishing firm, depending upon whether you read Freedland or Goldman. Either way, he decided to interpolate "My Mammy" into his show when it reopened. That was in late 1920 or early 1921. Freedland makes it seem as if *Sinbad* reopened on Broadway, but Goldman writes more convincingly that Jolson first sang "My Mammy" "when *Sinbad* reopened at the Shubert-Majestic Theatre in Providence, R. I., on Monday evening, January 31st [1921], and for the remainder of the tour stopped the show with it" (see Freedland 78, Goldman 114–15). This late interpolation of "My Mammy" into *Sinbad* explains the published song's date. It was an instant hit, though Jolson didn't record it till seven years later. Freeland says of "My Mammy," "Jolson made it his theme song. Today it is the one song that every mention of Jolson recalls" (78). I'd go further to say that now, if people recall *any* mammy songs, this is the one they are likely to remember, perhaps even with images of blackface Jolson on one knee, half-singing/half-speaking the final lines as if his heart would break, "I'd walk a million miles for one of your smiles my Mammy." Kiner's Jolson discography (see Bibliography) confirms he first cut the song, verse intact, with Abe Lyman's Orchestra on a 1928 Brunswick disc; it's on the Internet.

The phenomenal success of "My Mammy" in 1921 and succeeding years didn't end the writing and performance of mammy songs by Alleymen and entertainers; the genre persisted through 1933. While most of the songs were nothing to write home about, two had clever enough concepts, memorable enough words, and catchy enough melodies to become moderate hits when they were written, though neither stood the test of time beyond then. With Harry Link's music and Bob Nelson's spelling gimmickry not just in the title but in the lyric too, "No One Loves You Any Better Than Your M-A-Double-M-Y" (Fred Fisher, 1923) falls into the class of tune labeled a novelty song. Yet this novelty song had heart. After a verse addressed to "all you rolling stones" about how things will look better back home than the world they set out to see, the chorus details mammy as comfort zone: "No one loves you any better than your M-A-Double-M-Y, / And when you start to cry, / She'll dry each tearful, make you cheerful / . . . M is for the mince-pies that she used to make / A is for the apples in her apple cake, / Double M is for the many miles you had to roam, / And Y is that you're yearning just to get back home, / And though you've roamed this whole world over, / Say! A love like her's [sic] you can't buy, / 'Cause no one loves you any better than your M-A-Double-M-Y." On February 26, 1923, The Virginians, directed by Ross Gorman with a vocal by Billy Murray and Ed Smalle, recorded this jaunty tune, which is on the Internet, for Victor. Though there is no way to prove this, as I read, reread, and listened to Harry Pease's words to "That's My Mammy!" (Leo Feist, 1928), with music by Abel Baer and Ed G. Nelson, I became convinced that the singer and his biological mammy in this song are both white. The scenario is of a man up North asking a friend about to travel to the South to say hello to his mammy for him if he should see her, so he spends the chorus describing her. In the verse—the only place his mammy's home in Tennessee is named—the singer uses expressions that strike me as particularly "white" like "Say old pal, by the way, old pal" and, later, "If you'll allow, I'll try somehow." In the chorus, the singer describes his mother as "If you should see a soul that's happy / Strollin' with a grey hair'd pappy, / That's my mammy!" and "If you should see a silver haired old lady, / Sittin' with her knittin' where it's shady." Neither image seems to jibe with that of the usual black mammy waiting alone, miserable, and anxious for her prodigal son to return. Pease, Baer, and Nelson's tune captures the Jazz Age when it was written. The Internet has the 1928 Columbia disc by the Radiolites (a.k.a. the Ben Selvin Orchestra) with a vocal of the chorus by Irving Kaufman.

"Pick Me Up And Lay Me Down In Dear Old Dixieland"

Tin Pan Alley's Dixie homesickness tunes are almost as old as the Alley itself, the first written by lyricist Andrew B. Sterling and composer Harry Von Tilzer just a year after the two had their first multimillion seller with "My Old New Hampshire Home." In 1899, Shapiro, Bernstein & Von Tilzer published their "Where The Sweet Magnolias Bloom." On May 2, 1901, Addison Dashiell Madeira and Harry Macdonough cut a successful Victor Monarch record of it, which is on the Internet. Still, with lines like "I long to be with mother, in that old log cabin room, / 'Way down South in dear old Georgia, where the sweet magnolias bloom," the piece is pretty pedestrian, especially given what Sterling and Von Tilzer went on to write together and with others. Yet "Where The Sweet Magnolias Bloom" started the trend for close to 190 songs about homesickness for Dixie up to 1946. (I made a more manageable selection of about thirty to discuss or briefly mention in this section of the chapter.)

Once we eliminate songs solely about yearning to return to a sweetheart, two thematic threads run through Dixie homesickness songs, sometimes knotted together in a single piece, but more often one of them alone forming the fabric of an individual song. The more prevalent theme is the singer's homesickness for his own family home and relatives long ago left behind, but also well represented is the alternate theme of homesickness for Dixie as a whole or a part thereof (say, a city or state), almost always envisioned as idyllic in the mind and feelings of the singer. The very early "'Mid The Fields Of Snowy Cotton ('Round My Dear Old Southern Home)" (Weser Bros., 1906), with words and music by Otto and John Heinzman, demonstrates, however clumsily, the two threads coexisting in a single song. In the first verse, the homesick singer's focus is on "a little home forever dear to me; / With a lonely heart I'm sighing, for the loved ones kind and true, / Sadly longing by their sides once more to be." In the second stanza, he sees as idyllic the South and his early days where "There the days were never lonely, and the skies were ever clear." In the Moonlight and Magnolias Myth pervading so many Dixie tunes, the sun *always* shines by day and the moon by night; birds always sing and flowers always bloom. In these songs, homesick-type or not, I can't recall even one in which it's raining. This is all part of idealizing the South, to be taken up more fully in Chapter 9. We will start with the smaller group of homesickness songs, those about missing an idyllic Dixie, and move to the larger set about home and family, though, as will be seen, some major hits and all-time classics came from both types of homesickness pieces.

Eddie Leonard was one of the last—and one of the greatest—blackface performers, his career spanning actual minstrel shows into vaudeville in the early twentieth century, rivaling Al Jolson and Eddie Cantor for popularity. Leonard also wrote songs' words and music, often of special material for himself, employing a slight darky dialect, as seen in his "I Want To Go Back To The Land Of Cotton" (Jos. W. Stern, 1913), which mentions the singer wanting to see his "Ma" and "Pa," but mostly catalogues those idyllic things about Dixie that make it the place he wants to be: "Where de moon am shining bright, / . . . And the birds are singing in de trees: / And the darkies am a-humming all de day, / . . . That's where the sun forever shines." Four years later Al Jolson had a hit record with a Dixie homesickness song with a memorable melody by Jean Schwartz and clever words by the most prolific Dixie tunes lyricists, Sam M. Lewis and Joe Young. "I'm All Bound 'Round With the Mason Dixon Line" is a tune that only glances at the singer wanting to be back with "Oh! mother mine!" but otherwise wants to be in Dixie because "Dixie is the finest place on earth" and "I've read a lot about Heaven, / But give me Dixie all the time." Jolson cut the first verse and chorus of his impassioned encomium to an idyllic Dixie on a 1917 Columbia record (despite the YouTube entry saying it was 1919), which is on the Internet. When they were in top form, Lewis and Young found multiple ways to say the same things in their many Dixie tunes, as seen in their different take on an ideal Dixie in "Away Down South" (Irving Berlin, Inc., 1922), with Harry Akst's music, which is more legato, even mournful in spots, than Schwartz's tune for "I'm All Bound 'Round." In keeping with that quality of the music, Lewis and Young compare Dixie to the burdens of the rest of the world: "Ain't this a weary place to live in? / Far away from WAY DOWN SOUTH. / Oh, how I've struggled and I've striven, / Far away from WAY DOWN SOUTH . . . / I'm too many miles away from Heaven, / Far away from WAY DOWN SOUTH." The Peerless Quartet recorded the song, which is on the Internet, for Victor on June 21, 1922.

The year 1922 was big for songs of homesickness for idyllic Dixie, with two besides "Way Down South" that had more success, one of those becoming a perennial classic of American popular song. But first, the other one. The prolific team of Bert Kalmar and Harry Ruby wrote the words and music of the piece that gives its title to this section of Chapter 7, "Pick Me Up And Lay Me Down In Dear Old Dixieland" (Waterson, Berlin & Snyder, 1922), a cheerful number with a few home references but mostly idealizing the South, and a melody that's anything but mournful. Typical of the singer's sentiments about the South are the lines "Pick me up, and lay me down in dear old Dixieland, / The sun shines there each morn / That's where the sun was born, / My heart's been all wrapped up in that land of magic charms." The Peerless Quartet sang it on their February 23, 1922, Victor record that's on the Internet. Yet whatever fleeting success "Way Down South" and "Pick Me Up and Lay Me Down" may have had, the Dixie homesickness song for the ages, published in 1922, was lyricist Gus Kahn and composer Walter Donaldson's "Carolina In The Morning" (Jerome H. Remick, 1922). I make an exception here to my "no sweetheart songs" rule partly because of this tune's classic stature, but also because, though the young lady is central to the lyric, she's not a focal point of the idyllic Carolina Kahn's clever and intricate words paint. Incidentally, speaking of Carolina, with the exception of a single song—"Just A Little Bit South of North Carolina" (Porgie, Debin & Friedman 1941), with words and music by Sonny Skyler, Bette Cannon, and Arthur Shaftel—no Dixie tunes that mention "Carolina" designate whether "North" or "South." Be that as it may, Kahn with his usual mastery narrows his focus even more to concentrate on what is so idyllic about Carolina specifically "in the morning," ignoring whatever its charms may be during the rest of the day and evening. After an inconsequential verse, the chorus begins by generally idealizing Carolina before noon, "Nothing could be finer than to be in Carolina in the morning," after which the lyric gets minutely specific about things occurring in the a.m., such as "Where the morning glories / Twine around the door," those flowers known for opening their blossoms only in the early hours of the day. Most often Kahn expresses his idyllic picture of the minutiae of a Carolina morning in tricky, sometimes triple, rhymes, such as "Strolling with my girlie where the dew is pearly early in the morning / Butterflies all flutter up and kiss each little buttercup at dawning." Kahn doesn't generalize about the sun always shining and other clichés, but includes such little specifics, which is one likely reason, along with Donaldson's infectious melody, for both the initial hit status and perennial success of the song. Van and Schenck's recording (which is not on the Internet) was #1 in 1923, but not far behind at #8 in April was Billy Murray and the American Quartet's on Victor—with the verse, all on the Internet.

Two years later, in a song with music by Milton Ager that can be described as homesickness in ragtime, Jack Yellen's lyrics detailing why "I Want To See My Tennessee" (Ager, Yellen & Bornstein, 1924) are almost as specific as

Gus Kahn's in "Carolina In The Morning," although the Yellen-Ager tune never achieved the popularity of the Kahn-Donaldson piece. Still, through two verses, a chorus, and a patter break, the song is crammed with what the singer finds so appealing about Tennessee in his idyllic vision of the state and why he wants to return there. Nor does Yellen skimp on some pretty fancy internal rhyming, as in the phrase (emphases added to show where the rhymes fall with the music) "I know that *when* I see *Ten*-nessee *then* I see Paradise." Images comparing Tennessee favorably to Heaven and Paradise abound, side by side with earthly details of such things as "little chicks a-peckin' on the ground" and "the dew upon the waving corn." On October 20, 1924, Billy Murray and Ed Smalle cut the song for Victor, which is on the Internet. In 1931 Leon and Otis René and Clarence Muse wrote the words and music of "When It's Sleepy Time Down South" (Mills Music, 1932), a piece not introduced by Louis Armstrong but recorded by him that year and, it's said, close to a hundred times thereafter, Armstrong adopting it as his theme song. It has also been said that this homesick lyric is sung from the perspective of a southern black displaced in the North during the Great Migration, but the date of the piece puts it so much at the outer edge of that historical event that I find that notion less than credible. Aside from a slight mention of home and mother at the end, "Sleepy Time" mostly pictures Dixie as the idyllic place the singer wants to be, sometimes in rather tired phrases made effective by the song's haunting melody enlivening such lines as "Pale moon shining on the fields below / Darkies crooning soft and low / . . . Soft winds blowing thru the pinewood trees, / Folks down there live a life of ease," and "Dear Old Southland with its dreamy songs / Takes me back there where I belong . . . / When it's Sleepy time down South." The first recording by Louis Armstrong and his Orchestra, with Armstrong on vocal, was on Okeh in 1931, which may be heard on the Internet.

The last representative homesickness song of the type creating an idyllic vision of the place the singer wants to return to was strictly tied to the time it was written and recorded. "I Wanna Go Back To West Virginia" (Hollywood: Vanguard Songs, 1942), with words by Bill Crago and music by Grace Shannon, is the lament of a draftee in World War II who was taken from his West Virginia country home to fight in the war. There are slight references to wanting to go back to his sweetheart, but mostly the country boy yearns for his idyllic mountainous state: "Where the skies are blue / And the birds sing, too. / . . . Where the fields are filled with clover, / And the mountains reach the sky / Where the flowers bloom all over / Till they make you want to cry." The only references to his military status are oblique: "They took me away from West Virginia / They took me away from my home sweet home," and then much later in the song, "When the world is free, / That's the place for me, / Take me back to West Virginia." Entertainers as diverse as Eddie Cantor and Freddy Martin and his Orchestra performed the song, but the hit record was by Spike Jones and His City Slickers, with a vocal by Del Porter and The Boys in the Back Room. Despite Jones's band accompanying the vocal with its usual goofy instruments from goose-horns and cowbells to washboards and whistles, the song's sincerity comes through, as the recording on the Internet of Jones's 1942 Bluebird disc reveals.

Before I turn to homesickness songs about one's own home and family, three songs don't exactly idealize the South but for the singers emotionally *evoke* the places in Dixie they long to return to. Taking them out of order (thus saving the perennial standard for last), Jack Owens, Ted McMichael, and Leo V. Killon wrote the words and music of "By-U By-O (The Lou'siana Lullaby)" (Hollywood: Owens-Kemp Music, 1941), a tune now largely forgotten but which in 1941 was a Top 10 record on Decca for Woody Herman and His Orchestra with a vocal by Muriel Lane, and was popular enough that other artists such as the three-guys-and-a-gal group The Merry Macs (also on Decca), and Kay Kyser's Orchestra (on Columbia) recorded it too. The words of what is actually an up-tempo lullaby are sketchy at best, on their own offering little by way of a description of an idyllic Louisiana, except for the occasional phrase like, "It's blue, I know, / It makes the weepin' willow cry," referencing the lullaby's melody itself. More often the song's emotional appeal beckons the singer to return: "Southland's callin' / Dixie wants me." But what makes the piece work effectively is the symbiosis of the words and music to create a feeling of Louisiana's bayou country, as can be heard on the one recording of the song on the Internet, that by Kay Kyser's Orchestra, with a vocal by Harry Babbitt with Trudy, Jack, and Max in 1941. Born and raised in Savannah, Johnny Mercer was the one true white son of the Deep South to become a prominent Alleyman. Mercer's homesickness lyrics to "Deep South (In My Heart)" with music by Archie Bleyer and himself (Bolton Music, 1932) are significant for their seemingly personal and genuine sentiments of the kind seen elsewhere only in the words of southern black songwriters who came to the Alley, which are discussed under "Displaced Darkies" at the top of this chapter. Typical lines that sound like Mercer himself speaking are "I'd swap the Gulf Stream / For all that I've won. / Leave the town that gave me my start; / I've got the Deep South / Deep down in my heart."

The legends are legion about how Hoagy Carmichael's "Georgia On My Mind" (Peer International, 1930) came to be, but one thing is sure: the lyrics were written by Stuart Gorrell, who had been Hoagy's roommate and fraternity brother at Indiana University. After writing those lyrics, Gorrell went on to become a financier and never wrote another song in his life. As for how and wherever it happened, all that's certain is that Gorrell and Carmichael were living in New York City when Gorrell heard Hoagy playing the melody of what became "Georgia On My Mind," was inspired to write words to it, and—to drag out a cliché of sorts—the rest is Tin Pan Alley history. Aside from one concrete image—"Georgia, Georgia, a song of you / Comes as sweet and clear as moonlight through the pines"—the remainder of Gorrell's lyric is pure evocative emotion, coaxing the singer to return to his Georgia home. Which brings up the squabbles that have continued ever since the song was written over whether the song is in fact about the state of Georgia or a girl with that name. Well, if anyone took the time to read the line in the verse (or listen to it on the original Mildred Bailey recording) that says, "I'll go back to Georgia 'cause that's where I belong," the argument should be settled in favor of the state once and for all. And the state of Georgia definitely agreed on this point, making "Georgia On My Mind" its official state song in 1979. In 1930 Hoagy Carmichael and His Orchestra with Hoagy singing just the chorus cut the song for Victor as may be heard on the Internet. Mildred Bailey's 1931 Victor recording *with* the verse can be heard on the Internet too.

Alley songs of homesickness for one's own home and/or family go back even farther than those about yearning for an idyllic Dixie more generally if we count Sterling and Von Tilzer's 1899 "Where The Sweet Magnolias Bloom" (see above). After that one piece ten years passed before these more personal homesickness songs began to appear in anything like a steady stream, starting with one by the schmaltz king of the early Alley himself, Charles K. Harris, "'Mid The Blue Grass of Kentucky" (Chicago: Chas. K. Harris, 1909). Harris's first verse is totally home-and-family-centered: "'Mid the blue grass of Kentucky, / 'Tis the place where I was born, / How I long to see the old home once again, / Just to sit around the fireside with the old folks as of yore, / How the thought just fills my aching heart with pain." The second verse switches entirely to the singer's yearning for his sweetheart Genevieve, and so is out of bounds here. Newton Alexander's "New Orleans" (Edgar Selden, 1912) includes a longing for all of that city as "home" but zeros in on the singer's family home in such lines as "If I could lay my head / On my old Southern bed / I'd be contented there / Until the day I die; / Because it's Home, Sweet Home." "Caroline I'm Coming Back To You" (Boston: D. W. Cooper, 1916) had Jack Caddigan's words and music by James McHugh, who likely was the 22-year-old Bostonian who "grew up" to be Alleyman Jimmy McHugh. One image of home is quite specific: "Each day love for home grows stronger, / I see my Pop popping corn / Down there where banjoes were born."

Whatever Caddigan and McHugh may have done in a minor way up in Boston in 1916, that same year in New York established Alley professionals began to hit their stride with the publication of three home-centered Dixie homesickness songs, exhibiting the striving for maturity that would be seen in such pieces over the next two decades. There's no easy way to establish the chronology of their sheet music, so I will treat these songs in the order of their recording sessions and subsequent release to the public as discs or cylinders, the earliest thus being "Down Where The Swanee River Flows" (Broadway Music, 1916), with words by Charles McCarron and Charles S. Alberte and music by Albert Von Tilzer (Harry's younger brother), which Al Jolson recorded on Columbia on February 28, 1916. The persona yearning to return to Dixie could be white, but more probably black given his wanting to see "My little sister Flo,' keepin' time with Uncle Joe, / Singing a song and raggin' on his old banjo." This plus the sentiment "I see my dear old Mother / Oh, Lordy, Lordy, Lordy how I love her" puts home and family squarely at the center of the song's lyric about going back "Down where the Swanee River flows." Jolson, singing the entire first verse and the chorus on a 1916 Columbia recording, may be heard on the Internet. Jack Yellen and Albert Gumble, respectively, wrote the words and music for the other two homesick-for-home songs published in 1916, and Gumble's rousing ragtime melodies for each make these two of the most cheerful homesickness songs to come from the Alley. After some general feelings like "I'm kind o' lonesome for my family," in "Welcome Honey To Your Own Plantation Home" (Jerome H. Remick, 1916), Yellen matches Gumble's tune with deliciously detailed lyrics about the home the singer longs to return to: "Down home a rooster wakes you ev'ry morn / To tell you when it's breakfast time, / You come down stairs and get your buckwheat cakes, / While mammy's makin' / Some eggs and bacon; / And in the ev'ning, / . . . There's a musical treat, / And you shuffle your feet / To a good old ragtime tune." The Peerless Quartet recorded both verses and the chorus for Victor on August 1, 1916, all of which are on the Internet. The scenario in Yellen and Gumble's "How's Every Little Thing In Dixie" (Jerome H. Remick, 1916) is of a southerner who has been up North for some time meeting a friend from his hometown in Tennessee and grilling him about how everyone back there is, in such lines as "How's my Maw? / How's my Paw? / Brother Bill and all the friends I'm longing for?" (Some dour literalist with no sense of fun could ask why the singer doesn't just go home and find out for himself.) Yellen's "Maw" and "Paw" suggest the singer is white, since "Mammy" and "Pappy" were the more usual terms for parents in the mouth of a southern black, but the singer also asks about "Bill Green, long and lean / Who used to play the bones and shake the tambourine," instruments more often associated with darkies than with southern whites. Either way, Yellen's eye for the comforts of home are as specific here as in "Welcome Honey," seen when the singer asks, "How's my dear old mammy? Oh how she could bake / Pumpkin pie and nice delicious angel cake!" The American Quartet (as Premier Quartet) recorded the piece on an Edison Blue Amberol cylinder in 1917, which is on the Internet.

The year 1919 saw the publication of four very varied homesickness songs about one's own home, ranging from a topical novelty number early in the year to one that wasn't recorded until 1920 but, once it was, became what might be considered the be-all and end-all of Dixie homesickness tunes, although such songs didn't literally cease being written until after 1946. In Harry Fox's "There's An Old Oaken Bucket Way Down In Tennessee" (Jerome H. Remick, 1919), the singer is homesick for the well on his family property in Tennessee, and especially for the "old oaken bucket . . . always flowing for me / With sweet liquid melody." What initially seems to be a piece of charming nostalgia turns out to be a song just for its day, prefaced by the lines "And you can take Budweiser / And old Anhäuser / But I'll take that well for mine," and culminating late in the chorus with "If the U. S. A. goes dry / . . . I can always quench my thirst / At that old oaken bucket way down in Sunny Tennessee," referencing the ratification of the 18th Amendment ushering in Prohibition on January 16, 1919. Harry Hamilton's lyrics to "My Swanee Home" (Broadway Music, 1919) are more mainstream than Fox's song, if we consider a certain sub-genre of homesickness songs to be mainstream—those in which the singer virtually wishes to infantilize himself by not just returning to a loving home but retreating to his younger self as a child or infant cared for there. This can be seen in such lines of Hamilton's as "Sweet mem'ries of childhood hours come back to me," "Then ev'ry day was filled with joy for Mammy, Daddy and me," "That's where Mammy sang a slumber song," and "Longing for those olden days when on my Mammy's breast / I heard the song I always loved the best." Such songs of yearning to return to infancy or childhood were not uncommon, although I don't include too many for discussion here. What *was* uncommon was Hamilton's choice of a musical setting for the song; it's not in ragtime nor a two-step, but in waltz-time, as can be heard on the June 3, 1919, Victor recording of the first verse and chorus by Vivian Holt and Lillian Rosedale, which is on the Internet. Ubiquitous lyricists Sam M. Lewis and Joe Young come close to Hamilton's infantilizing, but not quite, in their home-centered "Bless My Swanee River Home" (Waterson, Berlin & Snyder, 1919), with Walter Donaldson's music, in such lines of the dreaming singer as "It's my mammy's sweet caress, / Kind o' guides me there I guess" and "Oh! I could be so cheerful, / With an earful of my Mammy's lullaby." But for most of the song, the singer asks for blessings on his family home in his absence: "Bless that little Dixie shack, / Where the sunshine gleams; / . . . Won't you bless ev'rything that's worth blessing, in my Swanee River Home." The Peerless Quartet cut the song for Victor on November 4, 1919, but it's not on the Internet.

Whatever topical, historical, or aesthetic interest the first three home-and-family-centered homesickness songs of 1919 may have, they were ephemeral successes at best. The fourth was anything but. The story goes that in the summer of that year, 20-year-old composer George Gershwin and 23- or 24-year-old lyricist Irving Caesar were riding on a bus in Manhattan and began sketching out a tune, which they then dashed up to George's apartment to finish, completing the brief song—both verse and chorus—in ten or fifteen minutes. Whether the details of this tale are entirely true or not, they help account for the breezy, impromptu spontaneity of "Swanee" (Harms, 1919), which, once it got into the right singer's hands, was on its way to becoming the most immortal Dixie homesickness song of all. "Swanee" originally appeared in the Broadway revue *Demi-Tasse,* which debuted on October 14, 1919, to herald the opening of a new palatial movie house, the Capitol Theatre. Famed Ziegfeld choreographer Ned Wayburn staged "Swanee" in a mammoth production number for "sixty chorus girls wearing electric lights on their slippers" (Jasen 149), but for all the glitz and glitter, Caesar and Gershwin's song went nowhere. It was only when it was brought to Al Jolson's attention and he interpolated it into *Sinbad* just about in time for the show's national tour that "Swanee" took off like the proverbial shot. Jolson cut "Swanee," verse and all, on January 8, 1920, on a Columbia record that's on the Internet. In 1920 "Swanee" charted for eighteen weeks, as #1 for nine. The sheet music sold over a million copies and the record over two million (see Jasen 149), and no other song in their extensive careers made more money for Jolson, Caesar, or Gershwin. As for the song's homesickness content, it may seem at first that the singer mostly just wants to return to his homeland near the Swanee, but at the heart of the song are his own home and family, as seen in one of Caesar's most clever lines, "I'd give the world to be / Among the folks in D-I-X-I- / E-ven know my Mammy's / Waiting for me, Praying for me / Down by the Swanee," a sentiment reiterated in the brief "trio" section, with "I love the old folks at home."

The unprecedented success of "Swanee" didn't put an end to the writing and performing of Dixie homesickness songs. In fact it may have had the opposite effect, inspiring other Alley writers to write more of them for another decade and a half, perhaps hoping to emulate Gershwin and Caesar's achievement or at least come close, and a few songs, a *very* few songs, almost attained that goal. But to continue looking at representative songs chronologically, regardless of their success, in 1921, 21-year-old Mitchell Parish for his first published lyric wrote the words to the homesick-for-home "Carolina Rolling Stone" (Joe Morris, 1921), with music by the husband-and-wife team of Eleanor Young and Harry D. Squires. It's a lyrical ballad with music in two-four time, and Parish's lyric, though short on warm fuzzy details, is definitely home-centered: "I want to be, / With the folks I call my own, / It seems the fields of snowy white, / Are calling me tonight, / And I can see my dear old Mammy waiting by the window light." Charles Hart and Elliott Shaw cut it for Columbia on January 16, 1922, and it's on the Internet. Also published and recorded in 1921 was the much more upbeat "Kentucky Home" (Jerome H. Remick, 1921), with words and music by Abe Brashen and Harold Weeks, a song with nicely personal home-centered lines about "a dear old gray hair'd mammy" and "those yellow sweet potatoes [that] / Melt like honey in your mouth." Henry Burr with a male quartet recorded "Kentucky Home" on a 1921 Columbia record, which is on the Internet. That same year three writers with longer, more successful careers than Brashen and Weeks— lyricist Bert Kalmar and composers Herman and Harry Ruby—collaborated on "My Sunny Tennessee" (Waterson, Berlin & Snyder, 1921), a homesickness piece with a very catchy tune, as the Peerless Quartet's September 21, 1921, Columbia recording on the Internet reveals. Eddie Cantor introduced and popularized the song in the Shuberts' revue *The Midnight Rounders of 1920,* which ran from July 12 through November 27 of that year, but he seemingly didn't record it. The lyric fuses an idealized Tennessee with images of the singer's own family: "I wanna be in Tennessee in my Dixie paradise / An angel's voice I hear, / I mean my mammy dear." Composers Eleanor Young and Harry D. Squires in 1922 teamed again with lyricist Mitchell Parish, this time on "Rock Me In My Swanee Cradle" (Joe Morris, 1922). Parish's words are perhaps the most overt example of self-infantilizing among Dixie homesick tunes. In the first verse the singer recalls that when he was a child and "used to cry, / Into my cradle I'd creep, / And mammy rocked me to sleep." Now that he's grown "How I miss that little cradle, / And the one who dried my tears." In the second, "in my fancy I stray, / Where first I saw light of day, / I'm a child once more, / Like in days of yore." In the chorus the desire to return to infancy comes out most strongly: "Just rock me in my Swanee cradle, / ... Let me be right near my mammy if you want my eyes to close." The Peerless Quartet cut the first verse and chorus for Victor on April 28, 1922, which are on the Internet.

What the final three songs in this relatively small sampling of Alley numbers about home-centered homesickness for Dixie have in common is that each was a big-selling phonograph record in its day, and each was recorded by at least one major artist, yet only one of them went on to become an all-time standard, mostly in jazz circles. "Swanee Shore" (Jerome H. Remick, 1927), with Cliff Hess's words and Charles Bourne's music, is an upbeat number that's totally about the singer wanting to return to his or her home by the Swanee, rich in homey details not so much in the verse and chorus as in the four stanzas of the lengthy patter section, with such lines as "I can taste the chicken stuff-stuff-stuffin' / As it oozes from the end / ... I can hear my old dog wuff-wuff-wuffin' / When I reach the garden gate," and "Things are peaceful there outside of Pappie's snore." In all, it's a specific, loving picture of home. The legendary Ruth Etting recorded it for Columbia on July 13, 1927, but at this writing it isn't available on the Internet, so we have to settle for a 1927 Brunswick recording of a big band arrangement (which whoever uploaded it on YouTube wrongly credits to George Gershwin) by Ben Bernie's Hotel Roosevelt Orchestra, with an unnamed vocalist singing just the chorus.

As a part of the clutch of Dixie tunes lyricist Mitchell Parish and composer Frank Perkins collaborated on from the early to mid-1930s and which included "Sentimental Gentleman From Georgia" and their classic "Stars Fell On Alabama," there was also the homesickness number "Cabin In The Cotton" (Mills Music, 1932). Lines such as "When I think of ol Virginny and those pickaninny days" indicate the persona singing is black, a supposition borne out by almost the entirety of the song's chorus, with such phrases as "We took the good and we took the evil, / Laughter and song and the ol' boll weevil," and the lines that reference the song's title itself: ". . . wishin' that I only knew / How to wake up in the mornin' in the cabin I was born in, / Little cabin in the cotton, I have not forgotten you." Two very different recordings had considerable success, both in 1932. Cab Calloway and His Orchestra recorded the chorus for Brunswick, with Calloway singing and another unnamed singer performing a kind of obbligato, as can be heard on the Internet. Also, in a more mainstream rendition, Bing Crosby recorded the chorus with Lennie Hayton's Orchestra, also on Brunswick, and also available on the Internet. The final song in this group, Eddie De Lange (words) and Louis Alter's (music) "Do You Know What It Means To Miss New Orleans" (Louis Alter Music Pub. Co., 1946), had its public debut in the 1947 motion picture *New Orleans* in which it was performed by Louis Armstrong and His All-Stars, Billie Holiday, Woody Herman, and Dorothy Patrick. It differs from the other songs in this category since it doesn't focus on the singer's family home, but on New Orleans itself as home, yet without idealizing it, rather just describing it as it is—or, at least, as it was then, since the Big Easy was pretty idyllic without any additional idealizing from the Alley. This quality is illustrated in such lines as having the singer "Miss the moss covered vines, the tall sugar pines," and say how he'd "like to see the lazy Mississippi a-hurryin' into spring. / The moonlight on the bayou, a Creole tune that fills the air . . . magnolias in June." These are all realities, not ideals, of the New Orleans the singer is homesick for, and together with Louis Alter's melody, they make for one of the most lush and lovely of all the Dixie homesickness songs, as can be heard in Louis Armstrong's slightly reworded yet classic rendition on a 1947 Victor recording on the Internet.

Dreaming about one's Dixie home and yearning to return to it is one thing, but getting there is another. Yet with all the homesickness songs Alleymen and women wrote through the decades, they turned out even more about traveling home and also a few about arriving there.

"Alabamy Bound"

If we add the baker's dozen of tunes in which a previously absent singer has actually arrived in the South again to the many more in which a person is still heading there, between 1901 and 1954 Alley songwriters wrote around 225 pieces about traveling home to Dixie. As with the songs about homesickness, I had to ruthlessly cut down to size this unwieldy group of what some have come to call back-to-Dixie songs in order to come up with a manageable yet still representative quantity of them for a comprehensive and illustrative overview of their scope and variety. My final cut left thirty-one songs from between 1909 and 1947, and just a glance at them reveals that back-to-Dixie tunes have much more variety than do homesickness pieces. Some are similar to homesickness songs in having either an idealistic vision of the South or a desire to return to one's home and family at their core, but several of the latter go deeper to look upon home as a sanctuary from an unfair or abusive world. Yet in others the singer has unusually realistic expectations about going home. Some songs range farther afield, especially those describing the activity of traveling home and the ones in the catchall group of novelty songs, often on the humorous side. I still follow my rule not to include songs in which the singer is going home *solely* to be with his girl (except for one novelty song), but I'm more forgiving of songs in which a sweetheart plays a secondary role in the singer's desire to return to Dixie.

Songs with the central motif of an idyllic South are fewer in the back-to-Dixie category than in the homesickness group because such a vision would be more in an absentee's reveries than in the thoughts of someone about to board a train, or already on a train, bound for home—since that view could be easily modified or shattered when the traveler arrives at his destination. Still, four early Alley songs, admirable enough to say something about, concern a person going back to Dixie and suggest the traveler's idyllic vision of the South was a prime motive for doing so. In 1909, "Just For An Orange Blossom," with Ruby L. Hescock's words and Nellie L. Brazer's music (Maurice Shapiro, 1909), sings in the first verse of a boy who rejected the South and left his mother: "I felt no love for Dixie with her fields of cane and corn, / And I longed to leave forever the land where I was born." By the second verse, he has been away for a number of years and become disillusioned, so "Now, I'm going back to Dixie, to my mother gray and old, / . . . Where the sun is ever shining, where the sweet magnolias grow." In the chorus, starting with the title phrase, "Just for an orange blossom, for a glimpse of cotton white; / Just for a sweetheart's greeting, for a mother's smile so bright," the singer concludes he's ". . . going back to Georgia, to her cotton, cane and corn; / For the fairest land and dearest, is the one where I was born." The singer is comparing Georgia's positive values to the negatives he found elsewhere.

In 1912, the Ted Snyder Company published "I Want To Be In Dixie," with words by Irving Berlin and music by Snyder himself, and that same year published precisely the same song under the title "I'm Going Back To Dixie," a mystery I've not yet solved. While the number is mostly an upbeat one about a traveler's eagerness to return by train to his Dixie home, in one line Berlin pictures an idyllic South through comic hyperbole as the place "Where the hens are doggone glad to lay / Scrambled eggs in the new mown hay." Collins and Harlan recorded the tune for Victor the year prior to its publication on November 22, 1911, and it's on the Internet. Also in 1912, a look at the idyllic South similar to "Just For An Orange Blossom" appeared in "I'm Going Back To Old Virginia" with Gene Buck's words and Albert Von Tilzer's music (York Music, 1912). It idealized the state in the title by comparing it to other places; in the verse "There's a certain fascination clings about the old plantation, / And the homestead where you spent your younger days, / Where your pals were on the level in their friendship you would revel, / Where everyone would greet you with a smile. / I have been to Italy, England, Spain, and gay Paree, / But Virginia's got those places beat a mile"; and in the chorus, "Where skies are blue and friends are true, / And ev'rybody treats you as they ought to do."

Last, Douglas Bronston (words) and Rennie Cormack's (music) "I'm Going Back To Alabama In The Spring" (Joe Morris, 1913) has enough descriptive phrases and hyperbole about Alabama to fill two or three songs: From the first verse—"There the sun is shining almost ev'ry day, / And birds are singin' nearly all the time. / That's the greatest place in all this world I know." From the second—"When there's such a Paradise on earth my dear, / Then what's the use of going to Heav'n at all? / . . . I'll never leave that sunny southern clime." And from the chorus—"Alabama that's the state 'what am' a state, / The finest spot I know." 'Nuf said, I think.

In all but one piece from the 'teens and earlier, an idyllic vision of Dixie drove the homeward-bound traveler. The exception was "In Alabama, Dear, With You," with words and music by Ellen Orr and Harry De Costa (M. Witmark, 1915), an up-tempo piece about a boy returning home to his mother in Alabama as a kind of sanctuary, since he discovered up North that "I'm tired of all the life that don't ring true," so "no more I'll roam but stay at home, In Alabama, dear with you!" The Peerless Quartet cut the piece for Victor on September 27, 1915, and it's on the Internet. Starting in the 1920s and '30s, back-to-Dixie tunes regularly featured a singer whose motive force is returning to his or her southern home and/or family. The '20s began with Clarence Gaskill's upbeat traveling-home song, "I've Got The Blues For Old Kentucky" (M. Witmark, 1920). The singer wants to be back with the family and have all the comforts of home. After singing in the chorus, "I long to kiss my Mammy, I miss my Daddy too," s/he gets down to what a Dixie home's all about in the second verse: "I can see them smilin' when they pile in the chicken fricassee. / When my sister Mabel sets the table / She'll fix a place for me, / I'll be in Kentucky, if I'm lucky, / With my family." More of the same is in the patter, like lines about finding an old school chum, Bill, who "now they say . . . owns a little private still." Singing comedienne Aileen Stanley cut the song for Victor in 1920, which is on the Internet.

Successful at the time but little remembered since was yet another song with lyrics by Sam M. Lewis and Joe Young and music by George W. Meyer, "Tuck Me To Sleep In My Old 'Tucky Home" (Irving Berlin, Inc., 1921). The image of wanting to be tucked to sleep in his old home suggests the tune is at least on the fringe of those with the sanctuary motif, viewing home as a haven away from the cruel world the singer has experienced while away. This is borne out by such lines in the chorus as, "I ain't had a bit of rest, / Since I left my Mammy's nest, / I can always rest the best in her lovin' arms." Al Jolson introduced the song, according to Lissauer, without naming the show it was in (Lissauer 877), but the Jolson discography reveals he never recorded it. Still, the song's popularity is suggested by at least three other artists who did, Ernest Hare on Pathé, Billy Jones on Okeh, and Vernon Dalhart with the Criterion Trio on Victor (Lissauer 877), all in 1921, the last of which is on the Internet. Also written, published, and first recorded in 1921 was a ragtime back-to-Dixie song that became what might be called a delayed classic. Lyricist L. Wolfe Gilbert wrote his own music for "Down Yonder" (L. Wolfe Gilbert Music, 1921), so insouciant in its seeming spontaneity that, like Gershwin and Caesar's "Swanee" two years earlier, it looks and sounds as if it could have been dashed off in under twenty minutes, tops. The piece has a forgettable set of two verses no one remembers and no one recorded, so, cutting right to the chorus we find the singer expressing his desire to return to his family home in the opening phrases, "Down yonder someone beckons to me, / Down yonder someone reckons on me," but then his mind embraces his love of Greater Dixie as his home as well: "I seem to see a race in memory / Between the Natchez and the Robert E. Lee / Swanee shore I miss you more and more / Ev'ry day, My mammy land, you're simply grand"; then, at the end he returns to the personal again with "There's daddy and mammy, / There's Ephraim and Sammy, / Waitin' down yonder for me." While the number achieved some temporal popularity when it was written, as on the 1921 Victor recording by the Peerless Quartet, which is on the Internet, "Down Yonder" didn't exactly set the world on fire then. Only thirty years later when female ragtime pianist Del Wood rediscovered and recorded "Down Yonder" as a piano solo selling over a million copies did Wolfie's happy back-to-Dixie tune gain the recognition it deserved. Wood's instrumental was followed in 1951 by a best-selling vocal of the piece by Champ Butler on Columbia, which is on the Internet. Gilbert, who didn't pass away until 1970, was alive to hear his song from thirty years before rise up for a second life and huge popularity.

Such popularity did not await "I'll Be In My Dixie Home Again Tomorrow," with words and music by Roy Turk and J. Russel Robinson (Waterson, Berlin & Snyder, 1922), yet the song is notable for a nice domestic image of where the singer is heading when he says how he'll know he's home again— "When I get a familiar sight, / Of the fuzzy old cat sneakin' from the stable, / Lickin up milk on the kitchen table," and, at the end, for his solution to his eagerness for getting there as soon as possible—"Somehow I just can't wait for a choo-choo train, / I'll hop right in an aeroplane, / And be in my Dixie home again tomorrow." Of the small group of songs in which the traveler has reached his desired destination, the only one worth mentioning is the jaunty "I'm Sitting Pretty In A Pretty Little City," with words and music by Lou Davis, Abel Baer, and Henry Santly (M. Witmark, 1923). After a verse that simply says, "There's no place like home, you never learn that till you roam," in the chorus the returned traveler tells the world how happy he is to be back home, the gist of his feelings summed up in the lines, "I'm sittin' pretty in a pretty little city down Georgia way / There are no angels near, / But it seems like heaven here." Arguably the best recording was by Irving Kaufman with Ben Selvin's Orchestra on Vocalion in 1923, and it's on the Internet. For Brunswick on November 19, 1924, Al Jolson cut "Hello, 'Tucky" with words by B. G. De Sylva and music by Joseph Meyer and James F. Hanley (Harms, 1924), well before he introduced the tune at the Winter Garden on January 7, 1925, in the show *Big Boy*. That recording of the entire song, including the verse, is on the Internet. The verse is the most important part of the tune since it makes the point, "Like all Kentucky boys, / Longing for city joys, / I left the farm and started to roam," but then "Like all Kentucky boys, / Sick of all city noise / I heard Kentucky calling me home," setting up the lyrics of the chorus—sketchy as they are—to vent the singer's feelings about Kentucky as a sort of sanctuary from the rest of the world: "I'm glad I went a-straying / To get the kick of saying 'Hello, 'Tucky, Hello.'"

In 1926 Jo' Trent wrote the words and Peter De Rose and Harry Richman the music of the popular "Muddy Water (A Mississippi Moan)" (Broadway Music, 1926), which Richman himself featured on stage and popularized through his own recording of it on Brunswick in 1926, as may be heard on the Internet. It's impossible to tell from Trent's lyric whether the song is about the literal geographic area in the northwest corner of Mississippi between the Mississippi and Yazoo Rivers called the Mississippi Delta, or what people familiarly refer to as the Mississippi River Delta at the mouth of Ol' Man River where it empties into the Gulf of Mexico. Personally I would go with the latter since the surrounding land is the muddier of the two places, even though when in the verse the singer says he's "Headin' home-bound just once more, / To my Mississippi delta," the phrase is ambiguous. Wherever he's going, his home turf is sloshy, but in the singer's eyes and mind it's a welcome sanctuary, as the chorus repeatedly proclaims: "Muddy water 'round my feet / Muddy water in the street / Just God's own shelter down on the delta / Muddy water in my shoes / Rockin' to those low down blues / They live in ease and comfort there, I declare. / . . . I don't care it's muddy there, but still it's my home / . . . My heart cries out for muddy water." Speaking of crying, "Cryin' For The Carolines" (Remick Music Corp., 1930), with words by Sam M. Lewis (here credited without the "M.") and Joe Young and music by the fabled Harry Warren, is one of the most gut-wrenching lyrics by this pair in their vast corpus of Dixie tunes, as the singer virtually wails about how New York City life nearly destroyed him (or her) and how he (or she) is seeking refuge and sanctuary back in the Carolines. I put the feminines in parentheses above because of Belle Baker's brilliant 1930 Brunswick record of the piece in which she wrings every nuance of painful emotion from Lewis and Young's words and Warren's music, as may be heard on the Internet. From the first verse's lines, "Big town you lured me / Big town you cured me . . . / I'm leavin' but I'll never sigh for you / Big town you robbed me of every joy I knew," through the patter's virtual wail, "Lord did you ever hear of Broadway / . . . Good Lord no you've never heard of Broadway / That's the place, that's the place where the sinners go," the entire song expresses the theme of the soul-killing effects of big-city life, especially in New York City. This is contrasted throughout by the contrapuntal theme of the Carolinas as a soul-healing sanctuary: "Small town you gave me all that I'll ever get." Lewis and Young's masterfully constructed lyric is flawed only by placing the Swanee River in the Carolinas, perhaps necessary to contrast it with wicked New York's Hudson in the patter, since no actual river in North or South Carolina would have been familiar enough for audience recognition. The last notable back-to-Dixie song with at least an implication of the sanctuary motif was "In The Hills Of Tennessee" (Southern Music, 1932), with words by Sam M. Lewis going solo and music by Ira Schuster. The lyrics are beautifully crafted—with the singer apostrophizing to a "Sycamore tree," which apparently was right in saying he never should have roamed from home in Tennessee. The scenario is the familiar one of the boy who left for adventure coming to realize, after hard knocks in the real world, that there's no place like home, and is now returning, in words that suggest home as shelter and sanctuary: "I know I'm goin' to find my Paradise lost IN THE HILLS OF TENNESSEE. / I know I'm goin' to find my Seventh Heaven, / It's just a cabin, my Seventh Heaven." This song by two established Alleymen was published by Ralph Peer's Southern Music Company, a firm noted primarily for publishing blues and country (then often called hillbilly) music, and the lead recording was by the very popular early country singer, who died much too young, Jimmie Rodgers. What we have, then, is an early crossover tune between the Alley and country music, long before Nashville was even a glimmer in Roy Acuff's eye. Jimmie Rodgers's 1932 Victor record is on the Internet.

For all the songs the Alley produced about southbound travelers anticipating returning to the embrace of home and family, whether as a sanctuary from the rest of the world or not, a few maverick tunes (from which I've chosen four) appeared in which the singer had more realistic expectations of what to find or even goals for going back at all. In the second verse of Billy Johnson's "I Am Going Back To My Georgia Home" (T. B. Harms, 1901), the homeward-bound singer muses, "I am going back to see / If there's one to welcome me, / To greet me as she did long years ago; / . . . As the dear old home draws near, / I have but one thought of fear, / That one sweet face is missing from the scene. / If my mother old and gray, in the church-yard's laid away, I am going home to see her grave's kept green." Perhaps a bit morbid for a popular song, but still the thoughts of a dutiful son home to stay. Eleven years later, "I'm Going To Take The First Train (Back To See My Folks In Sunny Tennessee)," with words and music by Norma Gray and Jack Coogan (Chicago: Will Rossiter, 1912), was a cheerful tune that took a wry swipe at homecoming Dixie songs in which the wandering boy is met by the hometown band, the mayor, and a parade. This singer isn't even rushing home: "No matter if the train is late, / If passenger or freight / I don't care as long as I get there, / . . . I don't expect a band, just a friendly hand, / Or a voice to say, 'We're glad to welcome you today.' / My Pa' and Ma' and all our friends and neighbors will be waiting there for me / Gee! I'm satisfied to live and die in Tennessee."

"We'll Have A Jubilee In My Old Kentucky Home" (Waterson, Berlin & Snyder, 1915), with words by Coleman Goetz and music by Walter Donaldson, is a realistic, nonhyperbolic paean to the simple joys of southern living, sung by a man returning to "A quaint old bungalow / Where sweet magnolias grow," but one where there's no sign of any family members or even a sweetheart. Apparently, this fellow has returned to settle down in "a good old southern town" with only some darky hired help, as seen in the lines, "You can have your high-brow airs, / Just give me three good squares with the corn and 'lasses, served by Rastus." In the second verse, the singer also seems content to be a gentleman farmer in a small way: "I'll ramble here and there, / And never have a care / I'll have some pigs in pens, / Also some laying hens, / That lay by fives and tens." The inimitable Billy Murray with a chorus cut the tune on a 1915 Edison Blue Amberol cylinder, which is on the Internet. Yet of all the travelers roamin' home for whatever reason, the noblest roamin' of them all (I couldn't resist that) has to be the singer of "I'm Gonna Make Hay While The Sun Shines in Virginia" (Kalmar, Puck & Abrahams, 1916), with words by (in this order on the sheet music) Joe Young and Sam Lewis and music by Archie Gottler. Given the usual meaning of the phrase in the song's title of taking advantage of an opportunity, the title is misleading, since Young and Lewis's lyric employs the expression literally to refer to the altruistic motive of the homeward-bound traveler to help his ageing parents tend their farm in Virginia, and attend to them too, rather than go home out of personal motives: "I'm gonna make hay while the sun shines in Virginia, / The old folks need a lot of sunshine now, / I'm gonna be a farmer in Virginia / I'll plant a kiss on mother's wrinkled brow / (How I love her) / I'm gonna raise the mortgage from the homestead / I'll weed out all their sorrows and their tears / . . . I'm gonna brighten up their few remaining years." Marion Harris featured "I'm Gonna Make Hay" in vaudeville and cut it for Victor on August 31, 1916, as may be heard on the Internet.

Like virtually all Alley songs labeled novelty numbers, those in the back-to-Dixie group have only two things in common: they don't easily fit into any other sub-groups of traveling-home songs, and the best of them (and I believe I have selected five of the best) are eminently entertaining, as the name "novelty number" implies. The earliest one, "There's A Lump Of Sugar Down In Dixie" (Jerome H. Remick, 1918), with Alfred Bryan and Jack Yellen's words and Albert Gumble's music, shouldn't even be here since the entire piece violates my "no sweetheart songs" rule for homesickness and traveling-home songs, with the singer wanting to go south strictly to see his or her sweetie in a lyric riddled with sticky sweet comparisons like "Sweeter than the honey to the bee" and "that little lollypop of mine." What makes the piece a novelty number is a time-bound topical reference, first allusively in the opening lines of the first verse, "Sugar! Sugar! / Ev'rybody's cryin' / 'Cause it's mighty scarce up here / Buy it! / Try it! / Just go out to buy it / And you'll find it's mighty dear," and then very directly in the last lines of the first chorus, "She's a gal that Mister Hoover ought to meet / Puts her finger in the pie to make it sweet." The lyric wryly comments on the sugar shortage in America and President Wilson's appointment of Herbert Hoover as U.S. food administrator shortly after the country entered the Great War in 1917. Although sugar was never rationed, as it would be during World War II, Hoover encouraged the public to conserve this preciously scarce commodity. Even though Al Jolson cut the song for Columbia, Marion Harris's June 18, 1918, Victor recording was the best seller, a record that is on the Internet. The unique back-to-Dixie motive of the protagonist in "Ten Little Fingers and Ten Little Toes (Down In Tennessee)" (Leo Feist, 1921), with words by Harry Pease and music by Ira Schuster and Ed. G. Nelson, may be briefly summarized. The singer has an unspecified job—perhaps as a traveling salesman—away from his home in Tennessee, but he has just gotten word that his wife has given birth to their first child, and so, rather than continue working on the road, "At Home Sweet Home I'll linger for they'll need me there I know / . . . For I've got ten little fingers, and ten little toes, Waiting down in Tennessee for me." Billy Murray and Ed Smalle recorded the tune for Victor, on August 19, 1921, and it's on the Internet. Equally brief can be the summary of the rather hilarious "Seven Or Eleven (My Dixie Pair O' Dice)" (Shapiro, Bernstein, 1923), with Lew Brown's words and Walter Donaldson's music. The premise is simple. Up North a black guy named Rufus Johnson keeps going to the railway station to shoot craps with the porters to bankroll enough dough to buy a ticket to "see my Mammy, / Down in sunny Alabammy." He perpetually loses but keeps coming back for more in his goal to "be on my merry way back to Heaven, / With my Dixie Pair O' Dice." In the sheet music he's a serial loser, but in added lyrics on Margaret Young's 1923 Brunswick record Rufus finally wins and is on his way home to Dixie, as heard on the Internet.

Vaudeville performances and records often don't include the verses of songs. Yet the verse of "There Ain't No Land Like Dixieland To Me" (Leo Feist, 1927)—one of the few tunes for which Walter Donaldson wrote both music *and* words—categorizes the piece as a novelty number, and without that verse one line in the chorus makes little sense. Only Jane Gray's (pseud. of Peggy English) 1927 Harmony record with just piano accompaniment contains the silly verse, as may be heard on the Internet. That verse speaks for itself: "Rufus Lindbergh Chamberlain Johnson Jefferson Washington Lee, / Was a colored aviator man, / Rufus Lindbergh Chamberlain Johnson Jefferson Washington Lee, / Was flying high to Dixieland. / He didn't need a compass nor a radio, / He didn't need a navigator to tell him where to go, / Rufus Lindberg Chamberlain Johnson Jefferson Washington Lee, / Just shouted 'I know where I am.'" After which the chorus is just a typical "doesn't Dixie look wonderful" thing, yet with some delightful comic touches like "Doesn't that smell like ham and eggs? / No, that smells like bacon and eggs. / Bacon and eggs and ham and eggs," followed by those lines that make little sense without the verse, "Oh, Gee! / Mister Lindbergh made Paree, / But I made God's own Heaven you see, / And there ain't no land like Dixieland to me." Looking at this humorous tune seriously for a bit, Donaldson's piece is about another black thrilled to be back in the South. For the last of our small selection of back-to-Dixie novelty tunes we must jump twenty years ahead to a song that debuted in the Bing Crosby and Bob Hope film *The Road to Rio* and then became a 1947 Decca record featuring the Andrews Sisters and Crosby, and it's on the Internet. The song is "Apalachicola, Fla." (Burke and Van Heusen, Inc., 1947), with words by Johnny Burke and music by James Van Heusen. The premise of this bit of hilarity isn't so much that the singers are heading back to the place in the title because it's heaven on earth, but because every place else they've been is so much worse: "I never liked the frankfurters they served in Hamburg, Ark. / And Devil's Lake, N. D. is simply N. G. after dark. / . . . On Penobscot Bay it gets so cold you need a fur hat, / The Androscoggin River's even colder than that"—and that's just the tip of the iceberg of Burke's lyric of undesirable locales making the singers rush back to Apalachicola, Fla.

To conclude this chapter I have chosen eight examples from one of the largest and longest-lasting groups of back-to-Dixie songs—those about travelers still in transit, usually but not always by train, to get back home in the South, and this group produced more than its fair share of hits. The first such song to make a splash was Irving Berlin's "When The Midnight Choo-Choo Leaves For Alabam'" (Waterson, Berlin & Snyder, 1912), the piece I glanced at without mentioning it by title under the "Displaced Darkies" section above, and which Charles Hamm tried to show was at the nucleus of some songwriting abetting a political movement to get blacks to go back from the North to Dixie where they belonged. The problems with Hamm's thesis are that he fills half of page 93 of his book on Berlin's early songs with wasted words, faulty evidence, and specious arguments in a failed attempt to prove that the protagonist of the tune is in fact black—which he decidedly is *not*.

For example, Hamm maintains, "A white person would hardly use the term 'choo-choo' or 'Alabam'," and yet in "Alabamy Bound" (1925) the singer, who is surely white since he can't wait "To put my tootsies in an upper berth" of an all-white segregated Pullman sleeper, uses both of those terms, and one or the other is continually used by white personae in Dixie tunes right down to "Alabam'" in "Tuxedo Junction" in 1940 and "Chattanooga Choo Choo" the following year. Hamm further asserts that only a black would "grab a conductor by the collar and 'holler' at him," conveniently leaving out Berlin's qualifier "rusty-haired" before conductor, suggesting the trainman is a red-headed Irish-American as so many were, and only another white would hug a conductor and holler, "Alabam! Alabam!" with glee. Had the song's protagonist hugged a Pullman porter, dining car waiter, or baggage handler (porter, Red Cap), all of whom were invariably black, it might argue for him being black himself, but a black passenger hugging a white conductor would have been unthinkable. And as for the singer's taking the midnight train because it would be cheaper as further evidence that he's black, well, that's just nonsense and shows Hamm didn't know his history. If the singer were indeed black, he would have had to travel in one of the all-black "Jim Crow" coach cars at the rear of the train, where the fares were the same all day and night regardless of the departure time. Stephen J. Whitfield summarizes all this very neatly when he writes that "musicologist Charles Hamm detects the possibility of something sinister, 'hegemonic' advice from Tin Pan Alley's newcomers to job-seeking blacks to get back home. . . . But since Berlin's narrator has to be white, such an interpretation makes no sense; and nothing in the lyric hints at Alabama's alternative economic opportunities" (Whitfield 18). Besides, my own examination of the words of all of Berlin's eleven back-to-Dixie songs out of his corpus of nineteen Dixie tunes *in toto* shows that the protagonist or narrator of each of the other ten is demonstrably white, so why should the singer of "Midnight Choo-Choo" be otherwise? With the race issue hopefully settled once and for all, the song *as* a song makes a joyful noise about the pleasures of traveling home to Alabama and the happiness to be found there: "I'm goin' to overfeed my face, / 'Cause I haven't had a good meal since the day I went away. / I'm goin' to kiss my Pa and Ma / A dozen times for ev'ry star." Yet to be fair to Hamm, if he knew "Midnight Choo-Choo" less from the sheet music than from Collins and Harlan's November 5, 1912, cut on Victor, which is on the Internet, singing with their usual comic darky accents whether a piece called for them or not, one may see why Hamm decided the traveler was black even though all textual evidence argues against it.

There's nothing controversial about "All Aboard For Dixie Land" (J. Fred Helf, 1913; transferred to Jerome H. Remick in 1914), the traveling-back-south tune that gave its title to this chapter. It's all good fun in Jack Yellen's lyric and George L. Cobb's ragtime turkey trot melody when the singer, who could be either black or white but probably the latter, is excited to be going home to New Orleans by steamboat: "My baggage is waitin' / My heart syncopatin', / Now I hope there'll be no hesitatin' / I'm all excited, / I'm so delighted; / Feelin' like a clown, / 'Cause I'm Dixie boun'." Waggish twenty-one-year-old Polish-Jewish immigrant Yellen even slipped a slyly incongruous Yiddish-Americanism into the lyric for the sake of a rhyme: "That's the side-wheeler, / My homesickness healer, / Just hear that darky spieler cry! / Dixie! All aboard the boat for Dixie, Dixie!" Ada Jones with the Peerless Quartet cut the tune, a popular success in its day, for Columbia in 1914, as did the American Quartet featuring Billy Murray for Victor on January 13 that same year. Both discs are on the Internet. "Make That Engine Stop At Louisville" (Geo. W. Meyer Music, 1914), with Sam M. Lewis's words and George W. Meyer's music, though not a commercial success, is entertaining. So eager to see his folks, the singer boards a train that doesn't stop at Louisville. He goes through goofy antics to get the engineer to drop him off at his home town: "Can't you stop at Louisville on this here line / . . . Oh mister make this engine stop at Louisville / Don't you take me too far / I'll get off and walk if you stand still / There's my Ma and my Pa." In one of the funniest lines, the singer wails, "Mammy will be waiting for me I suppose / She'll be saying 'here he comes and there he goes.'"

"Dixie Highway" (Jerome H. Remick, 1922), with lyrics by the great Gus Kahn and music by the equally eminent Walter Donaldson, is a rare song in which the homeward-bound traveler is heading south by automobile. In fact most of the number is a paean to the singer's "Ford sedan," about which we learn in the second verse, "Ten more payments and it's mine." But for now all the singer wants to make sure of is that his car (or hers, in the case of Aileen Stanley's sprightly recording) is in good enough shape to get him/her down to Dixie, as the patter section declares: "My little flivver is a real good friend / All you have to give her is a twist and a bend / She isn't worth a nickel but I bet By Gee / She'll bring a million dollars worth of smiles to me / Needs new tires front and rear / The horn won't speak to the steering gear / A little lopsided / Lamps don't light / But outside of that ev'rything's all right." In the chorus the singer philosophically proclaims, "I'll bless each rattle in my flivver / Each little knock / When I ride beside that Swanee River / I reckon All my cares will fly 'way / When I'm wending my way / Down the Dixie Highway." Aileen Stanley's cute 1922 Victor record of this very cute song is on the Internet. Eddie Cantor introduced the perennially popular "Alabamy Bound" (Shapiro, Bernstein, 1925), with words by Bud De Sylva and Bud Green and music by Ray Henderson, as an interpolation in the musical *Kid Boots.* Cantor performed most of this show uncharacteristically in whiteface, but didn't record "Alabamy Bound" at the time. As noted while discussing "Midnight Choo-Choo," the southward-bound traveler in "Alabamy Bound" is demonstrably white, since he's looking forward to sleeping in the upper berth of a Pullman car, which was reserved for white passengers only. As for the rest of the lyric, the singer is simply thrilled to be on a "choo-choo" going back to where "I'll be in clover soon," and the whole song simply bursts with his excitement to "Hear that feller yelling 'Alabam' / Mammy, Mammy, / Get your kisses ready for yo' honey lamb." Blossom Seeley's jazzy 1925 Columbia recording, which included the verse and patter and which popularized the number, may be heard on the Internet. Three years after "Alabamy Bound," a bit of fluff appeared called "I'm Gonna Charleston Back To Charleston" (Jerome H. Remick, 1925), with words and music by Roy Turk and Lou Handman. It capitalized on the current dance craze as a fanciful, if preposterous, way to travel back to Dixie—which is the only reason it's worth mentioning. The song's rhythm and music are those of a typical Charleston dance tune, and its lyrics are the singer's rejoicing, "I'm gonna Charleston back to my old shack in Charleston Charleston / Hang my hat upon the rack in Charleston Charleston / I'm so full of joy today I could Charleston all the way / Till I land in someone's empty arms." The piece was written as a dance tune, yet it still proclaims Dixie to be a more desirable place to be than anywhere else. It gained some popularity thanks to the 1925 Victor disc by the Coon-Sanders Original Nighthawk Orchestra, with vocal by drummer Carleton Coon and pianist Joe Sanders; it's on the Internet in all its Roaring Twenties glory.

"Roll On, Mississippi, Roll On" (Shapiro, Bernstein, 1931), with words and music by Eugene West, James McCaffrey, and Dave Ringle, is an odd piece in a couple of ways. First, it seems rather late in time for a popular song (not one from a stage or film musical) to have been written, recorded, and achieved considerable success, that was about traveling to one's southern home by paddlewheel steamboat. Second, it's unusual since the singer is traveling not from the North to a home in Dixie but upriver from New Orleans to home in Memphis, Tennessee. The main lyric consists of little more than the singer urging the boat to go as fast as it can: "Come on you lazy steamer, move on," until "I'll be with the folks I adore," but the patter catalogues the towns the boat passes on its way upstream: "New Orleans, Hello, / Bye-bye, New Orleans, / Gettin' long, goin' strong, / Baton Rouge so long, / Say, Captain, tell me, what's the next big town we'll see? / I'm so excited, I forget my geography." Of several recordings, the Boswell Sisters with their unique jazz styling had the biggest hit for Brunswick in 1931, and it's on the Internet. From a twenty-first-century perspective, the first two lines of Mack Gordon's otherwise masterful words for the classic traveling-home number "Chattanooga Choo Choo" (Leo Feist, 1941), with Harry Warren's music, have racist overtones. But if we put the lines "Pardon me boy is that the Chattanooga Choo-choo / Track twenty nine, / Boy you can gimme a shine" in historical perspective (without necessarily forgiving them), they make it absolutely clear that the traveler singing the song is white. Otherwise, Gordon's lyric is the most detailed one about train travel back to the South, with lines like "Dinner in the diner, nothing could be finer than to have your ham'n eggs in Carolina." And his description of the Chattanooga-bound traveler being met by "a certain party at the station / Satin and lace, / I used to call funny face" is refreshingly original. It's probably a toss-up between two tunes with music by Harry Warren, Gordon's "Chattanooga Choo Choo" and "On The Atchison, Topeka, and the Santa Fe," with Johnny Mercer's lyrics (which has nothing to do with Dixie), for the best American railroad song ever. Glenn Miller and His Orchestra with vocal by Tex Beneke and The Modernaires immortalized "Chattanooga Choo Choo" on a 1941 Bluebird record, as may be heard on the Internet.

Looking back at the types of songs covered in this chapter—from those about blacks displaced in the North yearning for the South again and those about the homesickness of whites *or* blacks, to southerners longing to be with Mammy once again, and then the more active tunes of people heading from the North back to Dixie—only a mere handful of the more than 440 such Alley songs were touched on here. Yet it should be apparent that a single thread runs through all of them, no matter how low-lying it may be. Quite simply, the lyricists of these songs, through the voices of the tunes' protagonists or narrators, glorified or idealized Dixie as a desired and desirable place to go home to. Why else would so many people want to go there? With so many songs written on this theme over such a long span of years, these pieces in many ways form the nucleus of the myth of an idyllic, glorified, romantic Dixie in the popular imagination of Americans during the first half of the twentieth century.

8

GLORIFYING DIXIE
Southern Myths and Southern Pride

According to some of the best authorities, ever since there was a section of America that could be called "the South," southerners have been mythmakers— or, if not makers of myths themselves, then embracers of myths their myth-making compatriots made. For southerners more than people elsewhere past and present, reality and myth have been inextricably bound together. In *Myth, Media, and the Southern Mind,* Stephen A. Smith quotes historian T. Harry Williams saying of southern folk that "more poignantly than other Americans, they realize that the past impinges on the present, and more often than their fellows in other sections they relate the present to something in the past" (qtd. in Smith 5). George B. Tindall wrote in *The Ethnic Southerners* that "myths have a life of their own which to some degree renders irrelevant the question of their correlations to empirical fact. . . . we may say that social myths in general, including those of the South, are simply mental pictures that portray the pattern of what a people think they are (or ought to be) or what somebody else thinks they are. They tend to develop abstract ideas in more or less concrete and dramatic terms" (Tindall 23). Charles P. Roland suggested, "The ultimate distinctiveness of the South may lie, not in empirical dissimilarities from other regions, but in its unique mythology: those images of the region that give philosophical meaning to the ordinary facts of life" (qtd. in Smith 97). In *Southern Folk, Plain and Fancy,* John Shelton Reed points to the longevity of southern myths after any practical function they may have served: "If Americans have been willing to make do with the hand-me-downs of the plantation myth despite its diminishing *cognitive* usefulness (its diminishing utility, that is, as summary description of the Southern reality), these antebellum types must have something else to offer Southerners and non-Southerners alike" (65).

Before turning to the myths Tin Pan Alley disseminated or may have partially created about Dixie, we need to examine the three primary myths southerners developed about the South and its people in at least broad over-view: in the nineteenth century, the antebellum Plantation or Old South Myth and the postbellum Lost Cause Myth; and, in the twentieth, the varieties of the Agrarian Myth that were developed by and flourished among some intelli-gentsia loosely associated with Vanderbilt University around 1930. "Of all the mind-pictures created by the romantic Southerner," wrote T. Harry Williams, "the greatest, the most appealing, and the most enduring is the legend of the Old South" (qtd. in Smith 44). This legend or myth is unique in that those who created or embraced it—the antebellum southern planter aristocracy—lived the myth contemporaneously with the reality in which they lived their lives, trying to make those lives conform to the particulars of the myth as much as possible. Most scholars agree that the Plantation Myth had its ori-gins in the consciousness of educated antebellum southerners in the chivalric novels of Sir Walter Scott, sets of which might be "found leather-bound in ev-ery cultured household" (*1001 Things* Item #912). Of the dramatis personae in Scott's novels, in the Plantation Myth such a figure as the Cavalier gentle-man became a planter, and the damsel of a castle a Southern Belle (see Smith 14). Scott's code of chivalry in novels like *Ivanhoe* was transformed into some-thing peculiarly southern too, as Mary Boykin Chesnut noted in her diary: "For us, soon as one defamatory word is [uttered] pistols come at once to the fore. That is South Carolina ethics" (qtd. in *1001 Things* Item #914). Smith quotes Clement Eaton's summary of the Old South Myth, which is useful for defining the antebellum South and distinguishing it from the North: "It is to the aristocracy—the country gentlemen of the South that one must look for the most marked differences between North and South. They cherished a set of values that were different from those of the North" (14). This myth was of a *romantic* South, and expressions of it contained many images associated with the moonlight and magnolias vision of Dixie that carried over into the twentieth century, especially in its popular songwriting.

The Lost Cause Myth began to take shape after Lee surrendered to Grant at Appomattox Court House in 1865—or at least from the time of the 1866 publication of Edward Alfred Pollard's history of the war titled *The Lost Cause.* The myth developed and expanded its contents and influence chiefly during Reconstruction as a way to soothe southerners' pain after the Con-federacy's loss to the Union army. In content the Lost Cause Myth is similar to the Old South Myth (including images of moonlight and magnolias). Its rearward-turning hindsight makes it different. Rather than try to describe the Lost Cause and its effects on postbellum southern society, I'll let the words of two scholars in the field do it for me. First, Stephen A. Smith in *Myth, Media, and the Southern Mind* (1985): "Performing a remarkable rhetorical feat, the South reconstructed the antebellum myth of the Old South and embellished it to accommodate immediate psychological needs. The myth of the Lost Cause allowed Southerners to reaffirm the alleged superiority of their culture by declaring that it had indeed been an antebellum golden age of chivalrous gentlemen planters, magnolia-scented ladies, and plantation mansions. With the passage of time, it became easy to believe that the entire South had once conformed to the representation of the old myth and the rhetorical symbols became even more powerful" (Smith 21–22). Nina Silber in *The Romance of Reunion* (1993) expands upon Smith's description of the myth and its functions even more broadly and deeply: "In the post–Civil War period, former Confederates learned to accept their loss by turning the old South into a land of idyllic plantation settings, heroic men, and elegant women. They transformed the system of slavery into a happy and mutually beneficial arrangement which offered enjoyment and contentment to all of its participants. In short, an army of southern novelists, journalists, and dramatists assumed command of a far-reaching campaign which resuscitated many antebellum stereotypes and deployed a romantic image of the white and wealthy antebellum South throughout the cultural landscape. In creating this 'lost cause' ideology, they provided white southerners with an emotional vehicle that had profound religious, psychological, and social functions—functions that were especially suited for a society that suffered from defeat, humiliation, and internal dissension" (Silber 4–5). To Silber's listing of "novelists, journalists, and dramatists," John Shelton Reed and Dale Volberg Reed added, in the dissemination of the "cult" of the Lost Cause, painters and engravers of numerous popular prints of Confederate war heroes, writers and speakers of sermons based on the Lost Cause, and a legion of minor poets glorifying the fallen of the Confederacy (see *1001 Things* Items #332–#339). According to Waldo W. Braden, the Lost Cause Myth captured the hearts and imagination of southerners during Reconstruction because they found "the present unbearable and the future unpromising, [so they] retreated to that romantic past and preferred to live in fantasy" (qtd. in Smith 21).

Unlike the Plantation (Old South) Myth and the Lost Cause Myth, each developed and refined over time by anonymous southerners before and after the Civil War, respectively, the Agrarian Myth (or, as we shall see, myths) was the deliberate creation of twelve southern literati and intelligentsia all somehow connected to Vanderbilt University in Nashville. Thus, the name Vanderbilt Agrarians has come to be attached to the group, along with Nashville Agrarians, Tennessee Agrarians, Southern Agrarians, The Twelve, and, as Stephen A. Smith called them with wry humor while discussing their ideas, "typewriter Agrarians" (Smith 32). The twelve Vanderbilt Agrarians were an impressive lot: in alphabetical order, Donald Davidson, John Gould Fletcher, Henry Blue Kline, Lyle H. Lanier, Andrew Nelson Lytle, Herman Clarence Nixon, Frank Lawrence Owsley, John Crowe Ransom, Allen Tate, John Donald Wade, Robert Penn Warren, and Stark Young. In 1930, they published a collection of essays as their manifesto titled *I'll Take My Stand: The South and the Agrarian Tradition.* It's easier to say what the Agrarians were against than what they were for; to a man they opposed the business-progressive view of the South that had been growing during the first decades of the twentieth century, perceiving what they saw as urbanism and industrialism harming southern culture and tradition. John Crowe Ransom actually claimed that industrialism "is capable of doing more devastation than was wrought when Sherman marched to the sea" (qtd. in Smith 32). According to Smith, the aggregate of the Agrarians believed "The myths of the Old South and the Lost Cause were still prominent and powerful forces in Southern life and thought," and "They idealized the antebellum planter aristocracy or squirearchy" (32). Smith sees the Agrarians' thinking as alike as twelve black-eyed peas in a pod on combating industrialism in the South by returning to an agriculture-based society modeled on the Old South Myth (minus slavery, of course).

Yet John Shelton Reed points out there were key differences among The Twelve as to what past model the present South should emulate: "Some of them—Stark Young, John Donald Wade—were peddling the moonlight and magnolias or Old South Myth version of the South, but others—e. g., Andrew Lytle, Frank Owsley—were trading in a sort of yeoman farmer, plainfolk myth that is something quite different. They never really confronted the fact that they were defending different Souths" (Reed e-mail to the author, September 22, 2012). Whichever version any one of the Agrarians was hawking, he never got many takers, unlike the majority of literate southerners buying successively into the Old South or Lost Cause Myth; "neither did [the Agrarian Myth] capture the popular imagination of a national audience" (Smith 33).

Smith's final remark is especially telling for our purposes. The *cerebral* arguments in *I'll Take My Stand* against industrializing the South and for returning to a lifestyle similar to the agrarian past never caught on in the public imagination, but during more than thirty years before that manifesto was published, Tin Pan Alley songwriters wrote and its publishers published roughly 878 songs whose underlying theme is implicitly—and in some of those songs, overtly—the Moonlight and Magnolias Myth of the South. The songs conveyed that myth not cerebrally but emotionally through evocative lyrics and melody, regardless of what the stated topic of a given song may have been, whether celebrating a barbecue or describing the prowess of a womanizing scamp. And, too, within the Alley's Moonlight and Magnolias Myth, and especially in its many songs about homesickness and traveling home, is a very evident vision of a pastoral, bucolic, or in other words *agrarian* South. Its success in Dixie tunes can be attributed to its *emotional* appeal to audiences, rather than the dry, intellectual approach attempted by the Vanderbilt Agrarians, which failed. This modern implementation of the Moonlight and Magnolias Myth from imagery that had begun in the Old South and Lost Cause Myths—but with the antebellum chivalric elements weeded out of it—was the gradual, unconscious creation of numerous (and mostly *northern*) Alley lyricists over decades. They, in the aggregate, shaped the idyllic picture of *contemporary* Dixie as an ideal never-never land of endlessly sunny, cloudless days and equally cloudless moonlit nights, of lush foliage and fragrant flowers (not to mention cotton, sugar cane, and corn), of lovely Southern Belles, of happy darkies singing or humming in the background, and, at the center of it all, in nearly half the songs, of Home—a warm and loving family home in the songs about homesickness for Dixie or actually traveling back there again, whether that home be a grand plantation house, a cozy bungalow, a cabin, or a shack. To repeat and emphasize a point, in most of the songs all this describes a mythic South contemporary with when each piece was written and published, not a backward-looking or nostalgic glance at the unrecoverable past. After the Vanderbilt Agrarians wrote their manifesto, the Alley produced another two hundred such songs right up to 1958. This is the southern myth that is at least the subtext of nearly all the Dixie tunes we have glanced at so far and which comes to the fore as the main thrust of songs directly glorifying the South in Chapter 9, only preceded by some groups of tunes on topics or themes about aspects of Dixie myth and Dixie pride we'll examine here.

"And They Called It Dixieland"

The two great nineteenth-century southern myths—the Old South Myth and the Lost Cause Myth—each developed a wide-reaching picture of an ideal planter aristocracy-based society in the South, but the Old South Myth, aside from some perfunctory digging into the English chivalric and Cavalier myths, as expressed in Sir Walter Scott's novels, never offered a creation myth for that world. It was Tin Pan Alley, well into the twentieth century, that came up with a creation myth for Dixie—in fact, over the ensuing decades, not just one embracing a creation myth for the whole South but others for the creation of some of its parts, people, and aspects of its music. The Alley's Dixie was not the squirearchy of the Old South and Lost Cause Myths, but the South of the lush, lovely, and melodic myth of moonlight and magnolias. For the one myth covering the creation of *all* of the South, lyricist Raymond Egan and composer Richard A. Whiting partnered on a song titled on the sheet music "And They Called It Dixieland" (Jerome H. Remick, 1916) and on the recording "They Made It Twice As Nice As Paradise." In the tune a man recalls what his Mammy told him about Dixie's origin when he was a little boy: "She said the angels built old Dixie and I know that's not a fib, / For to me it looks like heaven / And I'll tell you what the angels did." The chorus details the angels' creation of this idyllic South: "They built a little garden for the rose / And they called it Dixieland, / They built a summer breeze to keep the snows / Far away from Dixieland / . . . Nothing was forgotten in the land of cotton, / From the clover to the honeycomb / . . . They made it twice as nice as Paradise, / And they called it Dixieland." Geoffrey O'Hara, who in 1918 wrote the World War I hit "K-K-K-Katy," on May 2, 1916, recorded "Twice As Nice" for Victor, and it's on the Internet.

After a fifteen-year hiatus, starting in 1931 the first of three songs appeared celebrating the creation of more specific people or places that were indelible parts of Dixie. "That's Why Darkies Were Born" (De Sylva, Brown and Henderson, Inc., 1931), with Lew Brown's words and Ray Henderson's music, is a piece that has made some modern commentators a bit squeamish, embarrassed that it ever really happened. One such case is the anonymous soul who wrote the Wikipedia entry on the song. This Wikipedist maintains, "The song was written as a satirical view of racism," yet even in the lines he quotes from it there is nothing at all satiric, racist, or even ironic. To the contrary, I have always felt that to appreciate this song on its own terms, we must keep in mind that in the 1930s "darkies" was not pejorative, but used as it is throughout this book and not as a racist slur like coon or nigger. Instead, it simply refers in an absolutely neutral way to African Americans or blacks, primarily in the South. Accordingly, I see the song as a straightforward account of, if not the myth of *how* darkies were born, then at least of the *reason* for their birth as the title maintains. But to be sure my thinking on this point was historically accurate I decided to get a second opinion and so e-mailed Philip Furia, who in turn put me in touch with popular music authority Michael Lasser, Phil's coauthor of *America's Songs* (Routledge, 2006) and the host of public radio's *Fascinatin' Rhythm: Songs from the Great American Songbook*, who, Phil said, is more conversant with "the historical context" of songs than he himself is. Happily, when Michael Lasser replied to me, he confirmed my interpretation of the song, writing, "I agree with your take on 'That's Why Darkies Were Born.' I think I have a decent ear for irony but I've always thought of the song as straightforward. I went back and listened to Everett Marshall's recording because Marshall sang it originally in *George White's Scandals of 1931.* I found it melodramatic but without a trace of satire. And nobody ever accused Kate Smith of having a gift for irony, especially about blacks. She was a southerner of her time—to the bone. So, for what it's worth, I'd say you're on the right track with it" (Lasser e-mail to the author, October 2, 2012). Looking carefully at Lew Brown's lyric, which no one seems to have done, I would say the song is more than just straightforward; it even borders on being an expression of black (or darky) racial pride, especially in a moment in the verse when the singer declares, "What must be must be! / Though the balance is wrong, Still your faith must be strong" and, late in the chorus, "Sing! Sing! Sing when you're weary and sing when you're blue, / Sing! Sing! That's what you taught all the white folks to do." This certainly sounds more like pride than satire to me. The great socially conscious black singer/actor Paul Robeson recorded the song, which he would not have done if he saw in it anything racially satiric. After Kate Smith cut it for Columbia on October

28, 1931, her recording became the top-seller. Her powerful delivery, which is on the Internet, should dispel any notion that the song is racist.

Irving Kahal wasn't one of the Alley's most prolific lyricists, but he was one of its most poetic, as seen in his 1938 song with music by Sammy Fain, "I'll Be Seeing You," which only gained real popularity in 1944 and became forever inseparably associated with World War II. Kahal's same poetic gift is seen in his lyric to "That's How Virginia Began" (Words and Music, Inc., 1936), with Oscar Levant's music, a number that never achieved much popular success but is still a charming mythical tale of how some birds, flowers, and trees got together to create Virginia. One is tempted to quote Kahal's whole lyric, but fair use laws being what they are, that's impossible, so a few excerpts will have to suffice: "A flock of song birds were traveling south, / In a winter caravan, / Said the thrush to the lark; / 'Here's the place where we park,' / THAT'S HOW VIRGINIA BEGAN / A nest of flowers were looking around / For an easy living plan, / Said the gay daffodils, / 'There is sun in them hills,' / AND THAT'S HOW VIRGINIA BEGAN." And on the song goes, through the lonesome pine trees, to the birth of the Blue Ridge Mountains, and the northern and southern breezes coming "to rest where they blended best," creating Virginia's temperate clime. In the early 1950s, near the end of the Alley's long, fertile history of creating all kinds of Dixie tunes, the last song about the creation myth of a particular spot on the southern map was written, recorded, and became a Top 40 popular hit. "Mobile" (Ardmore Music, 1953), with words and music by Bob Wells and David Holt, purports to sketch out the mythic origins of that Gulf Coast Alabama city and simultaneously idealize it. To hit just a few high points of the lyric, "They saw a swallow building his nest, / I guess they figured he knew best, so they built a town around him and they called it Mobile / . . . Pretty soon the town had grown 'til they had a slide trombone and a man who played piano and a swallow who sang soprano." Julius La Rosa made the hit recording of "Mobile" for Cadence Records in September 1954, which is on the Internet. It's telling that this last Dixie creation myth from the Alley used musical examples to explain the origins of Mobile, since between 1924 and 1940 Alleymen wrote at least five songs about creation myths showing how kinds or aspects of Dixie music came to be, thus illustrating how deeply music is rooted in southern life.

The African American team of Noble Sissle and Eubie Blake wrote for their 1924 all-black Broadway musical *The Chocolate Dandies* a piece called

"Dixie Moon" (Harms, 1924). The verse purports to show how the beginnings of southern darky music were influenced by the southern moon: "Our melodies in minor keys were first originated under the Dixie Moon / Those melodies in minor keys were first syncopated under the Dixie Moon / There's a rhythm swinging with 'em, that makes life seem dearer, under the Dixie Moon / Swinging with 'em, in that rhythm, makes paradise seem nearer under the Dixie moon." Far more famous is B. G. De Sylva and Lew Brown (words) and Ray Henderson's (music) "The Birth Of The Blues" (Harms, 1926), which debuted in *George White's Scandals of 1926* sung by Harry Richman, who also recorded the immediate hit and soon-to-be-classic for Vocalion in 1926, in, to modern ears, a strangely up-tempo rendition; it's on the Internet. The lyric's specificity of the elements that "some darkies long ago" mythically combined to create the blues is extraordinary, starting in the verse with how, lacking instruments, these folks "only had the rhythm / So they started swaying to and fro, / They didn't know just what to use." The refrain then catalogues what they cobbled together into the blues, beginning with, "They heard the breeze in the trees / Singing weird melodies / And they made that / The start of the blues," going on to an anguished convict's cry and "From a whippoorwill / Out on a hill, / They took a new note, / Pushed it through a horn / 'Til it was worn / Into a blue note," till finally "the Southland gave birth to the blues!" The song charted at #4 in its day and is the one enduring piece about the mythic origins of any aspect of Dixie.

Like their fellow black Alleymen Noble Sissle and Eubie Blake, neither lyricist Andy Razaf nor composer/pianist Thomas (Fats) Waller was born in the South, but one of their collaborations, "How Jazz Was Born" (Harms, 1928) concerned the mythic origin of jazz in Dixie. To abbreviate the story a bit, "One night in Dixieland / They say a colored band / Once started raisin' sand / With a simple 'two-four' strain / When old Napoleon Bone / Laughed in his saxophone, / Brought out a low down tone, Sounded like he'd gone insane. / . . . This started the fun and soon everybody got hot . . . / As they played 'off-beat' / . . . Now you know how jazz was born." Lyricists George Whiting and Nat Schwartz and composer J. C. Johnson in "That's How Rhythm Was Born" (San Francisco: Sherman, Clay, 1933) sang of how, mythically, the South didn't give birth just to the blues and jazz but to a fundamental element of both—rhythm. According to the myth in their song, it all came about because of what happened at darkies' outdoor revival meetings: "Down South the banjos all cry to, / Deep blues the darkies Hi, Hi to, / While the moonbeams dance on the bayou, / That's how rhythm was born. / They praised the mighty forgiver, / They washed their sins in the river, / Cold water made them all quiver, / That's how rhythm was born." So, mythically, the shivering of the soaking wet darkies accounts for setting the rhythms characteristic of the blues, jazz, and other Dixie song-types. The Boswell Sisters cut a successful vocal-jazz arrangement of the piece for Brunswick in 1933, which is on the Internet. The last Dixie musical myth to come from the Alley was "Rhythm On The River" from the Paramount Picture of the same name (Famous Music, 1940), with Johnny Burke's words and James V. Monaco's music. The verse, not sung in the film nor on either major recording, claims the chorus is an attempt to explain "the meaning of swing," yet the lyric reads more like a brief discourse on swing music's origin, not its meaning: "When you hear a real hep cat / Take a chorus in B. flat, / It's the rhythm on the river / You know what that means, / He comes from New Orleans," and so on, with further references to origins of swing on Basin Street, until the number concludes with "In New York or any town / When a band swings out low down, / It's the rhythm on the river / Not the Hudson, Bud, Just the Mississippi mud." In the film, Bing Crosby sang the number in a pawnshop accompanied by New Orleans–born trumpeter Wingy Manone and other musicians. Then Crosby and Manone each cut his own recording of "Rhythm On The River," and each was a success at the time, with Manone on his record not only playing a mean trumpet but his singing sounding rather like a white Louis Armstrong. On the Internet, Crosby is on a 1940 Decca disc and Manone on a 1940 Bluebird one. The fact that over several decades Alleymen wrote more songs about mythic origins of southern music than the creation of other aspects of Dixie suggests how strongly their imaginations associated music with their vision of a South that was not only idyllic but also uniquely creative.

Spinning Yarns

Following an age-old American—and, especially, southern American—tradition or pastime, a few, indeed very few, Alleymen told tall tales, recounted lore, or otherwise spun yarns about Dixie folk heroes real, mythical, or purely imagined in the minds of those who wrote the songs. In my gathering of Dixie tunes, I found only four such pieces, three very early and one very late, but all of them entertaining and recorded by popular entertainers of their times, with most of the tunes achieving some degree of popularity. "Dixie Dan" (Maurice Shapiro, 1907), with Will D. Cobb's words and Seymour Furth's music, is a cheerfully fanciful tale with an infectious melody recounting the almost miraculous birth and later career of a southern darky minstrel. Sung as a first-person narrative, Dixie Dan declares, "I saw the light on a Monday morn, / And they called me 'Dixie Dan.' / In an old burnt stump of an old burnt tree, / The doctor he discovered me, / And my mammy shook her sides with glee, / And she called me 'Dixie Dan.'" Dan explains that when he grew up he fell for a gal "with cork-screw hair" named Trixie Ann, but lost her since "I must have been slow, / When I let her go, / A traveling round with a minstrel show." Happily, in the second verse, he spies her in the audience of one of his shows, invites her to come to the stage door afterwards, and, presumably, the two live happily ever after in this charming tale of love found, lost, and found again. In the chorus, Dan describes his personal attributes, "Coal-black color all except my teeth, / With a loving disposition underneath," and declares his undying love for "the girl I left behind." The vaudeville and musical comedy star Blanche Ring made "Dixie Dan" the hit of the 1907 Broadway show *The Gay White Way*, but I find no evidence she recorded the tune. Still, two popular recording artists of the day did—Billy Murray and Arthur Collins, though each sings only the first verse and chorus on his recording. Murray's version, on a 1908 Edison record on the Internet, is well sung, but Collins appropriately employs the darky accent that became his trademark in duets with Byron G. Harlan, as heard on his 1907 Albany Indestructible cylinder, also on the Internet.

Earle C. Jones's "The Mississippi Stoker" (Jos. W. Stern, 1907) is a pun-laden yarn spun by the title character about himself and various not-so-seafaring relatives in four verses and choruses, each one sillier than the last. The piece has no plot but instead is a series of brief tall tales or flat-out jokes, and to make sure the singer or reader of the sheet music got all the outrageous puns and gags, Jones put every one of them within quotation marks. In the first stanza, for example, the stoker tells of how he was descended from a dubiously seafaring family, though he just stokes coal on a Mississippi river packet: "All my people liked the water, but they took it 'on the side,' / And my Uncle Hezekiah used to go upon a 'tide.' / Once he went into a tavern just to get a strong cigar. / And unloaded forty 'schooners' that were standing on the 'bar.'" Starting with the second verse, the gags get even more outlandish: "Once my brother threw a poker deck into the kitchen fire, / 'Cause I said that he was cheating, and he was an awful liar, / But I grabbed 'em out and stamped 'em 'till I had the blaze in check, / That is why I'm called the 'Boy who stood upon the burning deck.'" In November 1906, the great black vaudevillian Bert Williams recorded for Columbia the first stanza and parts of the second and fourth, plus ad libs about him dancing during the musical breaks, all of which are on the Internet.

Unlike the anecdotal structure of "The Mississippi Stoker," the darkly humorous tall tale of "Steamboat Bill" (F. A. Mills, 1910), with words by Ren Shields (author of "In The Good Old Summer Time") and music by Bert and Frank Leighton (who introduced "Steamboat Bill" in vaudeville), had a hilariously bizarre linear plot throughout its three verses and choruses. In the first verse we learn that ship's pilot Steamboat Bill commanded "the Whipperwill" [sic], a steamboat on the Mississippi River, and that "The owners gave him orders on the strict Q. T., to try to beat the record of the 'Robert E. Lee.'" In the second stanza a "gambling man from Louisville" enters the scene, trying to "get a bet against the Whipperwill." Billy flashes a big bankroll, the overheated boiler explodes, and both Bill and the gambler are blown straight up vertically from the wreck, the gambler saying, "I don't know where we're going but we're neck in neck [sic]." Bill then bets the gambler that he'll go higher than the gambling man. In the third stanza things settle down as the river is "in mourning now for Steamboat Bill," and his wife receives a telegram letting her know he died. In what is arguably the funniest line of the song, "She says to the children, 'Bless each honey lamb, the next papa that you have will be a railroad man.'" There's a discrepancy between one line in the final chorus as printed in the sheet music and as Arthur Collins sings it on the record. The published text reads "Steamboat Bill, missing on the Mississippi, Steamboat Bill, is with an angel band," but on the disc the second phrase is "Steamboat Bill, he's living in Japan," making no sense since the last line is "He's a pilot on a ferry in that Promised Land." Collins's 1911 Victor "Steamboat Bill" is on the Internet.

Since I found only these three tunes, songs of Dixie yarns and tall tales apparently fell out of fashion with Alleymen and their hearers after the first decade of the twentieth century, only to resurface for one spectacularly successful moment over forty years later. That occurred when a Walt Disney TV miniseries, followed by a film put together from the series' episodes, gave birth to "The Ballad of Davy Crockett" (Walt Disney Music Company, 1954), with words by Tom Blackburn and music by George Bruns. While lacking the whimsical or outright belly-laughing qualities of the Alley's earlier tall tales, "Davy Crockett" retained some aspects of their outlandish storytelling, as in the song's well-known first verse: "Born on a mountain top in Tennessee, / Greenest state in the Land of the Free, / Raised in the woods so's he knew ev'ry tree, kilt him a b'ar when he was only three." Fess Parker (Davy on TV and in the movie), Tennessee Ernie Ford, and Bill Hayes all cut records, with Hayes's the biggest seller, topping *Billboard*'s charts for five weeks. One may hear his 1955 Cadence recording on the Internet.

Reflections on the River

"Don't keep moanin', / Grumblin' an' groanin', / 'Bout Old Man River no more; / Hush that prayin', / Mumblin' an' sayin', / Ol' River stay way from my door. / Lis'en believe it or not, / That river's the best friend I've got." This first verse of "Mississippi River (Keep On Croonin')" (Edward B. Marks, 1932), with Frank Abbott's words and music by the great black composer J. Rosamond Johnson, is important as an explicit statement of a long trend in songs about the Mississippi. If not perhaps in reality, then at least in the imagination of Alleymen, the Mississippi River reached mythic proportions in the hearts and minds of those southerners who lived near its banks. Songwriters wrote around a dozen songs between 1914 and 1951 about these Dixie folks' devotion to and kind feelings toward the River despite its sometimes turbulent, even destructive behavior. The earliest Alley song to sing lovingly, if briefly, of the Mississippi was "The Good Ship Mary Ann" (Jerome H. Remick, 1914), with words by Gus Kahn and music by Grace Le Bow, which, in the sheet music, is about a southern darky girl waiting on a pier for the steamboat *Mary Ann* to bring her boyfriend home safely to her. Near the end of the chorus she sings, "Bless the captain, bless that crew, / Bless the dear old Mississippi, too! / For bringing back my lovin' man." The piece had an odd genesis from sheet music to recording by singing star Nora Bayes (nee Jewish Eleanor Goldberg), who yanked the piece out of Dixie, sang it with an Irish brogue, and changed "Mississippi" to "Atlantic Ocean" and "lovin' man" to "Pat McCann." I feel her rendition does violence to a perfectly good Dixie tune, but Bayes's Irish-American January 22, 1914, rendering of "Mary Ann" on Victor is on the Internet.

For the 1914 play with music *Pretty Mrs. Smith,* Billy Gould wrote words that can best be described as cute and Belle Ashlyn penned a sprightly 2/4 time march melody for the delightful "Mrs. Sippi, You're A Grand Old Girl!" (Leo Feist, 1914). As the title proclaims, the song is an unqualified paean to the River, and, in the second verse, to Mrs. Sippi's tributary daughter Miss Ouri too. (It seems "her husband Mister Sippi, / Well, he had to take a trip, he has to live far out at sea," and that's all we learn about him.) The verses are full of such whimsy, while the chorus gets down to the singer's feelings about the River: "Oh! you Missis Sippi, grand old lady, / Oh! you Missis Sippi, cool and shady, / Oh! you Missis Sippi, when you thunder; / Even when you blunder, ev'rybody knows that you're a wonder. / Oh! you Missis Sippi, grand old missy, / It's music to my ears to hear and see you whirl and twirl, / . . . Missis Sippi, you're a grand old girl." Ada Jones and Billy Murray's October 20, 1914, Victor recording captures all the fun of the piece and is on the Internet. "See Those Mississippi Steam-Boats On Parade" (Jerome H. Remick, 1916), with Joe Kelsey's words and ragtime composer and pianist Charley Straight's music, is a nostalgia piece in which the Mississippi is secondary, as the lyrics imagine the remaining paddlewheelers "with all their beauty" along with their "Gray haired captains still on duty" reunited for a parade on the River's waters somewhere in Dixie, and, as in the old days, crowds of white folks and darkies on the banks cheering them on.

Uncharacteristically for a Dixie tune, "Mississippi Ripples" (Shapiro, Bernstein, 1922), with words and music by James F. Hanley and Mary Earl (pseud. of Robert A. King), is a waltz with quite a lovely melody but very pedestrian lyrics. The singer sings of his lingering attachment to the Mississippi River, however far from it he may wander. The first verse simply states that he was "born along the Mississippi" and no matter where he is, memory takes him back there again. In the chorus he declares, "Mississippi, rippling on your way / Mississippi / I miss you more each day / In my dreaming / Stars are gleaming / On you beaming / Mississippi ripples, ripple on forever / Mississippi ripples, ripple on." And that's it. The song's rather banal words may explain why all the recordings of it I found on the Internet were instrumentals by dance bands of the day, such as that cut on December 12, 1923, by the International Novelty Orchestra conducted by Nathaniel Shilkret for Victor. Quite different from "Mississippi Ripples," a wonderfully moving piece describing the singer's lasting attachment to the river was "Mississippi (Here I Am)" (Chicago: Grossman-Lewis Music, 1928), with Bernie Grossman's words and Arthur Sizemore's music. The singer lets his feelings be known right from the first verse's opening: "I miss the river, / My 'Sippi river, / I long to see it flow, I used to watch it night and morn, / A rollin' by where I was born, / . . . Old feet please tote me down that way, / To that river shore I'll say; [in the chorus] MISSISSIPPI / Here I am, Won't you float me on your bosom to the levee, / I'm a wearied tired lamb, / And my heart's bowed down / My burden's growing heavy." His lament continues in this vein to the final phrase in which he beseeches the river, "Won't you take me home or take your child to heaven." Grossman's powerful lyric of the weary traveler's attachment to the Mississippi is matched by Sizemore's lyrical melody, especially as the first verse and chorus are sung by an artist known only as Creole Crooner, with just steel guitar accompaniment on a 1929 Columbia disc that is on the Internet. In the hands of a dance band on the brink near the end of the Jazz Age, the song has a different, and inauthentic, ring to it, heard in the fox trot arrangement on a 1929 Supertone Record by Carl Fenton and His Orchestra with an unnamed male vocalist singing just the chorus, likewise on the Internet. Also in 1928 two established Alleymen wrote a *comic* tune about the strong hold the Mississippi has on the imagination of southerners—well, on *some* southerners. "What'll I Do If The Mississippi Goes Dry" (A. J. Stasny Music, 1928), with words by Harry Pease and music by Ed G. Nelson, tells of Lovesick Al, a not-too-bright darky who's afraid he might lose his girlfriend since he took it literally when "what my sweetie told me gave me a scare, / She told me she'd love me, / As long as that river was there; / I got worries, I could cry, / 'Cause what'll I do if the Mississippi goes dry?" Some of this silliness is on the 1928 Edison Diamond Disc cut by B. A. Rolfe and His Palais D'Or Orchestra with vocal by Theo Alban, which is on the Internet.

The next two songs about how much the Mississippi was a part of the lives of Dixie folks were written for Hollywood films. "Father Mississippi" (Leo Feist, 1929) was the theme song for Universal Pictures' *The Mississippi Gambler.* Harry Akst wrote the music, and the lyrics were one of the weaker efforts of the usually clever, witty, or at the very least sweetly sentimental L. Wolfe

Gilbert. About the best one can say for his words to "Father Mississippi" is that they are serviceable in sketching out the singer's ambivalent feelings toward the ambiguously moody river: "I fear ya, / When I'm near ya, / Still I'm sad when I roam, / I hear ya, always hear ya, / You keep callin' me home." After a very brief verse, three choruses are filled repetitiously with such thoughts. The grande dame of Alleywomen, Anne Caldwell, and composer Harry Tierney wrote "Mr. & Mrs. Sippi" (Harms, 1930)—a considerably better piece—for the 1930 RKO Radio Pictures' musical *Dixiana* starring Bebe Daniels and Everett Marshall. This number should not to be confused with "Mister and Mississippi" from 1951, the final song in this section. In the earliest days of the Alley, Caldwell was one of very few women lyricists, primarily writing lyrics and librettos for Broadway shows with music by Jerome Kern through the mid-1920s, and afterwards with such composers as Vincent Youmans, Dave Stamper, Raymond Hubbell, Otto Harbach, and Harry Tierney, tunesmith of the song we're dealing with here. When it was founded in 1914, Caldwell became a charter member of ASCAP. Both in Caldwell's words and Tierney's music, "Mr. & Mrs. Sippi" is an operatic-sounding piece in which a Dixie black sings of how his life is bound up with that of the Mississippi River in the South, and, specifically, in Louisiana, as the opening line of the verse makes evident: "Black water flow along, carry me on / Over the lonely bayou!" The refrain is the heartfelt lament of the singer estranged from his beloved river: "Mister and Missis Sippi, / I miss you so, I'se just dippy. / One day you're so level and mild / As you flow down to the sea; / Next day you'se a devil, too wild for a pore black child like me." Despite those ambivalent feelings, "When I'se beside you I'm happy / Because I was born by you; I'se part o' you, / The heart o' you." Everett Marshall on the Internet sings the song from the film, in the apparent absence of a commercial recording of the piece, and while it is a powerful vocal performance, it is—to me—also problematic. In the film Marshall, a white actor, played the son of a plantation owner who falls in love with a circus performer played by Bebe Daniels (also white, of course), a relationship his family opposes. Why Marshall's character sings this number at all, and with an authentic black—not comic darky—dialect is a mystery.

During the Great Depression, hard times befell Americans in all regions, including those in Dixie, which may have had something to do with the fact that between 1931 and 1939 Alley songs expressing southerners' feelings for the Mississippi were all entirely positive, viewing the river as a constant source of comfort, stability, and sustenance, with none displaying even a shred of ambivalence in the singer or more than the slightest reference to the river's turbulent and destructive side. Just as Frank Abbott's 1932 lyrics to the verse of "Mississippi River (Keep on Croonin')," which opened this section, explicitly admonished against badmouthing the Mississippi, his words in the chorus comprise one of the most detailed expressions of positive feelings for the river in song: "I was raised on your bosom in the good old days, / While you kept on croonin' to me. / Right down your river on my lucky day, / My gal came sailin' / Said she'd come to stay; That was years ago my sweetest memory, / . . . You helped to grow 'taters cott'n an' corn. / Fed me with fishes, / Since the day I was born." From the 1936 20th Century-Fox Production *Banjo on my Knee* starring Barbara Stanwyck and Joel McCrea, Harold Adamson (words) and Jimmy McHugh's (music) "Where The Lazy River Goes By" (Robbins Music, 1936) is a love song, pure and simple, but one in which a tranquil Mississippi is very much front and center: "Ev'rybody knows that it's just a muddy river / But it seems like Heaven on High / When the moon is shining bright, let me dream away the night / Where The Lazy River Goes By / . . . Everything is still all along the Mississippi / Ain't no one as happy as I / Oh I never want to roam let me live and make my home / Where The Lazy River Goes By." Ray Noble and His American Orchestra, with a vocal by Al Bowlly, made a properly lyrical recording of this lyrical ballad in 1936 for Victor, which is on the Internet. Still, the Swing Era was then in full swing, and Phil Harris and His Orchestra, with Harris doing his own vocal, cut a swing rendition of the number the same year on Vocalion; it's also on the Internet. Late in the Great Depression years' songs about the river, "Shanty Boat On The Mississippi" (Shapiro, Bernstein, 1939), with words and music by Jimmy Eaton, Harry Carroll, and Terry Shand, depicted the Mississippi as providing a total safe haven from life's uncertainties despite its own occasional turbulence, which is mentioned in the second verse. Thanks to living on his shanty boat, the singer has not only found a way to avoid laboring for a living—"I think I'd be crazy / To work and slave all day / As long as there's a hungry catfish in the stream," and "No hay to mow, no corn to hoe / Never gonna work no more"—but his water-borne life protects him from other of life's exigencies as well: "Sit and laugh at the bill collector / Snoopin' round my door / Ain't scared of him, 'cause he can't swim / Never gonna pay no more." Louis

Armstrong and His Orchestra, with Armstrong on vocal, recorded the number for Decca in June 1939, which is on the Internet.

The last song extolling the Mississippi or praising it for giving the singer attributes similar to its own was a latecomer, Irving Gordon's "Mister and Mississippi" (Shapiro, Bernstein, 1951). Written in the form of a repetitive four-stanza folk ballad, the piece tells how the river was the only mother and father the singer ever had, and how it—or people on it, like a riverboat gambler—taught him everything he learned about life and love. Yet unlike the earlier songs about the Mississippi, some things the river taught the singer were not terribly admirable. For example, from the river's continual shifting and flowing he learned in the song's concluding verse to be unable to settle down himself: "I'd love a tiny village / A quiet country town / A house, a little garden / With kiddies running 'round / I'd be a faithful husband / I'd be a trusting friend / Until I heard that steamboat / Comin' round the bend." Hardly the kind of morally uplifting life lesson one wants to be left with, yet "Mister and Mississippi" was the most popular of all the tunes in this mini-genre of songs about the River, with discs by Patti Page, Dennis Day, and Tennessee Ernie Ford scoring high on *Billboard*'s Charts. All versions combined peaked at #6 in *Cash Box* for 1951. Perhaps the best, Dennis Day's on RCA Victor, is on the Internet.

"You Can't Take Dixie From Me"

Those words from the subtitle of Roger Lewis (lyrics) and Fred Rose's (music) "You Can Take Me Away From Dixie (But You Can't Take Dixie From Me)" (Hearst Music Pub., 1923) encapsulate Alleymen's view of southerners' pride in and love for Dixie or the individual states that comprise it. Fifteen songs written and published between 1904 and 1938 embraced this theme. Just over half of those songs praised an individual state rather than all of Dixie; Virginia and Kentucky tied at three, and Carolina followed with two. We'll begin with these eight pieces, reserving discussion of the tunes about pride in the entire South for the end of this section. Unlike songs about Dixie myths, very few about Dixie pride had much commercial success. The reason can't be the subject matter since it falls within the moonlight and magnolias theme that had audience appeal during this entire period. One must look to the quality of Dixie pride songs for their general lack of success. Some were as well crafted as other Dixie tunes, but others show that some of the Alley's brightest didn't put their best efforts into writing them.

D. A. Barrackman's very early "Virginia" (American Advance Music Co., 1904) simultaneously trumpets aloud the singer's pride in his home state and his love for his girlfriend with the same name: "For the State I love most dearly, Virginia! / She's the home of cultured statesmen, great gen'rals known to fame, / And has cradled many Presidents as well / There I first met my dear sweetheart and learn'd to love her name, / For her name it is Virginia, Virginia!" That's just in the verse. The chorus is packed with similar puffery for the Old Dominion and the singer's girl: "Dear old Virginia, home of my birth, / Home of our fathers, no fairer on earth; / Home of my sweetheart tender and true, / Dear old Virginia, Virginia!" My research turned up nothing to indicate whether Barrackman was a Virginian himself, a southerner of any other sort, or merely an Alleyman of dubious talent wanting to capitalize on the northern sentimental feelings about Dixie prevalent at the turn of the century and for some years thereafter. My guess is he was the last of these. The writer of the next song expressing pride in a southern state is as famous as Barrackman is obscure—George M. Cohan. For his 1906 musical *George Washington, Jr.,* Cohan wrote the tune "I Was Born In Virginia" for Ethel Levey, the actress who played opposite himself (and who was Cohan's wife), but it was so associated with her that it became known and was actually published as "Ethel Levey's Virginia Song" (F. A. Mills, 1906). After the verse establishes the singer was "born in a Southern state, / Where all nature's sublime," the chorus is braggadocio about Virginia: "I was born in Virginia / That's the state that will win yer / If you've got a soul in yer; / Ain't no Southern frown / In the city of Norfolk, / Home of beauties and war talk. / Reckon you'll like it, / If you should strike it, / That doggarn town." Typical Cohan bravado, even when someone else in one of his shows sings it.

Grant Clarke was an Alley lyricist who deserves to be better remembered than he is, not just as a prolific writer who lived a mere forty years and two days, but also as one who developed a distinctive writing style all his own. Clarke penned numerous hits in nearly every popular genre from comic novelty numbers like "Ragtime Cowboy Joe" to lovers' laments and ballads like "Am I Blue?" and "Second Hand Rose," while also turning out the words for fifteen Dixie tunes between 1914 and 1929. As mentioned earlier, in nearly all of his lyrics, Clarke found ways to sneak in something quirky, ambiguous, unexpected, and yet, upon reflection, entirely in keeping with the rest of the piece. This is perhaps no better seen than in his contribution to songs about love for southern states. "Back To The Carolina You Love" (Waterson, Berlin & Snyder, 1914), with music by Jean Schwartz, is a piece in which opposites play off one another as a boy laments his girl, Carolina, has married another man, at the same time he still loves the state bearing her name. In the verses (here the second), the boy sings of himself in the third person: "Carolina broke his heart / When she wouldn't wait / Tho' he must forget the girl / He remembers the State / Ev'ry year he loves to go / Down where the roses grow / Once he said 'I love her so / But I'm a little too late.'" One can almost see Clarke's mind being attracted to opposites in virtually every other line. Clarke's ambiguous kicker comes at the end when the singer switches to the first person: "And still I seem to hear her say, / 'Will you be back, / Will you be back to the Carolina you love.'" Al Jolson cut the song for Victor in 1914, changing the verse to first person and the final "Will you be back" to the more pleading "Won't you come back." A hit, charted at #2 in January 1915, it is on the Internet.

In 1917 Jerome H. Remick & Co. published a song taking pride in a southern state titled "You-All Got To Be Born And Bred In Kentucky." The premise is that one must be born there to really know the state and sing about it properly. That motif would have had some authenticity to it had the words been by Alleyman Haven Gillespie, who was born in Covington, Kentucky, but he didn't write the piece. While the lyrics ring with sincerity to unsuspecting listeners, some of the actual lyricist's Alley pals probably appreciated the inside joke behind the song, since the real writer of its words was no Kentuckian at all, but Gus Kahn, who first saw the light of day in Coblenz, Germany! Kahn emigrated from there with his family to the States at the age of five— but not to Kentucky, to Chicago, where right out of high school he began his long, illustrious songwriting career. By the time he wrote this Kentucky tune, he had married its composer, Grace Le Boy, who had previously written the music for several of Kahn's hits; this piece wasn't one. As for the song itself, the opening lines of the first verse sound like a description of the actual Tin Pan Alley: "Every day or two I hear a new Kentucky ditty / Written by someone who spent his life in Kansas City. / Folks write about it but what can they know / When they've never been south of Buffalo." After saying such people can't really appreciate the state, in the chorus the singer declares you have to be born there "to know what Kentucky means / You've got to feel the thrills of those Blue Grass Hills / Breathe the air the sunshine kisses there. / And then you'll sigh for, cry for, die for Kentucky, / You'll give your good right eye for Kentucky." Regardless of where he was born, Kahn could passionately express pride in and love for the state.

In 1921 Lew Pollack wrote a novelty spinoff of African American James A. Bland's 1878 classic "Carry Me Back To Old Virginny" in "They'll Never Carry Me Back To Old Virginia (Virginia's My Home)" (M. Witmark, 1921). The singer, a died-in-the-wool Virginian, declares he'll never have to be carried back to Virginia because "That's where I reside." And he's darn proud *of* it. Usually snappy lyricist B. G. (Buddy) De Sylva was off his game writing the words for "Born And Bred In Old Kentucky" (Harms, 1924), with music by Joseph Meyer and James F. Hanley. The lyrics for this piece from the 1925 Al Jolson musical *Big Boy* are trite and insipid. From the verse we get old-hat phrases like "From the day we're old enough to know it, / We all love the land that gave us birth," and from the chorus such unimaginative lines as "Born and bred in old Kentucky / No place else is quite the same" and "I'm lucky cause Kentucky's homeland to me!" The lyric's poor quality is suggested by the fact that the only recording I found on the Internet was a Victor instrumental by Waring's Pennsylvanians cut on February 27, 1925, when the outfit was still mostly a dance band. A further indication of the insignificance of De Sylva's lyric is that he's not even credited on the Victor label.

Ten years after Bud De Sylva wrote his disappointing words for "Born And Bred In Old Kentucky," his former frequent lyric-writing partner Lew Brown wasn't up to speed either in his words to "Carolina," with Jay Gorney's music (Sam Fox, 1934) from the Fox Picture of the same name. Yet by comparison to De Sylva's earlier Kentucky piece, some lines in the verse show a bit of originality and nicely personalize the singer, as when he says of "milk and honey sunny Carolina," "I'd rather live in a shack on 'taters there / Than in a mansion elsewhere." But in the chorus Brown's writing reverts to such hackneyed phrases for expressing love for the state as "Carolina no matter where I roam / When shades of night are fallin', / I know I hear you callin', / Callin' me home." The title of the last song about pride in a single state sounds like it's about bootleg booze. But in "Moonshine Over Kentucky," from the 20th Century-Fox film *Kentucky Moonshine* (Twentieth Century

Music, 1938), with Sidney D. Mitchell's words and Lew Pollack's music, the verse is a tribute to the state's beauty by moonlight. In the chorus the singer thanks Kentucky for all the state has done for him: "Moonshine Over Kentucky / I'm lucky under your spell / I can't forget I'm in your debt more than words can tell." In 1938, the bands of Jan Savitt on Bluebird, Charles "Buddy" Rogers on Vocalion, and Bunny Berigan with a vocal of just the chorus by Ruth Gaylor on Victor, recorded it; the last of those is on the Internet.

Alley songs taking pride in or showing love for all of Dixie were not long in coming after those about individual states. The earliest was "Dixie Land, I Love You" (M. Witmark, 1909), with A. Seymour Brown's words and Nat D. Ayer's music, the team that in 1911 gave the world the monster hit "Oh, You Beautiful Doll." While Brown and Ayer's Dixie pride piece never attained such success, it did find an audience, as exemplified in a lively recording Billy Murray made of it on August 16, 1909, for Victor, which is on the Internet. Brown injects into the song's first verse something close to a southern patriotic—though by no means neo-Confederate or Lost Cause—flavor: "When you recognize Dixie [the song] / Something thrills you through / That same feeling comes stealing, / When you see the Red White and blue [sic]." The chorus mixes the personal with much southern flag-waving: "Down in Dixie Land, I will take my stand, / That's where I long to be, / . . . Dixie, Dixie land, my old home so grand—I love you." The following year, the *Ziegfeld Follies of 1910* introduced the delightful "They All Were Cheering Dixie Way Up North" (Jerome H. Remick, 1910), with words by John E. Hazzard and music by B. Hapgood Burt, in which the congenial "Col'nel Lee from Tennessee / Of the Southern G. A. R." takes a trip up North mostly to visit bars and cafés, drink juleps, smoke Henry Clay cigars, and induce the house bands to play "Dixie," much to the delight of the Yankee habitués of the dives he frequented: "When the band got ready and they played Old Dixie, ev'ryone applauded; / They were on their feet, and they were on their seat, / And they all broke forth; / Oh, the land of cotton hadn't been forgotten! / How the dear old South was lauded, / For they all were cheering Dixie Way Up North." This unregenerate "real red hot old patriot" of an ex-Confederate colonel was doing his bit to help along sectional reconciliation. Similar, though more expansive and written by more recognizable Alleymen, was "The Whole World Comes From Dixie (When They Play That Dixie Tune)" (Shapiro, Bernstein, 1916), with Ballard MacDonald's words and James F. Hanley's music. The premise is that all peoples react strongly to their national airs, but everyone goes nuts for "Dixie" and, while it's playing, is a southerner: "Frenchmen lose their heads and rave about the 'Marseillaise,' / The 'Wacht Am Rhine' drives Germans wild when someone that strain plays, / An Irishman goes crazy to the 'Wearing of the Green,' . . . / But there's a tune that's mighty hard to beat, / Bound to bring the whole world to its feet." The chorus spells that out: "Your pulses quicken and you taste fried chicken when the band plays, / That melody so sweet from Dixieland, / . . . And you want to start Virginia reeling, / Banjos ringing and darkies singing in the cornfield, / . . . You want to grab a stranger by the hand, / Holler 'Do you hail from Dixieland?' / For the whole world comes from Dixie, When they play that Dixie tune."

After such songs flaunting public displays of pride in Dixie, a few came along in which the singer's love of the South was internalized and always with him no matter where he chanced to be. One need read only the title of "I've Got The Swanee River Flowing Thru My Veins" (McCarthy & Fisher, 1919) to get that feeling from this song with Ed Rose's words and Billy Baskette's music without reading a word of the lyric. The verse reveals that the singer not only carries with him his love of the South but also of its songs: "It seems that I must always sing a Dixie song, / Just a good old fashioned Southern song, / Because we all love a Dixie melody, / . . . And way down in my heart, I've always had a part of D, I, X, I, E." The chorus continues in this vein, explaining that his thinking of the Swanee "Brings to me once more, / Songs that my mammy sang to me, oh melody I can hear the banjos playing night and day," ending on a more personal note with "Altho I left my heart with someone down in Dixie, / I've got the Swanee river flowing thru my veins." A similar title showing how deeply imbued the South was in the song's singer was "You Can Take Me Away From Dixie (But You Can't Take Dixie From Me)," the credits for which I gave at the top of this section. The verses say little except that the singer asks why he ever left Dixie but at least he knows he'll be back. The chorus lists aspects of the South that remain with the singer wherever he is: "There's the South in my mouth when I'm talkin' / And Swanee smiles on my face you can see, / I still say 'You all,' and ev'ryone knows / There's nothin' but cotton in my best suit of clothes; / . . . Send me 'way up north where the snowbirds hum / And they'll know that I'm from Dixie when I say 'How come.'" Chicago's Jack Chapman and His Drake Hotel Orchestra, with vocal by Raymond Davis and Clark Myers, cut the chorus on March 31, 1924, for Victor; it's on the Internet.

Anne Caldwell was another Alley lyricist not up to her usual level of excellence in her words for "My Heart's In The Sunny South" (Harms, 1924), with music by Harold Levey. The piece was one of many Caldwell and Levey wrote for the short-lived (forty-seven performances) Broadway musical *The Magnolia Lady,* for which Caldwell not only wrote all the songs but the book as well. Sung by Ruth Chatterton as Lily-Lou Ravenel, this very short tune just expresses in several ways the character's love of her home "In the sunny South; / In the shade of the white Magnolia tree." That's all there is to it—not one of Caldwell's better efforts. The final Dixie pride-and-love song was a novelty tune, Fred Rose's "Any Place In Dixie Is Home Sweet Home To Me" (T. S. Denison, 1929). After a verse stating, "Ev'rybody has some place / They love to brag about / While speaking of their home state," the singer says he can claim any state in Dixie "as mine." The chorus is a list song, giving the singer's connections to various southern states, such as "my granny's down in sunny Alabama / My mammy's waitin' down in Tennessee. / . . . I've got cousins by the dozens, / Down Virginia way. / I got a letter from my uncle down in Georgia, / Just the other day," and more ending with "At 'most any railroad station, / I'll be welcomed by some close relation, / 'Cause any place in Dixie / Is home, sweet home to me."

"Mammy's Dixie Soldier Boy"

Wars inspired a special breed of Alley songs singing of pride in Dixie and her brave sons who went off to fight in whatever war each individual song may have been about. Given the timeframe of the heyday of the Alley, most of those songs dealt with the Great War (World War I), but one early number memorialized the boys in gray from the Civil War, another glanced at those who fought in post–Spanish American War actions in either Cuba or the Philippines, and two (along with one other we already looked at) concerned World War II. Seven of the twenty-three Dixie tunes inspired by wars are rather tangential to it, including a couple of love songs sung by soldiers away from their girls, one in which Yankees training in the South enjoy dancing southern dances with Dixie girls, another in which a dance party is thrown for southern black soldiers returned from "over there," and three more simply so poorly written they don't merit discussion. Hence, I focus here on the other sixteen more deserving war-related Dixie tunes. Before looking at specific Dixie war songs, I should say that not many became hits in their own day, nor did any become a long-lasting classic in the annals of American popular song. In fact, only one Alley song out of the hundreds that emanated from World War I, George M. Cohan's hastily written "Over There," achieved such status, so much so that some people think of World War I as a "one-song war." Conversely, World War II inspired thousands of songs, many of which became hits, and a few perennial standards (see Jones *passim*).

Alley songs about pride in the South during wartime began with two pieces in 1906, one looking backward, the other contemporary. The first verse of "Dear Old Dixie" (New York Publishing House, 1906), with words by Herbert H. Taylor and music by William Heagney, opens by acknowledging the "heroes who are covered with glory, / Who in uniforms of blue marched away" during the Civil War and whose stories have been recounted in song and story, but the lyric then quickly shifts to "names we love in Dixie just as dearly / And we're proud of their part in the fray, / So while cheering for the blue who are marching, / Don't forget there were heroes in gray." The second verse elaborates on memorializing the "flower of the South [who] wore the gray," fighting and falling for the Confederacy, and the chorus strikes a chord of reconciliation between the sections: "Dear old Dixie, we all love today / The heroes in blue and the boys in Southern gray; / For one flag, together, united we stand, / So we'll give the yell we know so well for Dixieland." Bartley C. Costello's lyric for "Fare Thee Well My Old Kentucky" (Leo Feist, 1906), with Joe Nathan's music, was about a military action so contemporary with the writing and publication of the song that he didn't even have to name it for listeners to know what the piece was referring to. The first verse, in the third person, merely states, "Old Kentucky's sons, bravely shoulder guns, when the band begins to play— / . . . Off to fight the foe, boys in blue they go, / Sons of men who wore the gray." The second verse echoes this with, "'till [sic] at last the vic'try's won / Then from far and near, comes the ringing cheer, 'Old Kentucky, Nobly Done.' / But there's sadness too, with the boys in blue, and they sigh for those who fell." The chorus shifts from this patriotism and pride to the voice of one departing soldier, in the first person: "Fare thee well my old Kentucky, / Fare thee well my Grass of Blue / Fare thee well / Sweet heart and mother / 'tis for Country and for you." Though the United States wasn't involved in any major wars in 1906, the U.S. Army intervened in Cuba to quell uprisings after the Spanish-American War and occupied that island until 1909; also in 1906, the Army was sent to the Philippines to control the Moro Rebellion. Listeners hearing of "boys in blue" (the color of U.S. Army uniforms during and after the Spanish-American War) leaving Kentucky in 1906 would have known the piece was referring to one or the other of those military actions that year.

The earliest Alley Dixie tune to come from the Great War was also the most peculiar. The piece, with Arthur J. Lamb's lyrics and Alfred Solman's music, was published by Joe Morris Music in 1914, three years before the United States even entered the war in April 1917. This may be explained by the song's protagonist, a boy from Tennessee, having volunteered to fight with the British Expeditionary Forces, singing to an Irish comrade-in-arms. The song's title, "It May Be Far To Tipperary—It's A Longer Way To Tennessee," shows it was a spinoff of the popular British war song "It's A Long Way To Tipperary" (written before the war by Jack Judge and first performed by him in a music hall turn in 1912), suggesting the piece would be a lighthearted novelty number. To some extent that impression is confirmed by the first verse and chorus: "Comrade, you have a sweetheart, / On Erin's isle you say / But my girl's across the ocean / My girl's in the U.S.A." Then with no warning, the second verse becomes a tearjerker as we find our protagonist has been mortally wounded: "Comrade, the sun is setting / My life is setting too / Comrade, don't be forgetting / What I have asked of you: / Tell her, I had to leave her, / Don't let it break her heart / For someday we'll meet in Heaven / Never again to part!" For contemporary listeners who knew the names of the writers, this abrupt switch from novelty to weeper may not have been as shocking as it was to me when I read the lyric. Arthur J. Lamb was publicly known as one of the most skilled writers of tearjerking lyrics; we looked at two of them under "Dead Virgins in Dixie" in Chapter 2: "The Heart You Lost In Maryland You'll Find in Tennessee" and "When The Birds In Georgia Sing of Tennessee." More famously (but not Dixie tunes), Lamb wrote the words for two sob-song hits with Harry Von Tilzer's music, "A Bird In A Gilded Cage" (1900) and "The Mansion Of Aching Hearts" (1902). "It May Be Far To Tipperary" suggests Lamb's weepers were still in vogue as late as 1914.

Once the United States entered the war in April 1917, most songs about the South's pride in participating in it were more mainstream. One of the first became a minor hit after Eddie Cantor introduced "The Dixie Volunteers" (Waterson, Berlin & Snyder, 1917), with words and music by Edgar Leslie and Harry Ruby, in the *Ziegfeld Follies of 1917*. Cantor recorded it that year for Aeolian Vocalion, and it's on the Internet. That the song remained popular not just in 1917 but into 1918 too is suggested by the Premier Quartet (the American Quartet when recording on Edison) also cutting a rousing rendition on an Edison Blue Amberol cylinder in the latter year. For comparison with Cantor's version, the Premier Quartet's version is also on the Internet. Little need be said about the lyric except that it's a tribute to white southern boys who enlisted, are about to ship out, are "anxious to get to France; / And you can bet they'll do their share, when they get 'over there.'" (How quickly George M. Cohan's phrase caught on!) The chorus picks up a familiar theme: "See those great big Southern laddies, / Just like their dear old daddies, / They are proud to go, / And they want the world to know, / They're coming! They're coming! / From the land of Old Black Joe; / Peaceful sons have shouldered guns, / And now they're going to be, / Fighting men like Stonewall Jackson and like Robert E. Lee."

The year following "The Dixie Volunteers" a song was published, not about a volunteer but about a southern boy who was drafted and soon to leave for the war. Although Norman H. Landman's "Mammy's Dixie Soldier Boy" (Chicago: Will Rossiter, 1918) is sentimental and didn't have much popular success, the lyric offers sensitive insights into the black mammy/white child relationship from the mammy's perspective and is therefore of interest beyond being just another Dixie war song. We know the young soldier is a draftee from the omniscient narrator's opening lines in the first verse: "One day a bugle blew in Dixieland to call the Southern braves away, / And as the boys were sayin' their last farewells I saw a mammy bent and gray." The narrator also saw the mammy was "cryin' as though her heart would break" and when she spoke it appeared as if "her heart just seemed to ache." The chorus switches to the mammy speaking for herself: "Honey, don't forget your dear old mammy / Back in Dixieland / Though you're goin' to fight for Uncle Sammy in a suit of khaki grand / I've loved you like you were my own, but now that you have grown / They're taking you away from your mammy old and gray, and from your dear old Southern home. / . . . if love and pray'rs will help you, / You'll return some day I know / Though they say a bugle call is music to a soldier's ear, / To your poor old mammy ev'ry single note's a tear, / Oh honey, how I'se goin' to miss you, / 'Cause you're mammy's Dixie soldier boy." The second verse reveals the soldier felt similarly, for after he "proved himself a hero" and his thoughts turned to Dixie, his mind first saw "his sweetheart waving to him" but then saw "his mammy cry, as he had said goodbye, / And in his fancy seemed to hear old mammy say" her words in the chorus again. "Mammy's Dixie Soldier Boy" articulates the mother/son bonding between black mammy and white charge perhaps better than more familiar mammy songs.

Two other Dixie war songs appeared in 1917. One, like Arthur J. Lamb's 1914 piece, had a title that spun off of "It's A Long Way To Tipperary," but the lyric had a happier outcome. "It's A Long, Long Way To Dixie" (Chicago: Tell Taylor Music, 1917), with words by Chicago lyricist and publisher Tell Taylor and music by Earl K. Smith, finds in the first verse a Dixie doughboy dreaming of his "Old Kentucky home where the mocking birds are singing all the day," and where the Swanee River shows up in the geographically challenged chorus. In the second verse, we learn his "Mother old and gray" (they always were in World War I songs, even though their fighting sons were eighteen or twenty) has just received a letter from her soldier boy in France—not that he's dying, but that he's on his way "back again to the dear Old folks at home there I'll meet the girl I love sweet Nellie Grey." He doesn't explain why his tour of duty was so short; he might have been wounded, but he doesn't say so in his letter. Another happy-ending number about a southern doughboy who *was* wounded was "Way Down There A Dixie Boy Is Missing" (Jerome H. Remick, 1917), with Stanley Murphy's words and Harry Tierney's music. In the first verse, a soldier from Tennessee, apparently in a field hospital, tells the nurse who "came round to dress his wounded head" of his dream of folks back home, the chorus describing that dream: "I heard them singing in the pale moonlight / 'Where is our wand'ring boy tonight' / My mother dear was standing near / Her head bowed down to hide a tear / The neighbors gathered 'round the dear old lady fair / They all knelt down and offered up a prayer / For a Dixie boy / They're missing Way down there." The dream seems to presage the soldier's impending death from his wound, but the second verse proves otherwise as we find him safe at home by the fireside with his mother as "He cuddles to the dear old lady fair / And tells her of his dreaming over there," implying the Dixie boy received an honorable medical discharge.

"I'm Goin' To Fight My Way Right Back To Carolina" (McCarthy & Fisher, 1918), with words and music by Billy Baskette and Jessie Spiess, is the Dixie version of the hundreds of songs from both world wars in which a U.S.

soldier is fighting for God, flag, country, and—first and foremost—sweetheart. The chorus makes it plain that the "Carolina" in the title is the doughboy's girl, not the state: "I'm goin' to run ev'ry Hun, ev'ry son of a gun I see, / Depend on me, / 'Cause I'm in this thing to win, / And I know that it's no sin, / To grab a little German, / Any little Herman and carve my name on him. / And I am satisfied that Carolina loves me, / I left my heart with her in Dixieland, / She'll understand, / That I may come back with something missin' / But that won't keep us from huggin' and kissin', / When I fight my way right back to my Caroline." It's a mystery why Vernon Dalhart cut the tune on a 1918 Edison Blue Amberol cylinder using a Dixie darky accent even though nothing in the song suggests the doughboy is black. Dalhart's well-sung but odd rendition is on the Internet. Unlike "Right Back To Carolina," four more Dixie war tunes published in 1918 did in fact focus on southern black troops in the Great War, some of them quite fanciful in their conceits, making them all the more entertaining. Yet the most straightforward, but cleverest, was "You'll Find Old Dixieland In France" (Leo Feist, 1918), with Grant Clarke's words and George W. Meyer's music. The premise was that there were so many blacks fighting in France that Dixie was depopulated. Clarke showed his skill with a lyric throughout the piece: From the first verse we get "No more darkies on the Swanee shore, / No more singin' round the cabin door, / Dixie ain't Dixie now, I vow, . . . / Doesn't seem to be a soul down there"; and, from the second, when the boys are in France, "Ev'ry ev'ning when the star shells gleam, You're in Alabama it would seem / . . . Billy Johnson with his pet banjo, / Doesn't mind it when the shells hit low / He simply sits and croons, / The strains of 'Over There.'" The chorus describes some Dixie darky doughboys, ending with "Don't forget 'Old Shimme Sam,' / Famous boy from Alabam', / He marched away in khaki pants, / Instead of pickin' melons off the vine, / They're pickin' Germans off the Rhine."—a tribute to Dixie's black troops' role in the war, if, regrettably, in segregated regiments.

Watermelons went from that one mention near the end of Grant Clarke's lyric to being the central focus of Alfred Bryan's words for "When The Boys From Dixie Eat The Melon On The Rhine" (Maurice Richmond Music, 1918), with Ernest Breuer's music, a silly—indeed wonderfully preposterous—piece that still managed to be a flag-waver for contributions of Dixie troops, and presumably black ones, to the American effort in the Great War. I say presumably because the song doesn't mention or even allude to race, but since, stereotypically, eating watermelon was a Dixie darky pastime and delight, the troops that are the happy recipients of "a steamboat coming this way, / Loaded down with melons, they say" may be presumed to be black. The image of a steamboat built for river travel making a successful voyage across the Atlantic is wacky enough, regardless of whatever its cargo may have been; but let's not even wonder about the freshness of all those watermelons once they reached France. Still, putting reality aside, the song is a delight with its images of U.S. troops on the Rhine feasting on the big juicy pink fruit and even using it as a "weapon" of sorts: "Just watch those Germans retreat, / They'll meet their waterloo, / They'll surrender all in a bunch / Just to get a melon for lunch." According to the Alley's fanciful Dixie war songs, melons weren't the only indigenous American product exported to France to support the war effort. So was ragtime music. Alfred Bryan again, now collaborating with Cliff Hess and Edgar Leslie, wrote the words and music of "When Alexander Takes His Ragtime Band To France" (Waterson, Berlin & Snyder, 1918). In this song, the Dixie darky ragtime band and their leader Alexander, which Irving Berlin created in 1911 and which wound up in the interim in various other Dixie tunes, find themselves in France boosting the morale of the doughboys and through ragtime tunes getting German soldiers to drop their guns and retreat: "When Alexander takes his ragtime band to France; / He'll capture ev'ry Hun, / And take them one by one. / Those ragtime tunes will put the Germans in a trance; / They'll throw their guns away, / Hip-hooray! / And start right in to dance. / . . . Old Hindenburg will know he has no chance, / When Alexander takes his ragtime band to France." Would it have actually been so easy! Marion Harris featured the song in her vaudeville acts and also recorded the piece on June 18, 1918, for Victor, as may be heard on the Internet. The last of the 1918 Alley songs about black southern troops in the Great War is easily the most outrageous. With words by J. Keirn Brennan and music by Paul Cunningham, "When The Robert E. Lee Arrives In Old Tennessee, All The Way From Gay Paree" (M. Witmark & Sons, 1918) is impossible on a number of counts. First, as was noted earlier, the riverboat *Robert E. Lee* burned almost to its decks in 1882. Second, had it in fact survived until 1918, as magnificent as this sidewheeler was, it was built for river travel and never could have survived Atlantic Ocean crossings, although the song claims "she's a transport sailing the sea . . . / [which] carried over thousands of men, / She'll bring them back home again." And finally, a small point, but the boat could not have departed for the United States from "Gay Paree." Given all that, the thrust of the song is that the boat is now shipping back to the U.S. southern black troops who fought in France, presumably after the Armistice on November 11, 1918: "And when each dusky yank, Stops on that old river bank, / Oh, how happy we'll be! / There'll be darkies parley-vooing all about the war, / There'll be chicken stewing they never had before, / When the Robert E. Lee arrives in Old Tennessee, / All the way from Gay Paree." As factually goofy as the song may have been about their mode of transportation home, it still praised the black Dixie troops in the war.

Two other Alley songs, both in 1919, celebrated the return of Dixie doughboys from "over there" in very different ways. Alfred Bryan wrote a less than lucid lyric for "I'm Goin' To Break That Mason-Dixon Line (Until I Get To That Gal Of Mine)" (Jerome H. Remick, 1919), with music by Jean Schwartz. It seems to be about a soldier from Dixie mustered out of the U.S. Army somewhere up North who is now ready to do whatever he must to get back to his girl in the South: "I'm goin' to break that Mason-Dixon Line / Until I reach that gal of mine / I'm goin' to go clean thru to Caroline / And I will be right there on time / You know I broke one over there / It didn't even muss my hair / And when I hit the old levee / I'll land on it heavy / I'll say this boy is there." The song is full of such thoughts, and in the second verse the discharged doughboy is reunited with "the little gal I love the best." And that's it. Much more celebratory was "Dixie Is Dixie Once More" (Shapiro, Bernstein, 1919) by white lyricist William Tracey and black composer Maceo Pinkard. The song finds southern darkies rejoicing in black troops' return from the war: "There's joy on the old Swanee shore, / 'Cause Dixie is Dixie once more." The chorus describes the activities of some of the boys just returned: "'Shimmee Sam' is doing a new kind of dance, / Called the 'Franco-Dixie,' / He brought it from France, Hey! / Alexander's got his ragtime band, / Back in Melody land, / Banjos are a-strummin' / So tuney, So Tuney / Darkies are a-hummin' / So crooney So crooney / Just the same as in the days of yore, / Dixie is Dixie once more." For Victor on July 25, 1919, the American Quartet with Billy Murray cut nearly the whole tune plus some added comic dialogue, as may be heard on the Internet.

Unlike the plethora of Dixie tunes about the South's participation in World War I, the Alley produced only three pieces linking Dixie with World War II. "I Wanna Go Back To West Virginia" (1942) was already discussed in

Chapter 7 as the homesick lament of a World War II draftee. Like "I Wanna Go Back," the other two songs were written in the mode of the currently popular country or hillbilly music, but since Nashville had barely emerged as a center for publishing such songs, and since Alley publishers produced the two other World War II Dixie war songs, they may be classified as products of Tin Pan Alley. Both published in 1943, one of the songs hardly made any waves at all, whereas the other had a delayed reaction and became a hit two years later in 1945. "When The U.S. Band Plays Dixie In Berlin" (Bob Miller, 1943), with words and music by Graham Prince, Fats Ryan, and Esther Van Sciver, is a brief tune about world peace and American patriotism but not much about Dixie per se, except for the U.S. band playing the song of that title: "WHEN THE U.S. BAND PLAYS DIXIE IN BERLIN / The whole wide world will be at peace again / What a happy time there'll be, / When the whole world will be free, / We'll all shout Hallelujah and Amen." I found no evidence the song was ever recorded. But in 1945 Bob Wills and His Texas Playboys cut for Columbia Ed Burt's "Silver Dew On The Blue Grass Tonight" (Leeds Music, 1943), and it's on the Internet. The first and third verses are sung by a girl left behind in Kentucky writing to her sweetheart fighting overseas, but the second is a patriotic anthem: "Stars of gold on the old flag tonight, / While you fight for a cause that is right; / You will keep that flag on high / For those boys who had to die; Stars of gold on the old flag tonight!" Wills's "Silver Dew" stayed fourteen weeks on *Billboard*'s "Most Played Juke Box Folk Records" chart, topping it as #1 for three.

9

MOONLIGHT AND MAGNOLIAS
The Alley and the Myth

As discussed in Chapter 1, the various denizens of Tin Pan Alley in the early years, often barely high school educated, predominantly white and urban, and frequently immigrant, were not likely to have encountered or even heard of the Old South or Lost Cause Myths. This suggests they had to have located their random and assorted moonlight and magnolias images elsewhere, even though those images were originally parts of southerners' own myths about their society and culture. The Alleymen stripped from the images such antebellum elements as gentlemen planters, hoop-skirted ladies, and codes of chivalry that would be anachronistic in songs that were almost always about the present-day South. The Alley's sources may have included a few popular nineteenth-century songs that employed such images, or local color novels or stories in magazines like *Collier's* and the *Saturday Evening Post,* none of which could be classified as highbrow "literature" but merely diversionary reading for mass popular audiences and the sorts of things Alleymen themselves, lowbrow commercial writers that they were, may be supposed to have read. But wherever these mostly northern songwriters found images of an idealized South and pruned from them their unwanted anomalous antebellum features (yet retaining those magnificent relics of a bygone era, sidewheeler steamboats), the Alley's lyricists, each on his or her own, used them independently—with no collusion or mass collaboration among them—to disseminate a myth of an idyllic Dixie in the here and now, not one looking back at a glory that once was but is gone forever. Once sifted off from the purely antebellum elements of the Old South and Lost Cause Myths, the essential moonlight and magnolias vision of the South was of a *contemporary* land of perpetually sunny days, moonlit nights, fragrant blossoms, Southern Belles, southern hospitality, and happy darkies singing soothing melodies, with all the lush and lovely trappings that go along with them.

From the Alley's earliest days, its songwriters were quick to grasp the power these images had to create pictures of an idyllic present-day South in the short space of a song, and they appropriated them not just tangentially in Dixie tunes on other themes, as we have seen throughout this book, but also in about ninety-five songs between 1902 and 1951 whose sole concern was idealizing or glorifying the entire South or parts thereof. But that's enough about this for now; more at the end of the chapter. As with other large groups of songs such as those about homesickness or traveling home, to discuss all ninety-five pieces idealizing or glorifying Dixie would make the book much too long. So again I had to do some judicious pruning, reducing that amount to just about half, or roughly fifty-five songs on the topic. This number gives a representative picture of how widespread was this theme as the core of some Dixie tunes for roughly fifty years, at the same time the individual songs show how varied and imaginative were the changes rung on it by the best of the Alley's lyricists. Rather than examining these songs in a single chronology, I look at them according to the geographic parts of the South they idealize or glorify, starting with songs about all of Dixie, followed by a subset of tunes equating Dixie with heaven, and then songs about specific states, cities, riverbanks, and streets, concluding with a few novelty tunes that don't really fit anyplace else.

In just the second year that the Alley was the recognized hub of New York's popular music publishing trade, a song appeared containing a few snippets of the modern Moonlight and Magnolias Myth—"Beneath The Sunny Southern Sky" (T. B. Harms, 1899), with William H. Gardner's words and Dorothy Vaughn's music. The lyrics contain such images or variations thereof that would go on to lie at the core of the myth as "the happy darkies singing," "the perfume of the roses," "'neath the sunny southern sky," "the night-wind whisp'ring thro' the pine-trees," and the "land of sunshine and the flowers." Yet the song's focus is on the singer's nostalgia to see the South again, not on painting an idyllic picture of Dixie or glorifying it. The first Alley tune in which idealizing Dixie was its sole concern came a few years later in "Under Southern Skies (A Song Of The South)" (Vandersloot Music, 1902), with Al Trahern's words and Lee Orean Smith's music, from the play *Under Southern Skies.* Since I discussed and quoted from it at length in the Prologue, nothing more need be said here except that this song launched about fifty more years of songs whose exclusive aim was to extol the virtues of an idyllic South.

Similar to "Under Southern Skies," "Dixie I Love You" (Chicago: Chas. K. Harris, 1906), with Will M. Hough and Frank R. Adams's words and Joseph E. Howard's music, is packed with archetypal moonlight and magnolias (hereafter M&M) imagery from front to back. Like the earlier song, it too originally appeared in a show, the Chicago musical, *The Time The Place & The Girl.* To skim over some of the tune's M&M imagery, in the first verse we find: "When the sunny skies of Dixie smile on you, / You will vow no maidens [*sic*] eyes are deeper blue," and in the second: "Ev'ry day's a golden day in Dixieland, / Ev'ry flower seems just made to kiss your hand, / Ev'ry girl seems twice as sweet down there to you"; and from the chorus: "Sunshine above you, / Always shining down on you; / . . . No skies are clearer, no girls are dearer." Before I write one word about another song, I must forewarn readers that they will be encountering a lot of repetitious imagery about sunshine, clear skies, pretty girls, green grass, and the like. While the reader may feel bombarded by these images all at once, historically they were spread out over many years and so would not have had such a deadening effect upon their hearers or readers. Moreover, such repetition is the stuff myth is made of, and what's going on here is at least the Alley's dissemination of the M&M Myth, if not its very creation of it. That said, such imagery next appeared in "Down South The Skies Are Brighter" (Savannah: Parke Music, 1908), a song solely extolling the South, with music by Nat E. Solomons and lyric by poet/lyricist Frank L. Stanton, raised in Charleston, South Carolina and writer of "Mighty Lak' A Rose," with music by Ethelbert Nevin. The early part of his lyric is a virtual list of components of the M&M Myth: "Down South the skies are brighter / Down South the Roses whiter / Down South the hearts are lighter ev'ry day. / With greener grasses springing / with birds of sweetest singing, / With Bells melodious ringing ev'ry day"—after which Stanton engages in some lofty hyperbole: "Down South the money jingles 'till your pocket fairly tingles, / And your house has silver shingles ev'ry day."— getting back to reality near the end of the song: "Her green fields ripe for sowing, / Her streams in music flowing, / And Heaven its smiles bestowing ev'ry day."

The earliest Alley song to center on idealizing the "moonlight" side of the M&M Myth—yet without mentioning the moon—was Irving Berlin's "When It's Night Time In Dixie Land" (Irving Berlin, Inc., 1914) from his musical comedy *Watch Your Step,* which opened on December 8, 1914, at the

New Amsterdam Theatre. In the two verses and chorus, Berlin employs some characteristic nighttime images of the myth, such as "Through the air float the wonderful tunes of mister whippoorwill" and "Listening to the crickets call / When the evening shadows fall," but he also idiosyncratically places special emphasis on the contented lives of both southern whites and blacks in the evening, in the latter instance using the term "coons" in a thoroughly nonpejorative sense: "On the ground dance the bow-legged coons, / They simply can't keep still / . . . Darkies strolling hand in hand / Southern melodies, / Floating on the breeze / . . . For when you hear those darkies harmonize / Tears of gladness fill your eyes / . . . Dixieland embraces the happiest of races." As for the southern whites, Berlin's tune sings of "Vet'rans of the civil war / Telling stories by the score / How they fought in sixty-four / Down in Dixieland." Indirectly, the piece implies new racial harmony in Dixie. In a similar vein, two years after Berlin's song, a tune appeared with a title like a travel brochure, "See Dixie First" (Boston: Walter Jacobs, 1916), with words by Jack Mahoney, lyricist of the enormous hit "When You Wore A Tulip And I Wore A Big Red Rose," and music by ragtime virtuoso and composer of "Are You From Dixie ('Cause I'm From Dixie Too)," George L. Cobb. The piece places as much emphasis on idealizing the behavior of Dixie's denizens both black and white—and particularly on their behavior toward visitors to the region—as it does on glorifying the South for its natural attributes. Not that Dixie's physical beauties are forgotten, with the inclusion of lines like "Where the Swanee is flowing and cotton is growing" and "Bright Dixie moonlight makes ev'rything grand." But mostly the number focuses on extolling southern folks and their treatment of tourists to Dixie: "They'll show you hospitality down there; / Ev'rywhere / They are square. / And Heaven can't be far away, that's true, / For all the girls are like angels to you. / . . . Old Black Joe treats you like a brother, / Mammy Snow cooks like your mother. / Dixie folks will meet you, they'll be glad to greet you, / See old Dixie first." If the song sounds like a tour guide hyping the attraction he's promoting, today, the original sheet music cover art looks like that of a travel brochure. It depicts a young northern tourist couple dressed in immaculate white for the warm southern clime, perched on a low hill, she sitting on the grass, he standing with binoculars to his eyes, both at some distance from the darkies they are watching picking cotton in a field below them. Ah well, we must remember this was still only 1916, after all.

The year 1919 saw the publication of three songs lavishly idealizing, praising, or otherwise creating pictures of an idyllic Southland, two making their
debuts in musicals, one a freestanding popular song, and all three authored
and composed by some of the Alley's top-shelf talent of the day. For the musical extravaganza *Hello, Alexander,* which opened on October 7, 1919, as a
vehicle for the popular blackface vaudevillian team of McIntyre and Heath,
lyricist Alfred Bryan and composer Jean Schwartz wrote "Give Me the South
All The Time" (Jerome H. Remick, 1919). For a short song in which the verse
mostly just describes the South as the "Land of honey milk and honey you
are ever near," Al Bryan packed a whopping lot of Dixie into the number's
very brief chorus, the entirety of which is "Give me the Georgia pine trees /
Give me a Dixie moon / Give me the darkies singing / Along the Bayou and
dreamy lagoon / Give me the orange blossoms / In all their bloom sublime
/ Give me forever give me / Oh you can give me the South all the time." Almost as succinct in its summation of the South was "I'll Sing You A Song
About Dear Old Dixie Land" (M. Witmark), the collaborative effort of the
great black team of lyricist Henry Creamer and composer Turner Layton.
The piece was originally an interpolation sometime in 1919 into the long-
running Al Jolson musical *Sinbad,* which had opened on February 14, 1918,
but there's no evidence that Jolson ever recorded this paean to Dixie. The
two rather unimportant verses tell listeners, "You've heard songs about Hin-
dustan, and its mystic nights," followed by other places they may have heard
songs about, leading into, "But here's one tune you never heard before!" The
chorus then lists what makes Dixie the most idyllic place on earth, including,
in part, "I'll sing you a song of the fields of cotton, / I'll sing you a song of the
Swanee shore, / I'll sing you a song that won't be forgotten / As long as banjos
ring, darkies sing 'round that cabin door." The amusing content in the freestanding "Anything Is Nice If It Comes From Dixieland" (Leo Feist, 1919) is
so different, I was tempted to include it with the novelty tunes, but it glorifies
the South so sincerely that I decided to put it with the other songs idealizing
Dixie wholesale. With Grant Clarke's words and George W. Meyer and Milton Ager's music, the piece praises Dixie states for a product each is known
for (including Maryland, as many tunes of this sort did). To cite a few, "Just
to make our clothes, the cotton grows, / In dear old Alabam', / Each hungry
mouth looks to the south, / For sweet Virginia Ham, / From Tennessee comes
melody / That's played by ev'ry band, / And if you're talking of chicken, /

Oh, Maryland!" The conclusion is "Anything is nice, / If it comes from Dix-ieland." The American Quartet cut the whole song for Victor on March 31, 1919, and it's on the Internet.

In 1921 Sherman Hoffman, Sam Coslow, and Edward Davis teamed up on the words and music of what at first seems to be a novelty song spoofing all tunes previously idealizing the South. Titled simply "Dixie" (Robert Norton Co., 1921), its first verse begins, "Song writers rave about they misbehave about Dixie *[Spoken]* dear old Dixie / Every one pines about writes many lines about Dixie / My own Dixie." But just when it seems the whole tune will continue to lampoon other writers' hyperbole about the South, the three collaborators do an about-face, declaring, "Let's add another one to it" and break into their own chorus glorifying Dixie: "Dixie—Oh Dixie— / There's no place in the world like Dixie—where the sweet juicy peaches are growing— / I'm going, going where the Mississippi is flowing / Dixie—Oh Dixie—I'm in heaven when I'm in Dixie— / I'm a rover / I've travelled all over— / But, Dixie, I love you." Which shows that writers can have fun idealizing Dixie, rather than be solemn or romantically poetic in the process. We'll see more of this fun approach soon. But first, mention must be made of "There's No Place As Grand (As Bandana Land)" (Harms, 1924) by the black musical comedy writers lyricist Noble Sissle and composer Eubie Blake, from their show *The Chocolate Dandies.* The lyric idealizes the almost wholly black-populated parts of Dixie (which covered a lot of it), hence the song's title. On top of loving Bandana Land for its "cotton fields so white," as "The home of hospitality / . . . Where a friend's a friend in reality," and as a place where "The sun shines bright the skies are clear; / The moon each night seems mighty near," the song reserves for the place of honor at the end "It's [*sic*] pretty girls / With their pretty eyes, / Ev'ry complexion can be found / From the lightest mulatto to the chocolate brown, / There's no place as grand / As Bandana Land." Though written for white New York audiences, the song presented two black writers' perspective on idealizing those parts of Dixie peopled by southern blacks.

In 1929 Jack Yellen jumped on the bandwagon with other lyricists idealizing all of Dixie in "That's The Good Old Sunny South" (Ager, Yellen & Bornstein, 1929), with Milton Ager's music. After an inconsequential verse about following birds southward, the chorus has the pattern of "When you see blue skies and fields of white, / And the sun is shining bright, / Yes, suh! / That's the good old Sunny South"—picking up on other typical southern items like singing robins and Dixie gals "who sweetly drawl, / 'Mighty glad to see you-all.'" From this lighthearted idealizing of Dixie in the chorus, Yellen turns to outright comedy in the patter section meant to suggest what the traveler to Dixie sees from the train window, including such nonsense as "Look at those pigs. Hey! Sam! / Future kosher sweet Virginia ham," "See that cabin on the Swanee shore; / That's Al Jolson's Mammy by the door," and "Uncle Tom right there before my eyes! / That might be Lon Chaney in disguise." Irving Kaufman recorded the first verse and comic patter for Columbia in 1929, which are on the Internet. In a more mellow mood, lyricist Johnny Mercer and composer Hoagy Carmichael teamed up on "Moon Country (Is Home To Me)" (Southern Music, 1934), a tune full of idyllic pictures of a rural, down-home South from Georgia "where the peach trees bear a harvest all the year 'round" to Kentucky "where an old grey mare eats blue grass from the ground." The chorus, cut by Hoagy Carmichael and His Orchestra, Hoagy on the vocal on a 1934 Victor disc, is on the Internet. To Mercer, Moon Country is the rural Dixie that's "possum and 'coon country, / That sycamore heaven back South. / . . . that good for the soul country, / Good for cookin' things that melt in your mouth. (Oh Lawd) / When my cousin, Cindy Lou, plays a twi-light hymn to you / She makes that ol' piano sound exactly like brand new." In short, he equates his idyllic Dixie with life's simple pleasures.

In "Is It True What They Say About Dixie?" (Irving Caesar, Inc., 1936), wordsmiths Irving ("Swanee") Caesar and Sammy Lerner and tunesmith Gerald Marks took the novel approach of idealizing the South by asking questions to verify whether what they'd heard of its special attributes was ac-tually for real. Their approach paid off, since "Is It True" became the biggest hit among all songs glorifying Dixie. The 1936 Decca recording by Jimmy Dorsey's Orchestra with Bob Eberly's vocal was on the charts for ten weeks, and in the #1 spot for four of them, but it's not on the Internet. Yet Rudy Val-lee and His Connecticut Yankees, with Vallee on vocal, cut a version complete with the verse and added patter for Victor in 1936, and it *is* on the Internet. The gist of the chorus is seen in just its opening few lines: "Is it true what they say about Dixie? / Does the sun really shine all the time? / Do the sweet Mag-nolias blossom at ev'rybody's door? / Do folks keep eating 'possum, / 'Till they can't eat no more?"—and from its conclusion, "If it's true, that's where I belong." Except for the pieces centrally comparing the South to Heaven next to be discussed, the last two songs extolling all of Dixie had histories that were at the least unusual and in one case controversial or still unresolved as of this writing. In 1924 Bennie Moten and Thamon Hayes wrote "South" as an instrumental jazz tune that Moten and His Kansas City Orchestra first recorded for Okeh records that year, and then for Victor in 1928. Over the years, other major bands picked up on it and recorded it, including Woody Herman and the Woodchoppers for Decca, Hot Lips Page also for Decca, Kid Ory for Crescent, and Pete Daily for Capitol. Yet it wasn't until 1941 that "South" got words, thanks to Ray Charles—not the black soul and rhythm and blues singer of that name, but the white composer and arranger best known as the organizer and leader of The Ray Charles Singers, regularly featured with Perry Como on records, radio, and TV, as well as with other variety artists in these media. Charles's lyrics simply show that the stock-in-trade images Alleymen had used in idealizing Dixie for roughly forty years were still alive in the early 1940s. For a sampling, take: "Where the sun is happy to shine. / Where a friendly face is common to see, / . . . Where the folks are happy and gay, / . . . Where the bees make honey all day, / . . . Where the moon shines mellow and bright, / And the breezes play tag with the night." Charles's version with lyrics was published in 1941 by Peer International, the Alley publishing house whose primary output was of country or hillbilly music, and, in its transformation from jazz instrumental to Dixie tune with words, "South" took on a country flair, in its mandolin, fiddle, and guitar accompaniment to the singing of the Shelton Brothers on their 1941 Decca disc of the number, which is on the Internet.

The few things certain about "That's What I Like 'Bout The South" (copyright by Andy Razaf, 1944) are that Andy Razaf, one of the Alley's most gifted black songwriters, wrote both the words and music, and that in the mid- to late 1940s, the number was a blockbuster hit idealizing the joys of southern living, country style—sincerely, if rather rowdily. Beyond those facts, some questions remain open regarding the song's writing and first and future performances. According to Razaf's biographer, Barry Singer (see Bibliography), Razaf wrote "That's What I Like" in 1933, in the unusual circumstance of a black songwriter writing a song for Dan Healy's *Cotton Club Parade,* specifically for the twenty-third edition of that show. Normally, the all-black revue at the Harlem venue was written by all-white writers and played to all-white audiences, but somehow Razaf's number was accepted and performed "during the show's lengthy opening by Cotton Club bandleader Cab Calloway, accompanied by Dusty Fletcher, Gallie Gaston, and a chorus line of Cotton Club girls" (Singer 270). Singer goes on very briefly, and without documenting any of his information, to say that Razaf's song "was picked up, in time, as something of a signature tune by entertainer Phil Harris" (270), and that Harris attempted to credit himself with having written the number until Razaf threatened to sue him. To all of this can be added the information from the totally reliable bibliographical tool *WorldCat* that Razaf copyrighted "That's What I Like 'Bout The South" in 1944 and may have recorded the number himself that year as well. The Cotton Club story has been challenged by others, however, mostly online, including by Michael Feinstein, maintaining that Razaf originally wrote the song specifically as a novelty number *for* Phil Harris in his radio broadcasts, nightclub performances, and records, but that Harris, by changing a few words, tried to copyright the song as his own and avoid paying Razaf. The mystery of the song's genesis has yet to be cleared up. But whichever version is accurate (if either), Razaf's piece remains one terrific song, right from its famous opening of "Won't you come with me to Alabamy / Let's go see my dear old Mammy / She's fryin' eggs and broiling hammy / And that's what I like about the South" to lesser-known but just as yummy down-home Dixie gustatory lyrics like "She's got baked ribs and candied yams / Those sugar-cured Virginia hams / Basement full of those berry jams / An' that's what I like about the South / . . . Aahhh, don't take one, have two / They're dark brown and chocolate too. / Suits me, they must suit you / 'Cause that's what I like about the South." Whatever Harris's legal rights to Razaf's song may have been, his 1947 RCA Victor record with his orchestra and Harris's singing remains a classic and is on the Internet.

It wasn't unusual for songs in the group idealizing all of Dixie to toss in a line comparing the South to heaven or paradise, as, for example, "This place is next to heaven" (from "I'll Sing You A Song About Dear Old Dixie Land"), "It's a perfect paradise" (from "Anything Is Nice If It Comes From Dixieland"), and "Don't you know you're right next door to heaven down South" (from "South"). Yet many Dixie tunes also made such comparisons their entire lyric's controlling metaphor or central conceit for glorifying the South. The first such number, though a bit thin, was the fairly early Jack Yellen piece "So This Is Dixie" (Jerome H. Remick, 1917), with Albert Gumble's music, in which a newcomer to the South is very impressed by his surroundings: "You don't mean to say it's Dixieland / That I've been longing to see / So this is Dixie / So this is Dixie / Well it looks mighty good to me / . . . You're sure it's Dixie, Why it looks like Heaven to me." From this start, the Dixie = heaven and/or paradise paradigm increased exponentially, next in "Dixieland Is Happyland" (Shapiro, Bernstein, 1919), with Alex Sullivan's words and Lynn Cowan's music. In the verse we get "You'll enjoy the cooking / Just because the cook's good-looking, / Paradise isn't half so nice I want you to know," and in the chorus, "When you hear those southern darkies harmonize / Shut your eyes imagine you're in Paradise." Also in 1919, the prolific Dixie-tune lyricists Sam M. Lewis and Joe Young brought the Dixie = heaven motif center stage for the first time in "I Always Think I'm Up In Heaven (When I'm Down In Dixieland)" (Waterson, Berlin & Snyder, 1919), with music by Maurice Abrahams. In the verse the singer tells how as a child he or she never understood the idea of "the Promised Land" where "Angels watch over you" since the child was convinced there was such an angel at home in the South. The chorus picks up with "I always think I'm up in Heaven when I'm down in Dixieland / I've got an angel of a Mammy of the good old fashioned brand," and says, "Ev'rybody loves somebody down in dear old Dixieland, / The pretty flowers in the garden, / Keep their heads a noddin', when you walk by hand in hand / . . . And ev'ry other lane's a lovers lane, / That's why I think I'm up in Heaven when I'm down in Dixieland." The lyric avoids the usual idyllic imagery for Dixie but idealizes it in its offbeat comparison to heaven.

In "Heaven Christened Dixieland" (Jerome H. Remick, 1920), lyricist Raymond B. Egan and composer Richard A. Whiting wrote a song explaining the presence of both whites and blacks in the South. In the first verse, a little girl asks why she is white while her mammy is "black as night." In reply the mammy—to me the epitome of folk wisdom—replies in the chorus with a fable about the origin of Dixie: "Heaven built this world in six short days / And don't let yourself forget / That they spent the six on Dixieland / 'Cause the rest ain't finished yet / They took all shades of the rainbow / Building woodland field and stream / And there had to be some shadows / In the angel's [sic] color scheme / They intended you for sunshine and they intended me for shade / And this old black skin you see me in / Is the one the angels made / If they wanted to they might / Have made your dear old mammy white / But I'm the shady part of a great work of art / Heaven christened Dixieland." More conventional, but no less detailed, was the imagery equating Dixie with heaven in "Away Down South In Heaven" (Shapiro, Bernstein, 1927), with Bud Green's words and Harry Warren's music. Even in the two verses, the piece never strays from its motif of the South being heaven. In the first the singer as a "little kid" comes to realize heaven is "here on earth / In the very land that gave me birth," and in the second observes, "There could never be a place that's half as nice / As the land I call my Paradise." The chorus gets specific: "Oh! The sun shines bright on the fields of white, / And the birds make music all day / I mean away down South in Heaven" and "Where the fireflies lighten up the skies / Where the ev'ning is born, / And the whippoor-wills from the distant hills / Wake you up ev'ry morn, / Where they say 'Hello' and they mean 'Hello' / And you get that longing to stay / I mean away down South in Heaven." Ted Lewis and His Band cut the chorus, Lewis singing (or rhythmically speaking, as was his wont), for Columbia in 1927, and it's on the Internet.

Written for the 1930 William Fox Musical Movietone *Cameo Kirby* (now lost), a brief song with words by Edgar Leslie and music by Walter Donaldson establishes a three-way equation among Dixie, home, and heaven. "Home Is Heaven—Heaven Is Home" (Donaldson, Douglas & Gumble, 1929) mentions Dixie only twice, both times in the verse, but each time pointing to the South as the wandering singer's home: "I guess I'll find my blue skies down in Dixie," and "If I only heard a blue bird, / If I heard that one I heard down in Dixie, / He told me"—leading into the chorus's opening of "Roam—wher-ever you roam / Home is Heaven / Heaven is Home." The rest of the chorus varies but little from that idea, as may be heard on Gene Carroll and Glenn Rowell's cut of the complete song (with the verse not at the beginning, but in the middle) for Victor in 1930, which is on the Internet. The last of the songs in which Dixie = heaven is central, "Where The Swanee River Flows Thru' Heaven" (Santly Bros., 1933), with John Redmond and John Lynch's words and Ernie Davis's music, varied the stock imagery in such songs: "Oh! the cotton fields are whiter, / Ev'ry darkies [*sic*] heart is lighter, / And the whole day long, / You can hear their song, / WHERE THE SWANEE RIVER FLOWS THRU' HEAVEN, / All the Angels there are dusky, / And they sing with voices husky, / But they make your soul want to reach its goal, / WHERE THE SWANEE RIVER FLOWS THRU' HEAVEN."

The remaining Dixie tunes idealizing or glorifying the South focus not on its entirety, but on smaller geographic divisions of it (plus a handful of novelty numbers). The largest group, from which I selected fourteen, concern individual states. The earliest, "I Hear You Calling Me, Tennessee" (Cosmopolitan Music, 1914), with Powell I. Ford's words and Ray Russell's music, is a bit of a homesickness song too, yet it is packed in both the verses and chorus with the kinds of imagery used to idealize the whole of Dixie, including such phrases as "Where it's summertime always / Where the birds in the trees / Keep the rolling hills ringing, / With their melodies," "Soft breezes blow," "I see the blossoms on the apple tree," and "Why I can even hear the droning of a bee / Just like a beautiful melody." In 1916, a song appeared in two shows (not uncommon then), *Ziegfeld Follies of 1916* and Lew Fields's *Step This Way,* Irving Berlin's idyllic vision of being "In Florida Among The Palms" (Waterson, Berlin & Snyder, 1916), "With its peaceful air of 'I don't care' and lazy atmosphere that calms." In other stretched rhymes, Berlin's idealizing goes on with, "I'd love to live among the bamboo huts, the cocoanuts, / There's something in the climate that charms, / Heaven's corridor is sunny Florida, home of the shelt'ring palms." Just as Berlin's rhymes are a bit wobbly, his melody isn't among his most deathless, as heard on the Sterling Trio's August 11, 1916, Victor cut of the tune on the Internet.

Two songs within two years extolled Alabama, each for a different reason. George Hamilton Green's "Alabama Moon" (Sam Fox, 1920) focused on romantic moonlit nights there: "Alabama moon, coming out so soon, / Shining thro' the trees where ev'ning breezes gently croon; / Cotton fields of white, swaying in the night, / Dreaming of an Alabama moon. / Darkies softly hum, banjoes gently strum / . . . Songs of Dixieland, songs you'll understand." Although its title bore some similarity, "When The Moon Is Shinin' Down in Alabam" (Triangle Music, 1922), with words and music by Al Bernard and Nat Vincent, was most concerned not with amatory but with gustatory matters. The lyric glances at "the old moon painted high" under which "all the young people sway" but abruptly turns to "And there is possum in the oven / It's the bestest in the lan' / Just smothered with brown gravy all around it candy yams," and the whole patter section extends the litany of home-cookin' in Alabam'—in part, "First you take old corn bread with sweet Virginia ham, smothered with Molasses, on the side some berry jam. / Next we'll take our chicken any style you wish, each one fat and tender oh! Lordy what a dish." A fitting tribute to Alabama, but not one well reflected in the song's title.

The verse of "You're In Kentucky Sure As You're Born" (Broadway Music, 1923), with words and music by George A. Little, Haven Gillespie (a native Kentuckian), and Larry Shay, begins with the Dixie = paradise equation "I've heard a lot 'bout Paradise / But Paradise ain't half as nice / As my Kentucky Home-sweet-home," but the chorus combines conventional images with some imaginative twists on idealizing Kentucky: "When you see a field where grass is blue, and ev'rything looks good to you / You're in Kentucky sure as you're born / When a million sunbeams light your way, says 'Come on stranger, won't you stay' / You're in Kentucky sure as you're born," and "When the shadows creep you can go to sleep / On a carpet of moonbeams." Vaudeville entertainer and radio star Frank Crumit recorded the piece with just Phil Ohman's piano accompaniment for Victor on February 15, 1924, and it's on the Internet. Another number with words and music by the same team of Little, Gillespie, and Shay, "That's Georgia" (Broadway Music, 1924), did for that state what their previous Dixie tune did for Kentucky, and it did so using something of the same syntactic pattern in the lyric of the chorus, starting with, "If the ground's so white that you believe it's snow / But the old thermometer's a shoutin' 'no' / And the cotton blossoms nod and say 'Hello' / That's Georgia." A later verbal string even engages in a tricky quadruple rhyme: "'Nif you feel old Swanee's glistenin' dew / Christenin' you while listenin' to the birds at dawnin' whistle 'n' coo in the sweet magnolia trees." Although this piece's lyrics are among the most intricate of all those idealizing Dixie or any part of it, no recordings of it with the words have appeared on the Internet as of this writing, only instrumental versions by three popular dance bands of the day, Paul Van Loan and His Orchestra, Fletcher Henderson and His Orchestra, and the Benson Orchestra of Chicago.

Another song glorifying Alabama—actually that tiny part of it on the Gulf Coast around Mobile, the rest of the state being pretty much landlocked—was "Bam Bam Bamy Shore" (Jerome H. Remick, 1925), with Mort Dixon's words and Ray Henderson's music. The song's two verses mention sights the singer has seen and things he's done in his travels around the world, but each slightly raucous—yet idealizing—chorus begins, "Oh a thousand miles I travel'd and a thousand sights I saw," the first continuing with "But there ain't no sight like a moonlight night / On the Bam Bam Bamy shore / Oh a thousand gals I met with that I never met before / But the gal I get is the gal I met / On the Bam Bam Bamy shore," and the second, sillier one, with "But there ain't no bill like the vaudeville on the Bam Bam Bamy shore / Oh a thousand jokes I laughed at but the ones that make me roar / Are the jokes they crack from the Almanac / On the Bam Bam Bamy shore." The tune goes on with goofier things for which to idolize a southern state, but it's a fun way to do it. The bands of Ted Lewis and Paul Ash cut instrumentals of this Roaring Twenties fast fox trot, but Mike Speciale and His Orchestra recorded it with a vocal of the first chorus by Arthur Hall on October 14, 1925, for an Edison Blue Amberol cylinder, which is on the Internet.

For an Alley lyricist born in Coblenz, Germany, and raised in Chicago, Gus Kahn not only wrote a whopping lot of Dixie tunes—at least twenty-one—but quite a few specifically about Kentucky, including, in addition to those we've seen already and some not included in this book, one idealizing the state specifically in the a.m., "Kentucky's Way Of Sayin' Good Mornin'" (Jerome H. Remick, 1925), with music by Egbert Van Alstyne. As he did in his great 1922 homesickness lyric "Carolina In The Morning," meticulous lyricist Kahn selects imagery associated only with morning to idealize Kentucky in this piece: "'Good Mornin' the bees are hummin, / 'Mornin'' 'a new day comin' / . . . see the sunbeams that come a peepin' / Sayin' 'no time for sleepin'." Before the Andrews Sisters, or even the Boswell Sisters and the Pickens Sisters in the '30s, one of the first and most popular real sister singing groups in the '20s was the Tennessee-raised Brox (born Brock) Sisters, now largely forgotten, who cut with just piano accompaniment the first verse and chorus of "Kentucky's Way of Sayin' Good Mornin'" in 1925 for Victor, and it's on the Internet. Hearing or reading just the chorus of "That's The Reason Why I Wish I Was In Dixie" (Shapiro, Bernstein, 1927), with William Tracey's words and Dan Dougherty's music, might suggest the song would idealize the entire South. Yet the line in the verse about "my home in Tennessee" argues otherwise, focusing the chorus's images on that state, in phrases such as "Ev'ry cloud has silver linin' / And the sun is always shinin'," and "Little song birds say 'Good mornin'." The second verse imagery is more original, with lines like "And the only blues you hear of / Are the blues they sing and play." The Four Aristocrats' 1927 Edison recording of the first verse and chorus is on the Internet.

Lyricist Edgar Leslie and composer Mabel Wayne partnered on a quite literate piece idealizing Kentucky in the a.m. in "When Kentucky Bids The World Good-Morning" (Leo Feist, 1930). Leslie's conceit is that Kentucky's beauties in the morning equal the work of a famous composer or artist: "Ev'ry bluebird in the tree / Sings a Chopin melody / When Kentucky bids the world 'GOOD MORNING.' / There's a Rembrandt painted sky, / That's a picture for your eye / When Kentucky bids the world 'GOOD MORNING.'" In 1931 Red Nichols and His Orchestra, with Dick Robertson on vocal, recorded the chorus for Brunswick, and it's on the Internet. Also in 1931 the Dorsey Brothers Orchestra with the Boswell Sisters cut for Brunswick Walter Donaldson's "An Ev'ning In Caroline" (Donaldson, Douglas & Gumble, 1931), which is also on the Internet. The song extols the virtues of that state and also shows Donaldson to be as fine a lyricist as he was a composer. The premise of the verse is that when poets praise Dixie, what they write is "not exaggeration / It's not imagination." The chorus then points to some of Carolina's joys: "If you wanna see the moon in all its splendor, / If you wanna see the way the stars can shine / If you wanna feel a breeze that's sweetly tender, / Spend an ev'ning in Caroline." Carolina continued to be glorified by lyricists Marty Symes and Al J. Neiburg and composer Jerry Levinson in "It's Sunday Down In Caroline" (Santly Bros., 1933), pointing out the state's Sunday pleasures: "Folks can stay in bed 'til anytime they please, / IT'S SUNDAY DOWN IN CAROLINE. / Four and twenty hours set aside for play, / Cotton is forgotten down old Dixie way, / Heaven comes a callin' ev'ry seventh day." Paul Tremaine and His Orchestra cut the chorus in 1933 for Bluebird with Tremaine on vocal, and it's on the Internet.

The following year, the same trio—wordsmiths Neiburg and Symes, and tunesmith Levinson—switched states to idealize "Twenty Four Hours In Georgia" (Shapiro, Bernstein, 1934). The tune stays completely focused on the object of its idealizing in both verses and the chorus, in the verses with lines like "If the skies are friendly overhead / From the time you rise till you go to bed / You're in Georgia, Southland's Paradise" and "If you see peach blossoms all around / And snow white cotton on the ground / Yeah, that's Georgia, right before your eyes"; and from the chorus, "Like the honey from the comb, your day is sweet, / Twenty Four Hours In Georgia / Ev'rywhere you go, you hear a song / That's the reason South folks live so long / They just sing their blues away when things go wrong / Twenty Four Hours In Georgia." In 1934 the San Francisco–based Griff Williams and Jimmy Walsh Orchestra, with June MacCloy on vocal, cut just the chorus for Titan records, which is on the Internet. The next song extolling a southern state—and the last worth mentioning—didn't come along until fourteen years later, and in fact "I Went Down To Virginia" (Jefferson Music, 1948), with words and music by Redd Evans and Dave Mann, didn't so much idealize the Old Dominion as the singer just told it like it was about that state in his or her eyes. For a change, too, the focus isn't on the state's natural beauty, but rather on its good-natured, warm-hearted natives: "I WENT DOWN TO VIRGINIA / And didn't know a soul / No wonder folks befriend ya, / Their hearts are made of gold / Why the civic minded citizens are all so kind, / They see to it you hook a fish on ev'ry line, / . . . Well, brother, if you ever plan a comin' down this way, / You'll find that things are just exactly like I say, / And you'll stay down in Virginia, / Virginia, U. S. A." The number isn't divided into verses and a chorus, but is in two stanzas that run the length of the song. Larry Clinton and His Orchestra, with Helen Lee on vocal, cut the first stanza for Decca in 1948, which is on the Internet.

The next smaller geographic area of the South that Alleymen glorified was Dixie's cities, and not very many of them nor in many songs altogether—just two about Tallahassee, the same number about Memphis, and one about Nashville—all spread out between 1914 and 1951. In 1914, lyricist Karl Morandi and composers James A. Murray and Walter Johnson in "Down In Dear Old Tallahassee Town" (Karl Morandi, 1914) lightheartedly idealized that Florida panhandle city. In the first of two verses, we meet Hazel and Charlie, an unmarried couple who have been "going around together . . . up and down Broadway . . . been out late at nights. / Wined and dined in every swell café." Finally Hazel decides it's time for them to settle down. Charlie agrees and suggests he take her back to his hometown, named in the chorus: "Back to Tallahassee, dear old Tallahassee / Where the sun is bright, / All the little birdies up in the trees / Sing 'bout you every night, / Where the Cocoanuts grow, and the warm breezes blow, / There is no ice and snow down there." By the second verse, Hazel and Charlie "have a cute little bungalow they do not want to know the news of New York town, / . . . They also [have] the cutest, little, neatest motor car, / . . . [and] both confess that they had a better time by far / Since they had left dear old Broadway." Thirty-three years later, one of the true giants and geniuses of American popular and theatre music (*Guys and Dolls, The Most Happy Fella*, etc.), Frank Loesser, wrote both the words and music of the other song extolling Florida's capital city, "Tallahassee" (Famous Music, 1947), for Paramount Pictures' *Variety Girl*. Just a snatch reveals Loesser's virtuosity: "When you see land / Kinda green and grassy / Beneath a moon / Bright beyond compare, / When you hear blue jays / Chirping high and sassy / And catch one sniff of southern cooking / Hanging on the ev'ning air, / . . . Get off the train. / You're in Tallahassee, / The Southland at its best." Loesser wrote the piece for voices responding to one another, as did the Andrews Sisters and Bing Crosby for Decca in 1947, as may be heard on the Internet.

The two songs idealizing Memphis, separated by twenty-six years, couldn't be more different in character. With Edgar Leslie and Bert Kalmar's words and Pete Wendling's music, "Take Me To The Land Of Jazz" (Waterson, Berlin & Snyder, 1919) celebrates Memphis strictly as the city that gave birth to the blues and other jazz. From the second verse we get the hyperbole, "There is music in each breeze / Even trombones grow on trees, / You hear 'em moaning and groaning their tuneful harmonies," and from the chorus, "Take me to the Land of Jazz, / Let me hear the kind of blues that Memphis has; / I want to step, / To a tune that's full of ginger and pep; / . . . Let me give you a warning, / We won't get home until morning; / 'Cause ev'rybody's full of Jazzbo; / In the lovin' Land of Jazz." Marion Harris, sounding a lot like Ethel Merman before there *was* an Ethel Merman, cut the tune for Victor in 1919, as may be heard on the Internet. A far cry from the razzmatazz of Memphis in "The Land of Jazz" was the vision of it as an idyllic sleepy southern town in "Memphis In June" (Burke and Van Heusen, Inc., 1945), with words by Paul Francis Webster and music by Hoagy Carmichael, from the R. K. O. Radio Picture *Johnny Angel,* in which Hoagy himself sang it. With images of easy living like "cousin Amanda's / Making a rhubarb pie" and "I can see old granny 'cross the street, still a-rockin', / Watchin' the neighbors go by," in 1947 Hoagy Carmichael and His Orchestra cut it for ARA Records with Hoagy on vocal, and it's on the Internet.

By 1951 Nashville was firmly established as the center of the country music industry, so it's rather surprising that not even a glimmer of a mention of country or hillbilly music is listed among the joys extolled in that city in "Down In Nashville, Tennessee," published by one of the oldest and most mainstream Alley publishing houses, Harms, in 1951, and with words and music by two equally mainstream Alleymen, Bob Hilliard and Dave Mann. The recording of the song was by an equally mainstream popular singing artist, Dinah Shore, but one who knew the territory, since she was born in Winchester, Tennessee, was raised in McMinnville, and attended college at Vanderbilt University in Nashville. Her rendition of the number for Victor in 1951 is on the Internet. With country music absent from the things to be idealized about Nashville, the lyric concentrates on the delights to be found there just as a good ol' southern country town: ". . . come with me / Down to Nashville Tennessee. / You'll find your kind of real home cookin' / Why keep lookin'? / . . . Oh, what a town! / There's never a frown! / The place even glows when the sun goes down." Thus ended songs glorifying Dixie cities.

The next, last, and smallest geographic units of Dixie that Alleymen idealized were some of its rivers, riverbanks, and streets. Since there were so few of each, I have lumped them together, bringing the total number to five. Like songs in other groups, these cover a vast swath of time, from 1903 through 1942. The earliest, "Moonlight On The Mississippi" (Jos. W. Stern, 1903), by two black southern-born-and-raised Alleymen, lyricist Bob Cole and composer Rosamond Johnson, I discussed and quoted from at length in Chapter 1 in the section introducing African American Alleymen. Little more need be said about it here except that this piece was not just the earliest tune idealizing a river or riverbank in Dixie but only the second song to make idealizing Dixie or any part of it its central theme. Fourteen years after Cole and Johnson glorified this tranquil stretch of the Mississippi, W. C. Handy penned both the words and music of a tune that idealized, by contrast, one of the raunchiest streets in the South when he wrote of a notorious, nefarious Memphis thoroughfare in "Beale Street Blues" (Pace & Handy Music, 1917). In the verse the singer says he's seen Broadway, Market Street in Frisco, and the Prado, but "Take my advice folks and see Beale Street first," advice not lightly given since, as the chorus says, "You'll see pretty Browns in beautiful gowns, / You'll see tailor mades and hand me downs / You'll meet honest men and pickpockets skilled / You'll find that bus'ness never closes till somebody gets killed." That's just in the *first* chorus, with two more to go!—including lines like "If Beale Street could talk, / Married men would have to take their beds and walk / Except one or two, who never drank booze / And the blind man on the corner who sings the Beale Street Blues." No precisely contemporary vocal recordings are on the Internet, but there is a 1921 Victor record by Marion Harris with some altered and additional lyrics.

With Joe Young's words and Bernice Petkere's music, "My River Home" (Irving Berlin, Inc., 1932) idealized the placid life in a cabin on the banks of the Mississippi, in contrast to the bedlam of northern big-city living with "Riveters drilling—noises are killing." In "MY RIVER HOME / I see a light thru the pines, / That shines on a rickety door, / The latch is always open, /

Breezes kiss MY RIVER HOME / . . . I love that sweet serenade while under the shade of the trees. / . . . I'm hearin' the darkies down on the levee, / Singin' in rhythm hallelujah." This idyllic world seems in harmony, as opposed to the maddening cacophony of city noises. Peter De Rose and His Orchestra, with De Rose on vocal of just the chorus, cut "My River Home" in 1932 for Electradisk, as may be heard on the Internet. Questions still remain regarding just when black bluesman Spencer Williams wrote "Basin Street Blues" and just what parts of the song are actually his. Though the only existing published sheet music, that of Mayfair Music Corp. in 1933, credits "Words and Music by SPENCER WILLIAMS," various published and online sources claim Williams wrote the instrumental as far back as 1926 and that Mayfair originally published it that year. Louis Armstrong recorded it in 1928, but the only vocal is Satchmo's scat singing, not actual lyrics. Moreover, David A. Jasen credits the song's words not to Williams at all, but to Jack Teagarden for a 1931 Columbia record of the piece that he, Glenn Miller, Benny Goodman, Gene Krupa, and others recorded as The Charleston Chasers directed by Goodman, with a vocal by Teagarden (see Jasen 431), a recording that is on the Internet. A variant on what already sounds like an urban legend is that the words of the refrain are Williams's, and Teagarden wrote only the lyric of the verse from "Won't-cha come along with me" through "This is Basin Street!" Whether Williams wrote the refrain's lyrics or not, he had the background to paint an idealized portrait of the main street of New Orleans's red-light district, Storyville, himself the son of a prostitute there, and, after his mother's death when he was eight, cared for by his aunt, a prominent madam. The lyric is ironic in saying, "Basin Street is the street, where the elite, always meet in New Orleans, / Lan' of dreams / . . . Yes, siree, / Where welcome's free, / Dear to me, where I can lose / My BASIN STREET BLUES."

The last song idealizing a micro-spot on Dixie's landscape featured a place most northerners probably hadn't even heard of in "Ogeechee River Lullaby" (Cherio Music, 1942), with words and music by Cab Calloway, Guy Wood, and Jack Palmer. The Ogeechee is a 294-mile river in Georgia, and as small as it is in the larger scheme of the South, this song lavishes the same kinds of idyllic images upon it that other pieces pour on the whole of Dixie: "The stars are bright, / Tonight on 'Geechee river, / The mellow moon is high / The nightingale will sing his tender love song / OGEECHEE RIVER LUL-LABY! / Magnolias bloom tonight along the river, / The weepin' willows sigh."

In 1942 Cab Calloway and His Orchestra recorded the piece for Columbia with Cab and "the Cabaliers" on vocal, as may be heard on the Internet.

The final group of Dixie tunes idealizing or glorifying aspects of the South are five that fall into that hard-to-categorize category of novelty songs. Three of these idolize southern girls, including one that became a major hit in its day and for some time thereafter, while the other two, both from the same year, are just rather outrageously comic novelty songs; I'll begin with these. How do you create an idyllic mega-myth? According to colyricists and composers George Fairman, Gus Van, and Joe Schenck, you combine in one song idealized images of the two most popular geographic areas that Alley songwriters glorified—Dixie and Ireland—into a single piece called "If Shamrocks Grew Along The Swanee Shore" (Harry Von Tilzer Music, 1921). The results of this oxymoronic pairing are both charming and hilarious: "If Shamrocks grew along the Swanee shore 'neath skies so blue they'd bloom forever more / And then when Uncle Joe picked his old banjo he'd always play an Irish reel / And I'd give a dollar to hear old mammy holler / 'Hello Mister McClusky how do you feel? / . . . I'll bet my dear old Ma and Pa would always be dancin' to the Wearin of the green around the cabin floor if Shamrocks grew along the Swanee shore." Tenors Charles Hart and Lewis James cut this silliness, with some added comic patter, on a 1922 Edison Blue Amberol cylinder, and it's on the Internet. Also published in 1921 was a tune in which the writers of both words and music, Jack Stern and Clarence J. Marks, turned the tables on the songs idealizing the South by comparing it to heaven in "Heaven Is Like Dixie After All" (M. Witmark, 1921), demonstrating that heaven possesses all the idyllic qualities Dixie is known for, in three long and detailed refrains. To select just some of the highlights, starting with the entire first refrain: "Right down the middle ran the Swanee River, / Following the Mason Dixon Line, / Old Black Joe was riding in a Flivver / Along with Mammy O Mine. / On ev'ry side the trees were sprouting cotton, / And ev'rybody had a Southern drawl. / And when St. Peter started yellin' for a slice of watermelon, / I knew heaven was like Dixie after all." For just a few other snippets, "all peaches up there weren't fruit / The other brand I saw that they were showin', / Were angels, each one a beaut," and when the singer asked "how they voted up there in heaven" he "got this answer from St. Paul, / Who said in accents most emphatic 'This whole place is Democratic,' / I knew heaven was like Dixie after all." To appreciate the humor of the number's punch line, we must recall that

Dixie party lines have shifted from solid Democrat—albeit old-school Southern Democrat—in the 1920s to conservative Republican today (though the ideologies of the two aren't very far apart).

The three songs idolizing southern girls were written within a year of each other in the late 'teens, all by major Alleymen. In not one of his greatest lyrics, Jack Yellen extolled "Southern Gals" (Jerome H. Remick, 1917), with Albert Gumble's music. The chorus ticks off examples of girls the singer met in Dixie after a verse in which he explains, "I've just come back from the South today / . . . I've never seen such gals as they have down there." His list begins with "Mary down in Maryland" and works its way through such other southern states as "sweet Virginia too," "You'll go dippy over Mississippi / And the gals named Caroline / . . . Then there's Lucy Anna with naughty eyes / And a peach named Georgia who takes the prize." That same year, similar to Yellen and Gumble's tune was "There's Nothing Sweeter Than A Girl From Dixieland" (Leo Feist, 1917), with Grant Clarke's words and Jimmie V. Monaco's music. In the verse the singer brags he's been "around the nation" and "made a study of pretty girlies," but "Dixie takes the prize," as the chorus shows: "There's nothing sweeter than a kiss from a Miss down in Mississippi / . . . I love to hear them say, 'I reckon and you all,' / . . . There's nothing half as cute, as each little peach from the state of Georgia; / Don't overlook Louisiana and Alabama." Clarke ends on an unexpected note: "Father and I say to one another, / Each time we look at my dear old mother, / There's nothing sweeter than a girl from Dixie Land."

Clarke again provided the words and Milton Ager and George W. Meyer the music for the one big hit among Dixie tunes idealizing southern girls, "Everything Is Peaches Down In Georgia" (Leo Feist, 1918). According to David A. Jasen, co-composer Ager came up with the song's idea when during the Great War he was stationed at Fort Greenleaf, Georgia, from 1917 to 1918, after which he got a job with publisher Leo Feist and proposed the number to Clarke and Meyer (Jasen 4). In Clarke's clever hands, Milt Ager's idea became a poem in praise of Georgia peaches, both horticultural and matrimonial, mostly the latter, in two brief verses and the chorus. The first verse sets things up with "Down in Georgia there are peaches, / Waiting for you yes, and each is / Sweet as any peach that you could reach for on a tree"; the second elaborates the metaphor with such notions as "Clingstone peaches cling right to you." But it's in the more familiar chorus that Clarke really shows his stuff as a lyricist: "Ev'rything is peaches down in Georgia, / What a peach of a clime, / For a peach of a time / Believe me, Paradise is waiting down there for you, / . . . There's a preacher preaches down in Georgia, / Always ready to say: 'Will you love and obey?' / I bet you'll pick yourself a peach of a wife, / Settle down to a peach of a life, / Ev'rything is peaches down in Georgia." Charting at #5 in November 1918, Billy Murray and the American Quartet had the hit recording of the whole song plus some patter not in the sheet music, which they cut for Victor on August 1, 1918, as heard on the Internet.

* * *

Having now examined individually several hundred of the 1,079 Dixie tunes written by Alley songwriters and published by Alley publishers between 1898 and 1958 that are in major library archives of sheet music—plus Phil Harris's RCA Victor recording of Andy Razaf's unpublished "That's What I Like 'Bout The South"—it's time for an overview of whatever conclusions may fairly be made about that large body of popular song unified in subject matter and theme over sixty years.

Other than the obvious fact that the subject matter of all Dixie tunes was one or another aspect of the South, virtually all the songs engaged to a greater or lesser extent in presenting an idyllic, idealized, romantic, or glorified vision of that region, and, more often than not, employed many of the images of the Moonlight and Magnolias Myth as described earlier. Further, as has been mentioned several times throughout the book, with very few exceptions all the Alley's Dixie tunes were set in the South of the time each individual song was written, or, in other words, the song and the moonlight and magnolias imagery were almost invariably contemporaneous with the Dixie of that day, not reflexive or nostalgic of a prior time such as the antebellum South. This is significant for just what kind of myth Alley songs were implanting in the national popular imagination for more than half the twentieth century. In this respect, Karen L. Cox, at the outset of *Dreaming of Dixie,* is partly right when she maintains "that regardless of the medium the image of the American South was consistent. Southern belles and gentlemen, mammies and uncles, white-columned mansions, fields of cotton and, literally, moonlight and magnolias were employed to suggest *Dixie.* One could certainly find such icons within the post–Civil War mythology of the Lost Cause, but southerners were not responsible for marketing and disseminating this imagery for national consumption. On the contrary, Madison Avenue's advertising agencies, Tin Pan Alley's music makers, Chicago's radio stars, and Hollywood's filmmakers were the ones who found profit in selling the romantic South to American consumers" (Cox [*ix*]). Cox is correct when she sees moonlight and magnolias as just *one* feature of the Lost Cause Myth, all the others belonging to the pre–Civil War past; and she's also on fairly firm footing when asserting that the ad industry, radio, and Hollywood were behind perpetuating the Old South to Americans for marketing purposes. But she seriously errs when trying to lump Tin Pan Alley in with the other media she lists. After correctly noting here that the moonlight and magnolias imagery was but one element of the Lost Cause Myth, throughout the rest of her book Cox uses "moonlight and magnolias" and "Old South" as indistinguishable synonyms for antebellum Dixie (see esp. Cox 50, 53, 54, 80). Furthermore, a remark of hers raises questions about whether she even read or listened to any Dixie tunes: "Fans of Tin Pan Alley music were familiar with songs set in the Dixie of the Old South" (Cox 71). This, as has already been shown, is utter nonsense, since almost all were set in the time corresponding to when each song was written.

The novel *Gone with the Wind* was published in 1936 and the film released three years later in 1939, each event causing a short-lived craze for the Old South. Yet from the Alley's beginning in 1898 through 1936, the year the novel was published, writers had written and publishers had published 991 Dixie tunes, the number increasing to 1,007 through the year the movie opened, and, as we have seen throughout the book, many of these songs were popular hits and financial successes for their writers and publishers. The early public, when many folks had a parlor piano, could purchase these songs as cheap sheet music, pay to hear them sung by buying cheap seats to a vaudeville show or musical, purchase phonograph records or cylinders—also an inexpensive transaction once one bought the "talking machine" on which to play them—or, starting in the 1920s, listen to them *free* once the family bought a radio. True, we have the box office receipts for how many people saw the 1915 *The Birth of a Nation* and the 1939 *Gone with the Wind,* and the numbers are huge. But there's no way to count the millions of Americans who listened to (or sang and played for themselves) the many songs idealizing present-day Dixie that the Alley turned out over so many years. After the year of the film of *Gone with the Wind* until the Alley's last year of Dixie tune output, 1958, Alleymen added at least 72 more Dixie tunes.

What all this suggests is that for well over fifty years of the twentieth century, the myth of the South that pervaded the national popular imagination had nothing to do with transient fads for the Old South, but with the idyllic, idealized, bucolic vision of present-day Dixie as evoked through the pure moonlight and magnolias imagery employed by Alley songwriters over many decades. I would never commit the heresy of suggesting that these largely urban, northern songsmiths *invented* the Moonlight and Magnolias Myth—its creation had originated as parts of the Old South and Lost Cause Myths. But, at the very least, successive generations of Alleymen and women, having extracted from those southern myths their moonlight and magnolias elements wherever they found such images, *reinvented* them to write songs proclaiming, "Nothing could be finer / Than to be in Carolina"—or anyplace else in Dixie—right now, in the present-day South, not in the antebellum era before the Civil War.

EPILOGUE

The Years They Drove Old Dixie Down

The disappearance of Dixie tunes from the output of Tin Pan Alley song-writers and the stock of Alley publishers wasn't an overnight event. Nor did it stem from a single cause. It arose from a complex tangle of interconnected factors, some dating even to the later years in which the Alley's production of southern songs was still pretty much in flower. As was noted near the end of Chapter 9, from the inception of the Alley as the center of the popular music publishing trade in 1898, through 1936 when Macmillan published Margaret Mitchell's novel *Gone with the Wind,* writers and publishers combined to produce a minimum of 991 Dixie tunes, adding another 16 through 1939 when David O. Selznick's epic film version of Mitchell's novel was released. After that the Alley produced seventy-two more Dixie tunes during the nineteen years before the writing, publication, and recording of southern songs vanished from Tin Pan Alley entirely after 1958. With no further embellishment, these raw facts make it seem there was a sharp, sudden, and radical drop-off in new Alley Dixie tunes, which was not the case. Additional clarification and explanation show the decline was slower and more gradual.

One might think the 991 Dixie tunes published between 1898 and 1936 could be accounted for by their rapid proliferation when the craze for them began in the 1900s and 1910s, but such thinking would be wrong. In the 1920s, Alley writers and publishers produced 350 of those 991 songs, or about 35 percent of them. Their yearly numbers remained strong until the last two years of that decade, when they tapered down quite a bit, as the following list shows: 1920–40; 1921–44; 1922–53; 1923–50; 1924–34; 1925–31; 1926–23; 1927–31; 1928–17; 1929–17. In the first half of the 1930s the yearly number of Dixie tunes stayed in the teens except for two years when they rose into the 20s; in the second half of the decade, the figures were in the single digits: 1930–14; 1931–16; 1932–20; 1933–24; 1934–15; 1935–8; 1936–9; 1937–6;

1938–3; 1939–5. After that the yearly number of Alley Dixie tunes never rose out of single digits again.

It could be supposed that the annual number of Alley Dixie tunes crashed after 1929 just as the Stock Market did in October of that year, followed by the Great Depression, which, most historians agree, lasted for a full decade until the recovery in 1939 and 1940. But this supposition won't work as an explanation, since, like Hollywood's studios, the Alley's music makers were only lightly touched by the widespread economic hardships that struck the nation as a whole in the Depression years. The production of popular songs both as sheet music and phonograph records continued during the Great Depression. This can easily be seen by merely flipping through the pages of Lissauer's "Section II" in his *Encyclopedia,* which lists songs by the year of their recording; Kinkle's annual listings of "Popular Songs" and "Representative Recordings" in Volume I of his work; and Jasen's briefer listing of Hit Songs of the 1930s (Jasen 201–05), all of which show the Alley was alive and reasonably well during the Depression (see Bibliography for works by Lissauer, Kinkle, and Jasen). Ergo, we must look elsewhere for the decline in the number of Dixie tunes during the 1930s, despite the great popularity of some occasional ones such as "When It's Sleepy Time Down South," which Louis Armstrong scored big with on Okeh Records in 1931; Mitchell Parish and Frank Perkins's romantic "Stars Fell On Alabama" in 1934; "Moon Over Miami" (1935–36); and "Is It True What They Say About Dixie?" (1936).

Once we start looking for reasons for the fall-off in Dixie tunes in the 1930s, all we can do is speculate and conjecture, and whatever data or hard facts exist to substantiate our conjectures hover somewhere between slim and none. The first almost-possibility is that audience and music listeners' tastes in songs' subject matter changed radically between the happy-go-lucky Jazz Age of the '20s and the dreary Depression years of the '30s. Yet why would the moonlight and magnolias of an idealized Dixie have appealed to the Charleston-dancing, bathtub gin–drinking flappers and their beaus— who were seemingly having as much fun as was humanly possible—whereas the same images of a romantic South of sunny days and moonlit nights would have had little or no appeal to Americans stuck in the gloom of breadlines, apple sellers, homelessness, the midwestern Dust Bowl, and all the other visible manifestations of a nationwide economic downturn, except in those rare cases when an individual song *as a song* caught their attention? So, overall, the outmoded content conjecture doesn't work very well from the perspective of audience appeal when escapist Hollywood films were wildly popular during the Depression. Nor does a parallel conjecture regarding shifts in tastes for popular musical styles. Throughout the 1900s and the 'teens, composers of Dixie tunes accommodated their melodies to the current craze for ragtime, and even in the 1920s to a great extent they adapted the current jazz rhythms and melodic patterns to express their lyricists' rhapsodizing on the South's idyllic desirability as a land of moonlight and magnolias. But come the 1930s and the advent of the big bands and swing, it would seem that this new music simply couldn't, with rare exceptions, embrace what Dixie tunes were all about. I mentioned above a few of the Alley's Dixie hits from the '30s, but none of these were "swing tunes." They fall instead into the other, opposite, category in the '30s and '40s, which many people tend to forget about: "sweet music," a far better vehicle for expressing visions of an idealized South. Yet the number of such Dixie tunes remained few. Early in the '40s, two notable big band swing tune Dixie hits emerged, with "Tuxedo Junction" (1940) and "Chattanooga Choo Choo" (1941), but as popular as these pieces were, it was a case of too little too late; the years of large numbers of Dixie tunes coming from the Alley annually as they had before the '30s would not and could not be replicated.

Another reason for the steep decline in Dixie tunes during the '30s may have to do with the Alleymen who had earlier written such songs, and for this we have a bit of evidence.

Timelessness vs. The Ravages of Time

In 1918, lyricist Sidney D. Mitchell and composer Archie Gottler were so sure that things in the good ol' slow-movin' South were impervious to change that they wrote a tune called "In 1960 You'll Find Dixie Looking Just The Same" (Waterson, Berlin & Snyder, 1918). The first verse of this snappy song lays out the premise that since everything in Dixie now in 1918 looks just as it did back in 1858, it's a sure bet Dixie will remain just as unchanged in 1960. The chorus illustrates this thesis with some examples of timeless elements of the South: "In nineteen sixty, you'll find Dixie, looking just the same, / Cotton blossoms hiding possums, / Still bring Dixie fame, / You'll find her bread and 'lasses, / Still surpasses, / Anything else you know; / You'll find colored Aunties, / In their shanties, / Singing sweet and low." The Sterling Trio, made up of Henry Burr, Albert Campbell, and John Meyer, cut the tune for Columbia in August 1918, and it's on the Internet. Yet of all Alleymen, Mitchell and Gottler were alone in their Pollyanna view of an unchanging Dixie. Others, all in the 1930s, saw the handwriting on the wall—that the charming ways of Dixie, even *postbellum* Dixie, weren't destined to live forever.

Lyricists Herb Magidson and Maurice Sigler and composer James V. Monaco teamed up on "Ole Mammy Ain't Gonna Sing No More" (De Sylva, Brown and Henderson, 1934), symbolic of the demise of the essence of the South with the disappearance of the traditional mammy from the scene. Magidson and Sigler expressed this theme obliquely through such lines as, "The cotton blossoms look so mournful tonight, / The moon is sad and he ain't shinin' so bright. / . . . Ole Mammy Ain't Gonna Sing No More. / The angels took her up above / For the cotton pickin', / . . . They wanted Mammy up above / For to make fried chicken / That's why they called her from below." That same year, in a less lugubrious mood, wordsmith Earle Crooker and tunesmith Henry Sullivan wrote "Lily Belle May June" (Harms, 1934), which treads the line between satire and telling things like they are. In the first stanza, Lily Belle May June, a genuine Southern Belle, is making a career for herself by singing on the radio "Of the sunshine down in Dixieland / . . . moonlight and roses / . . . [and] that life is romantic where the magnolias grow." In the second stanza, a boy's chorus takes over, telling Lily Belle to "come back home right soon / Something's happened down in Dixieland." Not just something, but a number of things: "On the old plantation / They've put up a comfort station, / And the roadside's just a grocer's stand / . . . Some dirty Yankee's puttin' a rest camp where the magnolias grow." A strong hint that some Alleymen who used to extol the idyllic South may no longer have much to extol in the 1930s and were disinclined to write more songs glorifying present-day Dixie.

Two more songs substantiate this supposition, both from 1936 and both by major players in the Alley's pantheon of songwriters. From the Columbia Picture *The Music Goes Round*, "There'll Be No South" (Irving Berlin, Inc., 1936), with Lew Brown's words and Harry Akst and Harry Richman's music, argues that if traditionally southern music or music associated with southern blacks should ever disappear or fuse with bland northern song, that would be the end of the romantic, idealized South as we know it: "When darkies 'round the cabin door, / Don't sing about the Swanee shore, / Or wail about their mammies anymore, / THERE'LL BE NO SOUTH. / . . .If we can't stroll 'neath Southern skies, / And hear those darkies harmonize / The songs that brought tear-drops to your eyes, / THERE'LL BE NO SOUTH ." The last '30s tune expressing disillusionment with the present-day South, "Dixie Isn't Dixie Any More" (Robbins Music, 1937), had lyrics by Johnny Mercer and music by Rube Bloom, and it debuted in the all-black revue *Lew Leslie's Blackbirds of 1936*. In the song, a southerner returns to visit "the sunny South" but discovers that "Nothing there is what it used to be" since there's "a trolley going by the cabin door. / And the famous old plantation / Is now a filling station— / Dixie isn't Dixie anymore." Also, "You won't hear those darkies in the fields. . . . 'Cause they're all too busy singing on the radio," and "On the spot where all the traders used to sell their cotton / There is now a Woolworth five-and-ten-cent store." Not satire, but a sad photo of Depression-era Dixie.

Of course the United States slowly recovered from the economic troubles of the Depression, thanks largely to the buildup of defense industries starting around 1939, but other circumstances prevented Dixie tunes from ever making a full recovery in Tin Pan Alley again.

The Music Goes 'Round

Musically, the years of World War II from late 1941 through August 1945 were an extension of the big band and swing era, during which popular male and female vocalists who sang with the bands came to the fore as radio and recording idols. Alleymen wrote nearly as many popular songs related to the war as they had written Dixie tunes in the roughly forty-five years before then (see Jones *passim*), as well as other romantic ballads, novelty songs, and dance tunes, to help take the home front's collective mind *off* the war. Yet the Alley's output of Dixie tunes during the war was just eighteen songs, of which only "Chattanooga Choo Choo" in 1941 was a hit—and that before the United States was fully engaged in the conflict.

But something else was happening during World War II that would, if at first gradually, turn Dixie away from the Alley forever. In Nashville, Tennessee, in 1942, country singer Roy Acuff teamed up with country songwriter/ singer/talent scout/publicist Fred Rose to form Acuff-Rose Publications, the first music publishing house devoted strictly to country (previously hillbilly) music. Not only was their venture a tremendous success on its own, but it was a magnet that drew other country-music publishing and recording ventures to Nashville as the '40s and, especially, the '50s went on. In the early 1950s the Alley was still able to produce an occasional hit Dixie tune idealizing the South in the old style, like "Shrimp Boats" (1951), "Jambalaya" (1952), and "Mobile" (1953), but most southern songs—different from the Alley's fare for over half a century—came out of Nashville and reached, by and large, very different listeners.

Yet in some respects, not so different after all. In 1980, Stephen A. Smith published an article titled "Sounds of the South: The Rhetorical Saga of Country Music Lyrics" (see Bibliography), in which he ran up some statistics on frequent subject matter or themes in country songs. According to his figures, a large number of them are about homesickness or a desire to return to the South (see Smith, "Sounds" 168), which, as we have seen, was the dominant theme among Alley Dixie tunes in terms of sheer numbers, so in this sense it would seem Nashville just carried on from where the Alley left off. Yet Smith found something entirely unheard of in Dixie tunes idealizing the South—songs that "indicated a dissatisfaction with life in the South, . . . The major regional shortcoming . . . was poverty, to which the singer saw an alternative in the more industrial North" (Smith, "Sounds" 167). Songs of this type don't just reveal unhappiness with life in the South, but, perhaps more importantly for our purposes, show their writers had abandoned the Moonlight and Magnolias Myth. This tough view of Dixie in country music appealed not just to folks in the South, but, thanks partly to whites moving north from Dixie to look for work during the Depression, to a much broader-based audience. By the '50s, country music had found millions of listeners nationwide, both urban and rural. Mostly, country music audiences were young adults and older folk. Starting in the mid-'50s, as we shall see, teenagers would find their music elsewhere. Regardless of where either group of listeners was finding it, they were no longer looking for it in the Dixie tunes the Alley used to give them in abundance.

There is some evidence the Alley may have been aware of this, for with the exception of the few relatively traditional moonlight and magnolias southern songs I just mentioned that still became hits in the '50s, other anomalous pieces suggest the Alley was rather enervated where Dixie tunes were concerned. Even the big hits like Patti Page's 1950 recording of "Tennessee Waltz" and Kay Starr's of "Bonaparte's Retreat" that same year—each discussed earlier—use Dixie mostly as a background for a song about lost or found love. Jack Holmes's "The Blacksmith Blues" (Hill and Range Songs, 1952) is an example of simply a rhythm number, its opening line of "Down in Ol' Kentucky where horseshoes are lucky" just setting the scene for the lyric describing a "village smithy" who "sings the boogie blues, while he's hammering on the shoes" and "is even got the horses cloppin' / Bop, down the avenue." Not a moonlight and magnolias vision of the South, but this 1952 Capitol record became a million-seller for Ella Mae Morse with Nelson Riddle's Orchestra, and it's on the Internet. That same year Jo Stafford recorded a piece that could have been set anywhere, but its writers chose to place it in Dixie for no good reason. With words by Jack Lawrence and music by Sammy Fain, "Raminay! (The New Orleans Chimney Sweep)" (Warock Music, 1952) tells of a slightly magical chimney sweep who not only cleans chimneys, but also chases away bad moods and figuratively lights lovers' fires: "Got any gray clouds to sweep away? / If you got worry, if you got gloom, / The chimney sweeper will push his broom, / . . . If you're a lover, he'll help you discover / Love's loveliest dreams." The only southern reference is near the beginning when we find that Raminay "walks the alleys of New Orleans," as is heard on Jo Stafford's 1952 Columbia record on the Internet.

The last two Dixie tunes to come out of the Alley also had music by Sammy Fain. Both were from the 20th Century-Fox Picture *Mardi Gras,* and both had words by the multi-Academy Award-winning black lyricist Paul Francis Webster, who wrote several of his award-winning songs also with Fain. Yet from a look at these two final Dixie tunes, it's amazing the lyricist or composer ever won anything. The first piece, a male torch song briefly touched on in Chapter 5, was "Bourbon Street Blues," and the second, "Stonewall Jackson" (both published by Leo Feist, 1958). The latter was a novelty tune about applying Stonewall's battle tactics to winning women, with gratuitous asides praising the state of Virginia. The piece seems like a desperate last stand for Dixie tunes before their ultimate surrender to other kinds of music.

I use other *kinds* advisedly, not just *kind,* for, other than Nashville's country songs, two more types of music encroached upon the Alley and its Dixie tunes in the 1950s, one in a relatively minor way, the other with an enormous impact that no words can exaggerate. The lesser of the two was a musical movement that swept the country starting in the late 1950s and that I like to call with a bit of facetiousness "synthetic folk music." Not that a great many of the songs sung by new groups like The Kingston Trio and Gateway Singers (both of which gained national prominence in 1957), Bud & Travis (1958), and The Limeliters (1959), not to mention The Weavers, who had been around since 1948, weren't authentic folk tunes. But they also sang and played newly written and composed "folk songs" like the Gateway Singers' "Ballad of Sigmund Freud." A good number of these "folk" groups wore suits and ties during live performance—a visual oxymoron if there ever was one! But the tunes were great, and the groups and their music attracted wide followings of listeners and audiences—including myself—that, from what I could tell at the time, crossed all lines among ages and ethnicities.

But this was nothing compared to what began to happen among white, middle-class teenagers starting in 1954—in three words, rock and roll (or rock & roll, or rock 'n' roll). Al Pavlow, my friend, discography expert, and author of *Big Al Pavlow's The R&B Book: A Disc-History of Rhythm & Blues,* assured me that if I tried to write a comprehensive treatment of how rock and roll emerged from black rhythm and blues to become the dominant musical passion among America's white teens for decades starting in the mid-'50s, it would take at least a chapter if not an entire book. So he suggested that for a brief Epilogue focusing on reasons for the demise of the Alley's Dixie tunes, I should focus on the two events falling almost precisely a year apart that caused rock and roll to take off like a shot among postwar, reasonably affluent, record-buying white teens all across America, altering both what would be the primary kind of popular music and the age group that listened to and bought it for decades to come.

First, The Chords, a black rhythm & blues vocal group, wrote and recorded on March 15, 1954, for Cat Records, a subsidiary of the R&B label Atlantic Records, their only hit, "Sh-Boom." Their record rose to the #2 spot on *Billboard*'s R&B chart and #9 on the popular music chart. Later that same year, The Crew Cuts, a white male singing group, cut a cover of "Sh-Boom" for Mercury, tailored for white teens. This version made history as the first R&B song, or doo-wop tune, albeit in a white group's rendition of it, to hit the #1 spot on *Billboard*'s pop charts, staying there for nine weeks during August and September 1954. This ushered in, if only in a small way, the start of the new genre of rock and roll.

Second, on April 12, 1954, Bill Haley and His Comets recorded Max C. Freedman and Jimmy De Knight's (pseud. of James E. Myer) rock and roll tune "Rock Around The Clock." When Decca released it, it was the B-side (or flip side) of "Thirteen Women (And Only One Man In Town)," thus garnering less notice than if it had been the featured side of the disc. Although it made *Billboard*'s pop charts, it wasn't considered a commercial success. Only after Haley's rendition was used under the opening credits of the 1955 film *Blackboard Jungle* did "Rock Around The Clock" shoot up on July 9, 1955, to become the first rock and roll song to reach the #1 spot on *Billboard*'s pop music charts, where it remained for eight weeks, catching fire with the country's white, middle-class teens as no previous rock and roll songs (and there had been some) had before. To paraphrase the title of a later one, with Haley & Co.'s "Rock Around The Clock," rock and roll was here to stay. Although some mainstream singers of the '40s continued into the '50s and beyond, like Perry Como, Frank Sinatra, and Dinah Shore, and later ones like Eddie Fisher, Patti Page, and Teresa Brewer appealed to older audiences, now teenagers were the majority of the record-buying public, altering the character of Tin Pan Alley songwriters and publishers, and driving Dixie tunes from the precincts of the Alley forever.

These were the musical reasons for the demise of Alley tunes idealizing Dixie. But one more reason remains, accounting for the death of the Moonlight and Magnolias Myth itself.

Lifting the Veil

In 1919, Tin Pan Alley songwriters and publishers produced sixty-four Dixie tunes, most of them idealizing the South in one way or another for its idyllic tranquility. Among the sixty-four pieces, those that stood out as popular successes that year were "Anything Is Nice If It Comes From Dixieland," "Dixie Is Dixie Once More," "I Always Think I'm Up In Heaven (When I'm Down in Dixieland)," "Mammy O' Mine," "Take Me To The Land Of Jazz," and the mega-hit "Swanee"—all in the aggregate creating for their audiences and listeners a vivid picture of the moonlight and magnolias vision of the South. Yet, as Stephen A. Smith observes of that same year, "there were eighty-three lynchings in 1919, and Congress, under threat of Southern filibuster, was unable to pass legislation making lynching a federal offense" (Smith 52). But who knew? Before the much later advent of the electronic mass media of radio and, especially, television, it was the rare white American in the North— or any other section of the country—who was fully aware of the deplorable aspects of life below the Mason-Dixon Line, and not just for blacks, but for poor whites as well. In the popular imagination of most Americans, or at least those who listened to popular music, the moonlight and magnolias image of Dixie had already taken hold by 1919, and, somewhat later, it would take more than novels and stories by Erskine Caldwell and William Faulkner, read by only a small percentage of the population, to shake this vision of the South loose from their minds in favor of such writers' depiction of the often poverty-stricken, sometimes depraved underbelly of Dixie, an image reinforced later still in the plays of Tennessee Williams.

No, what ultimately lifted the veil of the Moonlight and Magnolias Myth from contemporary Dixie to reveal an often ugly picture of its reality was *television,* and then only beginning in the mid-1950s. Starting in 1954, and in the comfort of their living rooms, Americans across the nation could witness up close the dramatic effects of *Brown v. Board of Education* on the South; in 1955 they could watch the Montgomery Bus Boycott set off by the spontaneously heroic action of black seamstress Rosa Parks, too tired to give up her seat to a white man; and as the early '60s unfolded they could view the scary riot at Ole Miss, Birmingham's Bull Connor with his police dogs and fire hoses, and the embarrassing antics of governors George Wallace and Orville Faubus (see Smith 50–52). No vision of a bucolic, idyllic South—not even one that had lasted in the creative output of the Alley for over half a century— could withstand images of a harsh reality such as these. And it didn't. Even if moonlight and magnolias Dixie tunes somehow managed to survive the new kinds of popular music that were accosting them, they had no chance of survival if the listeners that once bought into the myth that made such songs so appealing now had that myth shattered right before their eyes—literally. Granted, some classics among the Alley's Dixie tunes have achieved immortality *as songs* and will undoubtedly be listened to and even sung by those who continue to remember them. Yet with the myth that was its foundation destroyed, it is inconceivable that Tin Pan Alley's decades-long output of songs singing of a luxuriously idealized, romantic, imagined South could ever rise again.

BIBLIOGRAPHY

Abbott, Lynn, and Doug Seroff. *Ragged But Right: Black Traveling Shows, "Coon Songs," and the Dark Pathway to Blues and Jazz.* Jackson: UP of Mississippi, 2007.

ASCAP Biographical Dictionary. 4th ed. New York: R. R. Bowker, 1980.

Bargainnier, Earl F. "Tin Pan Alley and Dixie: The South in Popular Song." *Mississippi Quarterly* 30 (Fall 1977): 526–64.

Birchfield, Marilee. "Robison, Carson J." *American National Biography.* Ed. John A. Garraty and Mark C. Carnes. Vol. 18. New York: Oxford UP, 1999. 682–83.

Bordman, Gerald. *American Musical Theatre: A Chronicle.* 2nd ed. New York: Oxford UP, 1992.

Cox, Karen L. *Dreaming of Dixie: How the South Was Created in American Popular Culture.* Chapel Hill: U of North Carolina P, 2011.

Dorman, James H. "Shaping the Popular Image of Post-Reconstruction American Blacks: The 'Coon Song' Phenomenon of the Gilded Age." *American Quarterly* 40.4 (December 1988): 450–71.

Dunn, Jeffrey D., and James Lutzweiler. "Yellow Rose of Texas." *Handbook of Texas Online.* Texas State Historical Association. http://www.tshaonline.org/handbook/online/articles/xey01.

Emerson, Ken. *Doo-dah!: Stephen Foster and the Rise of American Popular Culture.* New York: Simon & Schuster, 1997.

Ewen, David. *Great Men of American Popular Song.* Englewood Cliffs, NJ: Prentice-Hall, 1972.

Foster, Stephen. *Stephen Collins Foster: Sixty Favorite Songs.* Ed. and rev. by Joanna R. Smolko and Steven Saunders. Pacific, MO: Mel Bay, 2009.

———. *Stephen Foster Song Book: Original Sheet Music of 40 Songs by Stephen Collins Foster.* Comp. and ed. with an introduction by Richard Jackson. New York: Dover, 1974.

———. *A Treasury of Stephen Foster.* Foreword by Deems Taylor. New York: Random House, 1946.

Freedland, Michael. *Jolson: The Story of Al Jolson.* Rev. ed. Portland, OR: Valentine Mitchell, 2007.

Furia, Philip. *The Poets of Tin Pan Alley: A History of America's Greatest Lyricists.* New York: Oxford UP, 1990.

Gilbert, L. Wolfe. "Sentimental Songs Live Longest." *Billboard.* 11 December 1926: 78.

Goldberg, Isaac. *Tin Pan Alley: A Chronicle of the American Popular Music Racket.* New York: John Day, 1930.

Goldman, Herbert G. *Jolson: The Legend Comes To Life.* New York: Oxford UP, 1988.

Gregory, James N. *The Southern Diaspora: How the Great Migrations of Black and White Southerners Transformed America.* Chapel Hill: U of North Carolina P, 2005.

Hamm, Charles. *Irving Berlin: Songs From the Melting Pot: The Formative Years, 1907–1914.* New York: Oxford UP, 1997.

Harris, Joel Chandler. *Life of Henry W. Grady, Including His Writings and Speeches: A Memorial Volume.* New York: Cassell, 1890. (Cited as Harris, *Grady.*)

———. *Uncle Remus: His Songs and His Sayings.* New and rev. ed. New York: Grosset & Dunlap, 1921.

Hobson, Fred. *Tell About the South: The Southern Rage To Explain.* Baton Rouge: Louisiana State UP, 1983.

Hundley, Daniel R. *Social Relations in Our Southern States.* New York: H. B. Price, 1860.

Jasen, David A. *Tin Pan Alley: An Encyclopedia of the Golden Age of American Song.* New York: Routledge, 2003.

Jones, John Bush. "Contradictions and Curiosities: Becoming Jewish on Chicago's North Shore—and Beyond." *Rhode Island Jewish Historical Notes* 15 (November 2007): 143–59. (Cited as Jones, "Contradictions.")

———. *Our Musicals, Ourselves: A Social History of the American Musical Theatre.* Hanover, NH: UP of New England, 2003. (Cited as Jones, *Our Musicals.*)

———. "Sing Two Songs of Rhody, Each by Jewish Guys." *Rhode Island Jewish Historical Notes* 15 (November 2010): 640–55. (Cited as Jones, "Sing Two Songs.")

———. *The Songs That Fought the War: Popular Music and the Home Front, 1939–1945.* Hanover, NH: UP of New England, 2006 (Cited as Jones.)

Kanter, Kenneth Aaron. *The Jews on Tin Pan Alley: The Jewish Contribution to American Popular Music, 1830–1940.* New York: Ktav Publishing House, 1982.

Kimball, Robert, Barry Day, Miles Kreuger, and Eric Davis, eds. *The Complete Lyrics of Johnny Mercer.* New York: Knopf, 2009.

Kiner, Larry F., comp. *The Al Jolson Discography.* Westport, CT: Greenwood, 1983.

Kinkle, Roger D. *The Complete Encyclopedia of Popular Music and Jazz, 1900–1950.* 3 vols. New Rochelle, NY: Arlington House, 1974.

Kirby, Jack Temple. *Media-Made Dixie: The South in the American Imagination.* Baton Rouge: Louisiana State UP, 1978.

Lissauer, Robert. *Lissauer's Encyclopedia of Popular Music in America.* New York: Paragon House, 1991.

McPherson, Tara. *Reconstructing Dixie: Race, Gender, and Nostalgia in the Imagined South.* Durham, NC: Duke UP, 2003.

Perry, Jeb H. *Variety Obits: An Index to Obituaries in Variety, 1905–1978.* Metuchen, NJ: Scarecrow P, 1980.

Pratt, John Lowell, ed. *Currier & Ives Chronicles of America.* N.p.: Promontory Press, 1968.

Reed, John Shelton. *Southern Folk, Plain and Fancy: Native White Social Types.* Athens: U of Georgia P, 1986.

Reed, John Shelton, and Dale Volberg Reed. *1001 Things Everyone Should Know About the South.* New York: Doubleday, 1996.

Riverboat Dave's Paddlewheel Site. http://www.riverboatdaves.com/.

Silber, Nina. *The Romance of Reunion: Northerners and the South, 1865–1900.* Chapel Hill: U of North Carolina P, 1993.

Singer, Barry. *Black and Blue: The Life and Lyrics of Andy Razaf.* New York: Schirmer Books, 1992.

Smith, Stephen A. *Myth, Media, and the Southern Mind.* Fayetteville: U of Arkansas P, 1985. (Cited as Smith.)

———. "Sounds of the South: The Rhetorical Saga of Country Music Lyrics." *The Southern Speech Communication Journal* 45 (Winter 1980): 164–72. (Cited as Smith, "Sounds.")

Tindall, George Brown. *The Ethnic Southerners.* Baton Rouge: Louisiana State UP, 1976.

Whitburn, Joel. *Joel Whitburn's Pop Memories, 1890–1954: The History of American Popular Music Compiled from America's Popular Music Charts, 1890–1954.* Menomonee Falls, WI: Record Research, 1986.

Whitfield, Stephen J. "Is It True What They Sing About Dixie?" *Southern Cultures* 8 (Summer 2002): 8–37.

Wilk, Max. *They're Playing Our Song.* New York: Atheneum, 1973.

Williams, Benjamin Buford. "Daniel Hundley." *Encyclopedia of Alabama.* encyclopediaofalabama.org.

Witmark, Isidore, and Isaac Goldberg. *From Ragtime to Swingtime: The Story of the House of Witmark.* New York: Lee Furman, 1939.

GENERAL INDEX

INDEX OF SONG TITLES

CPSIA information can be obtained
at www.ICGtesting.com
Printed in the USA
LVHW021315050322
712646LV00015B/1426

9 780807 177358